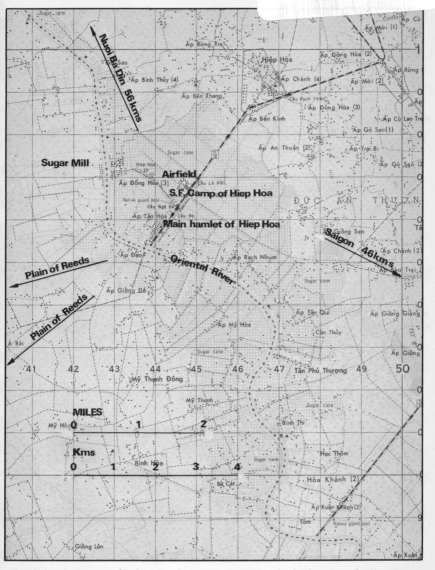

Sugar cane

Ấp Mới (1)
Ấp Cù

Núi Bà Đin 56 kms

Ấp Rừng Tre

Hiệp Hòa

Ấp Đông Hòa (2)

Ấp Rừng

Ấp Sao

Bình Thủy (4)

Ấp Chánh (4)

Ấp Mới (2)

Ấp Bến Thang

Cầu Rạch Thiệt

Ấp Đông Hòa (3)

Ấp Bến Kính

Ấp Cù Lao Tre

Ấp Gò Sao (1)

Ấp An Thuận (2)

Ấp Trại Bì

Sugar Mill

Sugar cane

Ấp Gò Sao (2)

Hiệp Hòa 10

Airfield

Cầu Lò Vôi

Ấp Đông Hòa (3)

S.F. Camp of Hiep Hoa

ĐỨC AN THUẬN

Native guard post

Cầu Nga Ba

Ấp Tân Hòa

Cầu Bé

Main hamlet of Hiep Hoa

Giồng Sao

Saigon 46 kms

Ấp Chánh (2)

Ấp Đạo

Ấp Rạch Nhum

Sào Trại

Plain of Reeds

Oriental River

Sugar cane

Ấp Giồng Đế

Ấp Tân Qui

Ấp Giồng Giồng

Plain of Reeds

Ấp Mỹ Hòa

Cần Thủy

Á Rắc

Ấp Giồng

Sugar cane

41   42   43   44   45   46   47   Tấn Phú Thượng   49   50

Mỹ Thanh Đông

MILES

Mỹ Thanh

Sugar cane

Mỹ Hò

0   1   2

Bình Thi

Kms

0   1   Bình Hòa   2   3   4

Học Thôm

Sugar cane

Bà Cát

Hòa Khánh (2)

Ấp Xuân Khánh (2)

Tôm

Native guard post

Giồng Lồn

Ấp Xuân

"Ap" is Vietnamese for hamlet; hence Ap Tan Hoa is the hamlet of Hiep Hoa.
"S.F." designates "Special Forces."

P.O.W.
TWO YEARS WITH THE VIETCONG

P.O.W.
TWO YEARS WITH THE VIETCONG

GEORGE E. SMITH

WITH AN INTRODUCTION AND EPILOGUE BY DONALD DUNCAN

Ramparts Press
BERKELEY

Published by Ramparts Press, Inc., Berkeley, California

Library of Congress catalog card number 74–172286
ISBN 0–87867–011–4

Trade distribution by Simon & Schuster, Inc., New York
Order number 67011

Manufactured in the United States of America

To Walter Brennan, Anus, Oil Can Harry, Suave,
Gidget, Pussy, Little King, and all the others,
with sincere appreciation from myself,
my wife Maureen, and Robin, Leslie, and
Trent, our three children.

CONTENTS

This book could not have appeared without the help and encouragement of Don Duncan, Dave Ransom, and Ramparts Press. Duncan's initial interest in my story and his straight-forward reporting provided the first factual account of my experiences as a POW and aroused the interest of a publishing house which wanted to bring the whole story to the American people.

Ransom and Duncan not only made a readable text out of many hours of tape-recorded interviews, but also provided the notes which help the reader see my story in the context of the escalating war in Vietnam and the growing anti-war movement within America. To them, and to Ramparts Press, I express my deepest appreciation.

George Smith

INTRODUCTION

In the fifties Ngo Dinh Diem coined the word 'Vietcong' to describe his enemies. The word was derived from the Vietnamese word for communist and has about the same ring as 'Commie.' No one knew better than Diem himself that his opponents were not just communists, but during his "exile" in New Jersey in the fifties, Diem had discovered McCarthyism. His invention of the term 'Vietcong' transplanted McCarthyism to Saigon. Diem's "communist menace" kept funds flowing in from Washington and diverted attention from his own regime's shortcomings.

Labeling Diem's opponents commies didn't stop the Vietnamese from supporting them, as Americans are beginning to realize, but it succeeded for a long time in stopping us from thinking about just who the Vietcong are. After all these years of war, few Americans—from officialdom down to the GI in the field—have even a remote understanding of the Vietnamese they support, much less of the Vietnamese they oppose. Above all, we do not understand how it is that the Vietcong continue to fight.

The morale of the U.S. Army in Vietnam has never been lower—yet our GIs have always had the advantage of not having to fight under a hostile sky. The American infantryman in Vietnam ventures forth knowing that no enemy planes will be bombing or strafing from above. If he runs into resistance, massive friendly air support is present or on-call. He knows he will not have to walk through thirty or forty miles of jungle to get to the battle area. If he is wounded he will be whisked away in minutes to a well-equipped surgical ward. If ammo gets low, choppers will bring more, or it will be parachuted to him. When the battle is over, he will return to a base camp with movies, showers, electric lights, warm food and cold beer—and in twelve months he will go home.

The Vietcong soldier has none of these things. He goes into battle after a long march, knowing the sky will soon fill with planes dropping napalm and fragmentation bombs. Rockets and cannon tracers will seek him out. There will be no chopper to evacuate him when he is wounded. The bombing will not stop because the battle is over. He will have to fix his own rice, and as he rests in his hammock the world can suddenly explode from the horror of a B-52 drop. And his "tour" is as long as the war—or until he dies. For many it has already been more than a decade; yet they fight on.

Those GIs who have been caught under a misplaced bomb drop know well the terror they felt, the rage and powerlessness they felt at not being able to stop it. Those GIs, for a few moments, have known what it is to be in a nightmare of deafening explosions, white-hot shrapnel seeking soft flesh, parts of bodies being tossed through the air, screams of agony unheard in the holocaust. They, and we, can only imagine what it would be like to live in such a nightmare day after day—and I doubt the imagination is equal to the task. Who are these people who can, and do, prevail under such conditions? Who are the Vietcong?

For several years every ambulatory American journalist worthy of the name has wanted to travel to the jungle camps of South Vietnam to answer this question. Quite a few have sought out officials of the National Liberation Front in Paris, Prague, Algiers, or Phnom Penh, seeking permission to enter the "liberated" zones. Although any number of Western journalists have been granted permission to visit Hanoi (and some allowed to travel far afield in North Vietnam), only a very few have been allowed into NLF-controlled areas of the South—and none of them Americans. Of those few who made it, only one made more than the briefest visit—the Australian-born Wilfred Burchett.

Permission is denied because of the obvious military need for security. There is also a problem of logistics—food, lodging, diversion of busy people to escort duty, etc. Equally, there is the almost obsessive Vietnamese concern with protecting a guest, to which any American visitor to North Vietnam can readily attest. Perhaps it has never been discussed, but if a James Reston were killed by American bombs while traveling with the Vietcong, would it be believed?

But even if one, two, or half a dozen American journalists had been granted permission, the most they could have expected was a two- or three-week tour—and inevitably a carefully guided tour at that. George Smith, however, lived with the NLF not for two weeks but for two years. A United States Army Special Forces sergeant, he was captured at Hiep Hoa, twenty-five miles northwest of Saigon, in November 1963. For the next two years he traveled and lived with the Vietcong in a series of jungle camps. Because he and his companion prisoners were not visiting VIPs, their tour was not a series of briefings and speeches with everyone putting on his best face for the occasion. Except on special occasions, Smith's contact was not with high-ranking officials, but with common soldiers, with the kind of soldier we hear about on the news every night: ". . . 147 Vietcong killed. . . ."

It would be difficult to imagine a worse position from which to develop a sympathetic picture of the Vietcong, but this is what Smith has done. He has given us for the first time in a long war a detailed picture of life in the National Liberation Front's safe areas and an intimate portrait of the people we call the VC.

Every war has its propaganda, and the war in Vietnam is no exception. As I've said elsewhere, however, this may be the first time we had the propaganda before we knew we had the war. Certainly we had the propaganda long before most people in the United States could locate Vietnam on a map. As always, the propagandists have endeavored to paint the enemy in the most diabolical terms possible. This makes it possible for a nation to send forth its sons to be killed, and allows otherwise normal young men to kill other people day after day and still retain some semblance of sanity. Do you remember the Japs, the Nips, the little brown monkeys who wore big glasses and displayed buck teeth? You knew every Nip soldier was an animal who raped, pillaged, and burned. Japanese-Americans spent World War II in detention camps lest that myth be broken. It took a generation to destroy the stereotype. Today, the Nips are our friends the Japanese, who make marvelous electronic equipment and fine cameras, and whom we woo as allies.

Today the pilot in the air and the soldier on the ground kills gooks, Vietcong, Comm-yew-nists, slopes, Cong, Charlie. And we all know about them. Those who aren't blowing up American bars in Saigon or assassinating village chiefs are out engaging in fanatical human-wave attacks against isolated outposts. After all, how would "leaders" get one group of young people to go out and kill other young people if the killers believed those they were killing had girlfriends or a young wife with a new baby; if they believed that the enemy soldier laughed, enjoyed a game of cards, enjoyed living—wanted to live? Would the people of this country expend so much of its wealth to defeat another country if they could not convince themselves of that country's evil?

In November of 1965, then–Vice President Hubert H. Humphrey, in great dudgeon because he was asked the question, stated that we (the United States) would never recognize or negotiate with the NLF because they were an "...

illegitimate ... band of wandering minstrels." Once that image of any enemy has taken hold of a national consciousness, terminating a war short of the annihilation of the enemy becomes difficult if not impossible. Negotiation implies compromise, but how can one compromise with evil?

The first hurdle has been crossed: in 1968 the United States sat down with the National Liberation Front in the Paris peace talks. But the talks have gone slowly. The Nixon administration persists in offering the issue of POWs as a justification for continuing the war. Hysterical charges of torture and cruelty are still being voiced to excuse the latest decision to prolong the war, to stall the Paris talks another week, month or year; and the grief of separated families is still being exploited to renew the old stereotype of the inhuman enemy. And so the feeling persists that negotiation is somehow a compromise with evil.

This feeling must change, and I believe George Smith's story is a step in that direction. Given what has gone before, the process will be neither fast nor easy. How to make the marine at Khe Sanh who lost a leg and most of his face believe that those on the other side who pulled the lanyard are really "nice guys"; or the GI who was the lone survivor of an ambush? How can it be explained to the widow and children of Sergeant Kenneth Roraback, who was captured with Smith and executed by the Vietcong while a prisoner? Will it be more, or less, difficult than explaining it to the parents or young wife or Nguyen Van Troi, a member of the National Liberation Front executed in Saigon, October 15, 1964?

DONALD DUNCAN

PART ONE: SPECIAL FORCES

ATTACK!

Jesus Christ! I was awakened out of a sound sleep by an explosion so close it left my ears ringing. I opened my eyes just in time to see the first burning white phosphorus spewing through the thatch where McClure slept.

The VC attacked the night after we split up the camp. With the area supposedly pacified, Captain Horne had taken six of the team and the only half-decent Vietnamese platoon out to where we were supposed to set up a new camp—some ten miles away. After dinner, Camacho climbed the observation tower with his bottle of VO, and Colby settled down to writing his book on bear-hunting. Roraback was puttering around somewhere, and McClure was just keeping to himself as usual. The flurry of excitement we'd had a few days before when one of our informers reported a VC battalion in the area had died down. Colby had commandeered a recon plane from Saigon and flown around some, but of course he hadn't seen them pitching their tents anywhere, and we figured it was a false alarm. With half the team gone, I couldn't even get our usual pinochle game going. "Hell," I decided, "I'll go to bed."

When I woke up, phosphorus rounds were falling all over the house, and tracers were cutting through the three-foot-high thatched wall. My carbine was hung up on the wall, with my harness of grenades and ammunition. "Shit, if I stand up, they'll probably catch me"—I'd be silhouetted against the glare. But I had to have my weapon. I nearly stretched my arm out of the socket to get the damned thing.

The camp was lit up like a night ball game. I could see Camacho scrambling through the house with his clipboard under his arm, heading for his mortar. As he went out, he kicked at something under the little table the interpreters used for translating. It was Roraback. "What the hell you doing under there!"

I was in my underwear, but I didn't take time for my boots or pants. The place was burning, and the rounds were still coming in. I remembered Can Tho, where a round had landed right above me, and I told myself, "Shit, it's just a matter of time until one lands right on my head."

I threw on my harness, grabbed my weapon, and ran out the back door. By this time the house was in flames, and I saw another round land just where I'd left. "Jesus Christ, this place is really going to get smashed!" I dropped into the closest mortar pit, right beside the house. It was sandbagged three feet high all around, and I got down on my hands and knees to get out of the way of all those tracers.

I decided not to open up the mortar's ammunition bunker because the sparks from the house would probably set the damned thing off. I didn't know what the hell I was going to do even if I *did* open it up and get the ammunition out, whether I was just going to drop it in the tube and hope it landed in the right place, or what. Hell, I might have blown up the sugar mill we were supposed to be guarding.

"I'll go over and help Camacho, then." But when I raised up, I saw flashes coming out of Camacho's mortar. Somebody must be helping him, I figured, maybe McClure. If McClure had run out his back door he would have been right next to the bunker.

The mortar fire began to fall off, but the small-arms fire was still intense. I was waiting for our Vietnamese strike force to repel the attack when I heard the bugle sounding and knew we were really in for it. We'd heard about bugle charges—if they used a bugle, by God they were serious; they were going to do what they had come to do.

By now sparks from the house were falling into the bunker and the concrete floor was so hot that my hands and knees were getting burnt. I took my carbine and my harness and flopped over the bunker wall into the mud. There was some barbed wire, just a couple of strands, and I crawled through it and in the process got mud in my carbine. I crawled into a little corner bunker that had two firing ports facing out of the camp and could see into the camp besides.

I could still see the flash coming from Camacho's mortar, but he was firing illumination rounds that lit up the whole damned area. I couldn't figure out why. Afraid the VC couldn't find their way through the barbed wire, maybe.

By this time the incoming mortars had stopped. There was a tremendous amount of small-arms fire coming into the camp. I was still waiting for the strikers to repel the attack, wondering what had happened to the Cambodian squad on the perimeter. I saw some people running between the camp and the dependents' housing compound and started firing at them. That seemed to make them run a lot faster, but I didn't see any of them fall.

Pretty soon I was looking out of the crawl hole, and over by the generator shack I saw half a dozen guys in black combat uniforms and camouflage helmets. "Christ, they're inside the camp!" The fire had dropped off to sporadic shots here and there, and here came one of the strikers, crawling along the wall with a BAR—a Browning Automatic Rifle. He dropped into the bunker and I told him, "Point that thing at those sons of bitches and shoot it!" But he motioned, "No, no, be quiet, they won't see us."

It wasn't such a bad idea. There were half a dozen of them in a little group just sort of standing around bullshitting. It would have been very easy to shoot them all—assuming I could hit them all quicker than they could get around to doing something to me. The mud in my carbine had jammed the mechanism for automatic fire, and it was stupid to try to shoot into them one shot at a time. Maybe I should have taken away the striker's BAR and fired it myself, but Camacho's mortar had stopped firing and the VC were in effective control of the camp. "Maybe he's got a point," I said to myself. "At least they won't know we're in here."

But apparently someone had seen him crawl into the bunker. Pretty soon a group of VC came over and got into Camacho's mortar bunker. The striker seemed to understand that they were saying something about us. They started firing at our bunker.

He threw his rifle out and then went out himself. They must have yelled to him to surrender, but I hadn't understood it. Colby had packed the house with all kinds of ammunition that shouldn't have been there, and as the fire burned further and further it was exploding—recoilless rifle ammunition, grenades, rockets. I didn't see what they did with the striker after he went out. Of course, I wasn't really worried about the striker. I was worried about myself.

It was a toss-up: stay in there or surrender. I could stay in there and shoot at them. It was close range, and they were shooting at me. I could hear the bullets hit the sandbag—*dup! dup! dup!*—all around the place. While I was peeking out, one went *phunk!* about an inch from my head. That's a funny thing, that inch. You're dead so easily, but you never think about that when you join the Army.

I could stay in there and shoot back at them and wait for them to throw a grenade. There wasn't any firing from our strikers or the ARVN* detachment at the sugar mill. I could have thrown a grenade at them too; that was possible. But it

* Army of the Republic of Vietnam.

wasn't going to change the situation, because they had already taken the camp. The only thing that would be different was that I would be dead.

"Oh, hell, what's the use." I decided that I might as well do what the striker did, throw the damned carbine out and surrender. And that's what I did: I threw out my weapon, and my harness for good measure, and went out after them with my hands up. They came and surrounded me, grabbed me, and threw me to the ground.

I was a prisoner of the Vietcong.

They were rough—it seemed like there were a dozen of them sitting on me while they tied my hands behind my back—but all things considered they really weren't too bad. After they tied me up, they took me over behind the latrine and sat me down. Then here came two more with Camacho. He was tied up as I was, and blood was running down the back of his neck. He told me that he had been shooting at one of the attackers when another came up behind him and whacked him in the back of the head with a rifle butt.

They could easily have killed us. They could have thrown a grenade into my bunker and that would have been the end of me. They could just as easily have shot Camacho. But I got the impression that the people who had taken us over by the latrine were guarding us. Some of the line troops were coming up and shouting, pointing their fingers and being very threatening with their weapons—as if to say, "Hey, son of a bitch! I'm going to shoot you!" But the people who had us were holding them off.

There was still some rifle fire, but the VC didn't seem to be worried about it. There were hundreds of them in their black shorts and shirts and camouflaged helmets swarming all over the camp. They kept Camacho and me behind the latrine until they rounded up all the ammunition and broke into the main bunker for our weapons. We had a tremendous stockpile of ammunition; we had just received a huge shipment, and Colby had stacked it all along the house, cases and cases of small-arms and mortar ammunition. We had a lot of weapons, too: Thompsons, shotguns, rifles. Camacho said he saw them taking his mortar down, and I imagine they got the other one as well. The mortars were real prizes—81s. All they had at the time were 60s.

When they were carrying everything they could, they got us up and told us to move out. They had come in by laying bamboo ladders over the barbed-wire apron, and they were going out the same way. As we started over the top, I heard what I thought was an incoming round and jumped in the machine-gun bunkers—right on top of half a dozen dead strikers. I never did see any VC casualties.

My jumping down angered the VC, and one of them whacked me with a rifle butt and told me to move down the apron. Then in three or four columns we started across the cane fields that surrounded the camp. The sugar mill was no more than half a mile away, but the ARVN battalion and their American advisers kept their two 155 mm howitzers silent—afraid of getting attacked themselves, I guess.

We were halfway across the cane fields to the river before the air strike began. It was a laugh. First a flare ship showed up and dropped its flares. That lighted up the whole cane field, so we didn't have to stumble along, just run like hell. It was handy for the VC, carrying all that heavy shit. Those little guys were running across the cane breaks carrying big, heavy cases of mortar rounds, along with their weapons and everything else they take into battle.

As the T-28s making the strike came in, Camacho yelled at me, did I think they'd use napalm? I yelled back that it probably didn't matter: the Vietnamese Air Force hadn't hit anything recently anyway. "I'm not worried about them hitting us on *purpose*!" he answered.

He was right. They made their runs *across* the columns instead of *along* them, and they generally dropped their napalm a thousand yards from where we were. As far as I could make out, the only thing they hurt was a lot of cane. It didn't seem to bother the VC much at all. "Little bastards sure are calm about it—talking and chattering away as if they didn't have a worry." The plane would dive, and we'd just jump in a ditch. As soon as the plane passed we were up and running again.

Then, when the air strike was over, the VC actually sat down in the middle of the cane and took a break, passing around thin wafers of rice. They gave us some, too: I guess that was their combat rations.

I tried to get my thoughts together. Here I was, still in my undershorts, barefoot, running across a cane field after an air attack, maybe fifteen minutes after being awakened by a mortar round next to my bed. But all I could do was wonder if they knew how we'd treated our prisoners at the camp and remember what they taught me at Bragg: "Guerrillas don't take prisoners."

They kept Camacho and me pretty close together while we were crossing the cane break. They had us tethered on ropes, and a couple of times I considered trying to dive into the cane fields to get away. The guy that was holding on to my rope was a puny character, and I could have thrown him in the damned ditch very easily. But there might have been more VC in the cane—at different points we would pass a guy sitting in a little hole in the cane, covering the retreat.

This is normal guerrilla warfare: you leave a secure route of escape, so that you will be able to get out without being ambushed. The VC had prepared the attack according to the book, and the thing had gone just perfectly for them. They accomplished their mission, captured the Americans, took all weapons and ammunition, and withdrew with few casualties —none as far as I knew.

At one point, after they had had their break, the guards dropped our ropes and told us to walk ahead. Then we heard them draw the bolts on their rifles—*clak! clak!*—as they chambered rounds. "Looks like they're going to grease us!" Camacho said. "Walk a little faster!"

I was in front, walking pretty fast already. I thought about running or diving into the cane. It looked like we had had it. Then somebody ran up shouting at the guards and grabbed our ropes again. I don't know whether they really intended to shoot us, or whether they were just testing to see if we would run, but when they pulled the bolts on their rifles, I really thought we were finished. Maybe we were just being spared so that we could be executed in public in some village. I wished I could stop shivering and wanted to piss. One of the things they told us at Bragg kept running through my mind. "As a member of Special Forces, you will be specially inter-rogated at a higher level. Try to hold out for at least twenty-four hours."

In a short while the column walked into a village on the river, and the people came pouring out of their houses. You could hear them laughing; spirits were very high. It was em-barrassing: the place couldn't have been more than a mile from our camp. This was supposed to be our pacified area, yet this village was open to the Vietcong. I'd never been there before, I didn't know whether any of our team had been there before. That's how professional we were: we weren't even aware of VC hamlets a mile from our camp.

The villagers came out into the town square, and they brought out big stocks of bananas and passed them around and gave us some. The VC seemed pretty happy and the villagers were chattering and milling around. "How'd it go?" they seemed to be saying. "Jesus Christ, we *smashed* that son of a bitch!"

They crowded around and patted us like we were strange pieces of merchandise. Camacho kept telling me, "Smile, be friendly; they're trying to reassure us." But dressed in my drawers and mud, I felt like public exhibit number one. They sat us down on a bench in the middle of the square and gave us bananas, more bananas than I could eat. And cigarettes. I'd puff one, and a guy would say, "Here, take another." And I'd puff his.

Camacho and I tried to get oriented a bit. "First thing I remember is a mortar round hitting the house," I told him.

"I don't think it was a mortar round," he said. "I think it was a demo charge."

"A demo charge—shit, they would have had to walk right into the camp to plant it."

"Or have somebody already in the camp plant it."

"You mean one of the strikers?"

"That's what I mean!"

LEAVING HOME

I went into the Army in 1955 when I was seventeen years old—more or less to get away from home. On my birthday, I took my mother by the arm and said, "Come on and sign for me." A week later I was on my way to Fort Jackson.

I went to high school in Steubenville. It was haphazard. I went part of the time, and part of the time I dodged school. A couple of times I ran away to Florida.

School was all right when I was younger, but when I got to high school I felt like I was wasting my time. I got through because I have a pretty good memory and could pass a test, but I was never really interested in it. It didn't lead to anything that seemed worthwhile. I didn't get along with the teachers and never tried to. I suppose I've always been defiant. I resented authority and didn't want to follow rules unless I considered them fair. The teachers didn't particularly put themselves out for me, either; there were about fifteen hundred students in the school and the classes were always overcrowded, fifty in a class.

The first job I ever had was in a hamburger joint. I was the flunky around the place, did everything the owner didn't want to, worked a whole day for a dollar. That lasted about three months, until we got into a fight and I told him to go to hell. I was about twelve years old. After that, I set pins in a bowling alley for a while for nine cents a line. I worked from six to eleven and could set about thirty lines a night. Not much money, but I thought that for a kid I'd arrived. I was making three times as much as the paper boys.

The first time I took off for Florida, I went alone. It was just defiance. I couldn't stand everyone telling me don't do this, don't do that. I'd take a beating rather than let anybody tell me what to do. One morning I packed my lunch and instead of going to school, I just went out and got on the highway and started hitching. That night I was about five hundred miles away.

My grandmother sent the money for me to come home that time. My grandmother doted on me; she kept me for a few years when my mother was working when I was very young—two, three, four, five years old—before my stepfather came along. She died a couple of days after I was released by the Vietcong. She hung on until I'd been released, and then that sort of relaxed her to the point where she went ahead and died.

I ran away from home a couple of more times before I turned seventeen and went into the Army.

The Army was what I had been waiting for. Even if I'd graduated from high school, there was no money for me to go to college, and the outlook for a job was very dim. The military was the only alternative. On high school "Career Day" all the recruiting sergeants come down and give you their hard sell, and to somebody who wanted to get away from home it seemed like a good way out. It would be a haven, and still I would be free to a certain extent—as much as you can be free in the military.

A week later I was on my way to Fort Jackson, right outside of Columbia, South Carolina. Fort Jackson was quite a shock. The second day I was there, they put me on KP for forty-eight hours at one of those consolidated mess halls where people were coming in and out from buses and trains all night long. I thought I would die.

Basic training was hectic too. I was still a little kid, seventeen years old and about a hundred and twenty pounds. When I'd finished eight weeks basic training at Fort Jackson, I got orders for Fort Campbell, Kentucky, which was the Eleventh Airborne's home base at the time. I had volunteered for Airborne when I enlisted in the Army because one of my friends had—he was a little tougher than I was and a little bigger. I was seventeen years and four months old the day I graduated from jump school.

We did physical training all the time in jump school. After you'd been working hard all day, jumping off mock airplanes and doing constant, hard exercise, they'd have half-hour runs in the July Kentucky heat. They'd tell you, "The only way you can fall out of this run is on your face; you don't drop out and walk." They made quitting a greater sin than anything else—you had to stay in there and suffer, even if you died in the process, and a couple of guys did. For me it was more a challenge than anything else, because I was trying to prove that I wasn't too little for it.

I grew up in the Army. It became my culture. Seventeen is

a formative age, and if you get into something like the Army at seventeen, and you begin to think like a soldier, then whatever they tell you is acceptable. You relate everything to what you learned when you were seventeen. When I was twenty-five I was still doing that—until I was captured.

From Fort Campbell they took us to Germany. In the Far East in World War II, the Eleventh Airborne had been quite a famous fighting unit. Even though there were only a very few veterans from the Far East, the whole division tried to retain the tradition of being the famous Eleventh Airborne. When they got to Germany, they wanted to show the Germans that they were the toughest people around, so they began beating the hell out of them. The Germans didn't appreciate that, of course, but we couldn't understand why not. We were there to protect them, and they shouldn't mind having a few beatings now and then. They were rough on women, too. Some of the prostitutes they paid, some they didn't. The Army didn't arrange any shotgun weddings; if a GI got a German girl pregnant, she was a prostitute, and the Army would go about *proving* she was a prostitute.

I got involved in a couple of fights. I was still a kid of eighteen, but I had the Airborne spirit pounded into me in jump school. "You are as good as five ordinary soldiers, and you are as good as maybe a hundred civilians." They take a little kid and make him think he's a really bad character. He believes he can go around and punch people in the nose, and that it's acceptable because he's a paratrooper. Paratroopers were *supposed* to get into fights, otherwise they didn't earn their wings. Kicking ass was part of wearing that patch and the boots. You couldn't go into a bar and drink a beer and just walk out, you had to start one or two fights, and if you could wreck the bar, that was even better, and if you could take a whole gang with you and completely level the place, that was the best.

About everyone I knew was involved in something like

that. Even the commanding general went along with it to a certain extent. He got up and made a speech in front of the whole division one day in a parade-ground assembly. "This is the finest fighting unit I've ever served with," etc., etc. Right after that he was relieved of his command and the whole division was scattered to the four winds.

I ended up in the Navy hospital at Portsmouth, Virginia, after getting cracked up in a car wreck while on leave in Italy. When I got out of the hospital, they sent me back to Fort Campbell. Then at the end of my tour they mustered me out and I went home.

When I got out, I was thoroughly pissed off at the Army. "Fuck the Army," I said. "I'll never come back." I walked out into civilian life totally unprepared. I came back to Chester, West Virginia—where my parents lived—with a couple of hundred bucks, no education, and no skills.

That was 1958, and employment prospects hadn't gotten any better. I got a job at the church supply company where my mother worked, but they fired me after a week. One day they told me to take the trash out and burn it, and I said, "Well, I see I'm on ash-and-trash again!"—Army slang for the garbage detail. One of the supervisors overheard me and turned me in for criticizing the job.

After the church supply company, I worked one day a week at Waterford Park Racetrack for a while, but it turned out that the house wasn't big enough for me and my step-father. I ended up packing my bongos and going to stay with my grandmother for a couple of months. They had passed a law allowing ex-GIs to draw unemployment based on their time in the Army and I got about four weeks' back pay from that and talked two of my friends into taking off for Tampa with me.

In Tampa I got a job with Pillsbury Mills driving a forklift.

It turned out to be one of the hardest jobs in the plant: you had to load the pallets yourself. Boxcars carrying twelve hundred bags of feed would arrive and they'd say, "We don't have any help right now, you go back and start on it yourself." I'd start on it myself and I'd finish it myself. When they cut out my overtime, I quit. They were paying a dollar an hour—minimum wage in Florida then—and when you cut out the overtime, you end up with nothing.

After that I drove a cab. Then I went to work for a building materials company. It wasn't an easy job, and I wasn't making any money. Finally, I just got disgusted and quit.

There was really no outlook for anything. I could continue to work as a dollar-an-hour wage slave, or I could go back into the Army. In the Army there would be people that I liked to talk with and run around with. If I wanted to blow all my pay on pay day, I could do it and still be fed the rest of the month. If I got sick, I could go to a free hospital. The outside world seemed tough, but I knew how to get around in the Army.

So I re-enlisted. When they asked me what I wanted to do, I told them, "Throw it in the computer"—I'd take pot luck. I went back to my grandmother's just long enough for them to process the papers, and then in November 1960 I was assigned to Fort Dix, New Jersey, as a movie projector repairman.

BRAGG

After running through Fort Dix's file of training films and the Army's "Big Picture" TV series, I became bored repairing movie projectors. There wasn't much to be gained by jauntily telling the girls at Atlantic City that I was a movie projector repairman. I tried getting back on jump status, but it turned out that none of the Airborne divisions needed movie projector repairmen either. But this was shortly after the CIA's Bay of Pigs invasion of Cuba in '61, and Kennedy was quadrupling the Special Forces. The sergeant suggested I try them.

With my Airborne background, I was in. They assigned me to radio operator training at Fort Jackson, but I couldn't stand it so I switched to medic training and off I went to Fort Sam Houston in dry and dusty San Antonio. There I spent almost a year in intensive eight-hour-a-day schooling. I liked medic training and I graduated in the top of my class.

The "Big Picture" films at Fort Dix had told me all about Special Forces: be a hero, have fun, make big money. Special Forces paid you per diem on missions—some places in South America it was forty dollars a day. Besides, all Special Forces were NCOs, something it would take you five or six years to get in a normal outfit.

In the adventure films, Special Forces skied, blew up bridges, jumped into previously unexplored areas, and conducted guerrilla operations in oppressed countries. That was the Special Forces mission: we would infiltrate (not necessarily with the permission of the government of the country), equip the people with weapons, and train them to fight guerrilla wars and overthrow unpopular or oppressive governments. We studied the tactics of Rogers' Rangers[1] and read Mao Tse-tung's handbook.

In Special Forces we weren't like the rest of the Army. When we went to the field, we didn't take a cook with us, we took chickens and rabbits and did our own cooking. We sat around and talked; we didn't wear uniforms. Rather than being regimented and riding around in jeeps, we hitchhiked rides with farmers. It wasn't like the Army at all. The officers were just like us—we would just sit down and bullshit together and eat out of the same rice pot.

Guerrilla warfare is what we volunteered for. Nearly everybody had the same attitude: we were going to be guerrilla fighters and overthrow unpopular governments. But somewhere along the line, they turned the whole thing around. "Since you are guerrilla fighters and are capable of training people to *fight* guerrilla warfare," they told us, "you should be equally capable of training people to *combat* guerrilla warfare." They wanted us to *combat* insurgency, and of course the application would be in South Vietnam.

This didn't seem quite what I had volunteered for. Nevertheless, I did have a green beret, we did get mission pay, and it would be sort of exciting to go to Vietnam. As one of our instructors told us, "It's all the war we've got." I'd never been in a war, and it seemed like a game. I felt as though I was in an overgrown Boy Scout outfit, as if this was my outlet for going camping. In those "Big Picture" films they didn't show anyone getting killed, only Special Forces training other people and sending *them* out to do battle.

We were arrogant, too. The Army is a separate society; it has its own hierarchy, and I could rise to a stratum in the Army that I couldn't attain in the outside world. They'd already driven arrogance into us in Airborne, which is a high level in the Army, but Special Forces was the highest level you could reach, the elite of the elite. Elitism was the philosophy they taught at Bragg: "You are professors of warfare, you shouldn't fight unless attacked. It costs thousands of dollars to train one of you and you're too valuable to send into battle."

I believed it. I believed everything the Army said. I never questioned anything they told me until I got to Vietnam, and then things didn't quite fit anymore.

The old-timers were particularly disgusted, not only about the changed role of Special Forces but also because they no longer gave the intensive training that Special Forces had been based on. They were just letting people slide through. I had few qualifications for Special Forces, except that I was a pretty well-trained medic. I didn't know how to climb a mountain, or rappel from a helicopter, or ski. I could swim, but not five hundred yards quietly underwater at night, or whatever the hell they wanted me to do. I didn't know any foreign languages, and I learned more Spanish in three weeks as a prisoner than I learned Vietnamese the whole time I was at Bragg.

I wasn't really qualified for the Green Berets and neither were the other new recruits. But the Special Forces were assuming this new counterinsurgency role, and therefore needed more teams to go into different countries—Laos and Vietnam and the Congo. My group, the Fifth, was initially assigned to Africa, and I thought we were going to the Congo.

In the end we went to Vietnam. "We've been invited to Vietnam," they told us. We would be supporting the government of the people, they explained, or at least training an army to defend the democratic government of South Vietnam against Chinese Communists. As far as I knew, that was true. Ngo Dinh Diem, the "George Washington of South Vietnam"—I didn't know who he was. I didn't know where Saigon was. Hell, I didn't know where *Vietnam* was. I knew where China was, though, and what Communists were. And I knew we had to stop them. Everybody knew that—we saw it on "Big Picture."

Communism is a magic word. Anybody who is a Communist, no matter what he does, is an enemy. Even if he lives next door to you, he's an enemy. The Communists were coming down from China to overthrow the legitimate government of South Vietnam, which had the support of the people but was helpless to defend itself—that's what they told us. It was even on the patch we had for Vietnam service—a picture of the Great Wall of China with a break in it and red streaming down: the Red Hordes of China streaming down into South Vietnam.

I got out of medic school in December 1962. In March or April, eight "A" detachments—ten men, two officers—were alerted to prepare for deployment to Vietnam to replace those about to come back. We would be the third wave of Special Forces in Vietnam. Even though I'd finished my training, I couldn't be assured a berth. Quite a few of the men on the teams were dropped out for any number of reasons—lack of training, personality conflicts, or because they weren't members of the sergeant major's clique. I definitely wasn't one of the sergeant major's favorites.

For one thing, he couldn't understand my kite flying. For as long as I can remember, I have always flown a kite in March. I made a point of flying a kite in March. Except in Vietnam—I didn't get to fly any kites there. I went down to the store with a friend I nicknamed Gnat and I said, "I want a kite."

"You want a *kite*?"

"Yeah, I want a kite, and I want some string, too."

She looked at me. "Is this for your little boy?"

"No, it's for me. I want to fly a kite. I fly a kite every year at this time. Charlie Brown flies kites. I fly kites."

"Yeah," said Gnat. "We fly kites."

So we went out in the middle of the parade ground and flew that kite. Some fellows from the Seventh came by and got mad. "Look at those bastards, we ought to go up there and kick their goddamned ass! Who the hell do they think they are, out there with their green berets on, flying kites. Dumb bastards!"

It was about this time, too, that I read *Catch-22*. Both at Bragg and in Vietnam I could connect almost every situation with *Catch-22*.

The Fifth Group commander at Bragg was Colonel Will. We called him Chill Will because he was just a mean, nasty, old colonel. He reminded me of Colonel Cathcart in *Catch-22*, the commander who thinks up stupid schemes for getting his picture in the *Saturday Evening Post*. Chill Will decided he would install a botanical garden at Fort Bragg. He had the whole Special Forces out there digging, raking, scraping, and planting grass and little bushes. It all died, of course—nothing grows in the sand hills of North Carolina. I spent several days spreading fertilizer, with my green beret on, as if it were my sole purpose in life.

It was Chill Will who told us, as we were getting on the plane to go to Vietnam, "Now, keep your powder dry." Despite my not being one of the sergeant major's best buddies, I was assigned as one of the medics in an "A" detachment.

By the time the teams were put together, it was hard to tell what criteria they used. One guy was dropped from our team because he spent too much time at the NCO club bar, but another team was given an alcoholic team sergeant complete with nervous tic. On my own team we had three blacks, but they gave us a redneck as team sergeant, a fellow from Alabama by the name of O'Neill. I believe his father owned some land down there and had some black sharecroppers. He was a real redneck, loud and vulgar, ignorant. He didn't like black people, and when they assigned black people to his team, he didn't like that. He made a habit of calling McClure, the demolitions man, a "cotton-patch coon."

Our team leader was a reserve captain from North Carolina named Horne. He was a very likable, easygoing fellow who enjoyed telling jokes. His father-in-law was in the diaper business, but he got tired of diapers and applied for active duty. He was in his early thirties and liked to get along with people. He wasn't trying to be a general, he was just making a living.

Colby, his executive officer, was the other kind—a real gung ho who thought he was Joe Stillwell and wanted to kick ass right up the ladder. He'd been to officer candidate school and had Airborne and Ranger training, and he never got over the combination. He was all for double-timing everywhere, a "stand-at-attention-and-call-me-sir" type who fancied himself a killer.

Horne was ready to kick my ass off the team until I got high score on the "pro-pay" test and he found out I could play a pretty good game of pinochle. Both were sort of a feather in his cap. They had pinochle games between teams, and if Horne met up with Leitz, another team leader who thought his team had some good pinochle players, he'd say, "I'll get Smith to come down and whip your ass," and he and I would go down and beat Leitz and his pinochle player.

But really he took me on his team because I got the highest score on the proficiency-pay test. If you passed the test with a standard score of seventy, it meant thirty dollars a month extra. It was a status symbol for his team that he had the "most proficient" medic in the company—and the best pinochle player besides.

With the exception of Morley, the team's other medic, and Camacho, who was our heavy-weapons man, most of us had been in Special Forces a relatively short time and none had been on any missions. Camacho came on in the very last weeks before we left for Vietnam. Given the pick-up nature of the teams, I thought we'd be eating, sleeping, living, and training together as teams until we left, trying to build cohesive units, but instead they sent us off helter-skelter for what they called "cross-training." I got a crash course in Vietnamese and another in heavy weapons. They weren't worth much.

In July they told us we were ready to go—though it was clear that we were only "ready" because they had to replace the returning teams, not because our training was completed. Ready or not, our team and three others from our company boarded the military version of the 707—no windows—and with Chill Will's "keep your powder dry" we were off to save Vietnam from the Communists.

CAN THO

The landing at Tan Son Nhut, outside of Saigon, was a letdown. Vietnam looked old and beat up, and it had a peculiar odor to it—the odor of an ancient and hard-worked country. I was depressed. The plate-glass window in the air terminal had a big crack in it. I went in and ordered what turned out to be a really nasty hamburger and a warm Coke. "Oh, Jesus," I said to myself, "this is going to be a real kick in the ass."

We were in Tan Son Nhut just long enough for the

hamburger and Coke and then they flew us north to Nha Trang. There they issued us new weapons—M-2 carbines, the automatic carbines that could fire seven hundred rounds a minute if you could load that fast. They took us out to the range and told us to test-fire our weapons. They told us, "Be sure and police up your brass, now; don't leave it lying around, or the VC will come down and pick it up and reload it and shoot it back at you." We thought that was bullshit, but we did what they said.

From Nha Trang we flew out over the beautiful beach and back across Saigon to Can Tho, the largest city in the Delta. Can Tho was muggy and hot, and a shimmer of pink dust seemed to hang over everything. They took us into town that afternoon. There was a tailor shop where you could have the sleeves of your uniforms cut off; that was allowed in Vietnam. Can Tho is a very crowded city, very dirty, very old. The houses are close to each other, and there were all kinds of people on the streets, not much vehicular traffic, just people walking.

I got a strong impression of tremendous poverty, first around Tan Son Nhut and then in Can Tho. The houses the people were living in were like shanties, very tumble-down, made of straw, cardboard, and tarpaper, with corrugated tin roofs. I've never seen anything quite so bad: even share-croppers' shacks in the South are quite a bit better than what the people live in in Vietnam.

They told us Can Tho was completely safe. We were even advised not to take our weapons downtown, and we didn't. The truck went down the little narrow streets, and every-where there were little kids running out and cheering. We assumed that the people of Can Tho must be on our side, or it wouldn't be safe to go downtown. But I suppose kids cheer anybody.

We were billeted at the end of the airstrip. The camp was a base for the "B" detachments—headquarters companies—that served all the "A" detachments in the IV Corps area, including the village of Hiep Hoa, where our camp would be.

When we got back to the barracks, they set up some briefings for us and made plans for aircraft to take us out to Hiep Hoa as soon as possible. After dinner and the inevitable pinochle game, I went next door to the NCO club and drank some beer. We were all pretty tired from so much traveling and not having caught up with the time change, so I came back, lay down, and dozed off.

Wham! The next thing I knew, something exploded right over my head and I felt a brutal slap in the leg. The safest area in the Delta was under mortar attack. Shells were falling all around—*bam! bam! bam!* I dropped to the floor and grabbed my carbine off the wall. I was trying to load the son of a bitch, when just as quickly the attack was over with, before I even got it loaded.

I don't know who I'd have shot at. I didn't even know which direction the mortar shells were coming from. It was complete confusion; guys were howling and yowling all around me. I crawled over to one black guy near me. He said, "I'm getting cold, man. I'm *cold.* I'm hit somewhere." I started feeling around him, and I felt the wet. It was down the small of his back, a nice little hole, big enough for me to put my finger in. I could feel the blood running out of it. "Shit," I said, "I can't do nothing for this guy, especially in the dark."

I felt something wet in my boot, and I found a big hole in my leg, and a big glob of blood. I pulled a chunk of metal out of my own leg.

By this time the people who were on the perimeter, supposedly guarding the place, were firing a few bursts with a machine gun, and then someone turned the lights on in the damned barracks and we could see what was going on. Colby came through and said, "Okay, everybody, turn the lights out and go back to bed." At that one guy just about lost his mind: "What the hell do you mean! We're under attack! And you're telling everybody to go back to bed?"

Fifteen or twenty rounds had come in; the first round knocked out the radio and every one of them hit something. Sometime earlier, the VC must have paced off the distance from every structure to where they set up their tubes.

It really shook us up. It was our second day in the country, and we weren't expecting anything. It was the first I knew that the Vietcong *had* mortars, and that they were hostile. We thought maybe we'd find some of them if we went looking for them; we didn't think *they'd* come looking for *us*. But in the second largest city in the area they were able to attack the airstrip, to come in and leave without being caught. That seemed to indicate that they had a lot of support from the local people.

The VC disappeared as soon as they set up their mortars and fired their rounds but it took five hours before I was gone. They carried us to a French hospital in town and then flew us out, back to an Army hospital in Nha Trang. It was three weeks before I rejoined my team in Hiep Hoa.

It was hardly an auspicious beginning, but our contingent was to be plagued for the entire tour. Of the four teams that flew out from Bragg together, one would be ambushed, another overrun, seven of us would be taken prisoner, and two of our number executed.

HIEP HOA

When my leg healed they flew me into Hiep Hoa to join my team. From the air, the flat countryside wasn't much to look at: a few scattered villages strung along a muddy river, the canals that fed into it, occasional palm trees, and what seemed to be endless miles of cane fields separated by dikes. As the plane went into a tight turn to line up with the short runway, I got my first glimpse of the camp itself. It looked like one of the stationary forts that had screwed up the French so badly.

Strange, I thought. "The guerrillas you're fighting are a fluid element that can move in and strike and move out again," they had drummed into us at Bragg. "To combat these people, you must also be fluid." But here they were doing exactly what they had told us not to do—dropping us down in these goddamned French forts.

Set at the end of the runway in the middle of the cane fields, the camp was diamond-shaped—about two hundred yards wide one way and maybe two hundred and fifty the other. Whoever had built it, us or the French, had surrounded it with a three-foot-high earth wall with a single apron of barbed wire extending out from it—not much of an obstacle to a determined attacker. The camp buildings had thatched roofs, with short reed walls supporting wire screening that extended to their eaves.

About half a mile south-southwest of the camp was Hiep Hoa's largest hamlet. From the Oriental River the hamlet ran for about a mile along a major canal. One or two thousand

P.O.W.: TWO YEARS WITH THE VIETCONG

people lived there in two-room thatch and bamboo houses with mud floors as hard as cement. The river and the canal were the roads for the farmers of the area; the canal was wide and heavily traveled, and there was a lot of commercial traffic on it. Small, skinny boats with little stern sweep paddles or primitive putt-putt engines moved up and down it continuously.

Some rice and vegetables were grown in the area, but most of the people worked either in the cane fields or at the sugar mill that sat beside the river, half a mile north of the camp at the far end of the airstrip. Later on, Horne told me that the mill and the cane fields belonged to Madame Nhu, Diem's sister-in-law. We were there to keep her sugar mill from being overrun by the Vietcong. Of course the French had a certain amount of stock in it too. It was run by a bunch of French supervisors who had a club in the mill where we would occasionally go and drink beer. There were a couple of MAAG* advisers up at the mill too, attached to the ARVN artillery unit billeted there in an old French housing compound. Sometimes they would fire their two 155 mm cannons at a VC village nearby.

Our own team house was a combination radio shack, kitchen, dining room, and sleeping quarters. It had a lot of added comforts—Camacho handed me a cold beer as soon as I stepped in the door. While I had been recuperating in Nha Trang, the rest of the team had thoroughly settled in. The preceding "A" team had shown them the ropes and already the atmosphere was relaxed, just short of lethargic. The kerosene refrigerator was well stocked, we had a cook and some "boys" to clean the house, and we had a routine.

Captain Horne welcomed me in and assigned me to Camacho's mortar as assistant gunner. "Hey Camacho," I asked when we were out in his bunker checking out the tube,

* Military Assistance Advisory Group—U.S. advisers.

44

"where are the damned VC?"

"Who knows?" he shrugged. He told me that one of the so-called "reliable informants" contacted by the team intelligence officer would report VC companies and battalions in the area, then the others would say there was no such thing. There hadn't been any attacks or contacts on patrols before I'd arrived. Nonetheless, Horne had jumped channels straight to group headquarters in Nha Trang for an airdrop of ammunition after Lieutenant Lieu, the Vietnamese commander, had said that he had received reports of a large VC force in the area preparing to attack.

"The ammo arrived all right," Camacho said. "But the attack didn't." Our "B" team at Can Tho got royally pissed off—not so much because Nha Trang was told about the attack before they were, but because Horne had panicked before confirming the reports. They sent Horne a letter saying that we were the "most unprofessional team" in Vietnam, but Horne laughed it off and we sympathized with him. We figured that the up-country team led by the alcoholic with a tic was worse than we were. (That guy got relieved, finally, but his replacement wasn't much better. He came back to the camp one evening so drunk that he couldn't drive the truck through the front gate—tried three times, knocked down the guard post, gave up, and walked in.)

Nevertheless, if I had to summarize what we were doing in Hiep Hoa, "nothing" would pretty much suffice. Of course, we found things to do—but for what nobody knew, and nobody seemed to care much either.

What time we got up in the morning was based on individual preference and metabolism. My day usually started between nine and ten with multiple cups of coffee and breakfast prepared by Mr. Loc, the cook. Some of the team might already be up and out, others would still be dawdling over coffee, perhaps one or two would still be in the sack.

Then Morley and I would check the camp's two small

dispensaries—one set up for the treatment of the villagers and supposedly run by the Vietnamese, the other for the strike force and manned by striker medics under our supervision. If we had enough supplies, we might take some strikers and an interpreter out to a nearby village and conduct sick call for three or four hours, coming back to camp for supper. After supper some people might go up to the sugar mill or into Hiep Hoa to drink beer. Four of us generally settled down for what became a marathon pinochle tournament. Back at Bragg, I'd make about ten bucks a night playing pinochle, but these guys wouldn't play for money. Morley and I always played together—he wasn't especially good, but we cheated, and that made up for it. If the others were in a good mood—determined by how badly they were losing—our game would go on well beyond midnight.

The days weren't much different for other members of the team. Roraback and Potter, one of the team's three blacks, busied themselves checking over their radios and sending and receiving the routine messages and reports. Weber and Camacho played with their tubes and expended a little energy training a generally unwilling Vietnamese strike force. Along with the demolitions men, McClure and Shannon, they would periodically check fortifications and recommend improvements which we could never do anything about. Horne met with Lieu, and sometimes went the rounds of the local villages inspecting the public works projects we were financing. Sometimes Lieu and Jasper, the black intelligence sergeant, would jaunt around from one "reliable informant" to another on the two motorbikes they had lifted from two VC "suspects." Lieutenant Colby was forever wanting to mount patrols and take some sort of offensive action, but few materialized. He was so frustrated that he would sometimes climb the observation tower with his M-1—with a maximum accuracy of maybe five hundred yards—and take pot shots at farmers a couple of miles away.

It wasn't that we were lazy or didn't know what should be done. To a man, we all had things that needed doing and wanted to do them, but we lacked the means and often the willing manpower to initiate real programs.

The strike force we were supposed to be training was part of what was called the Civilian Irregular Defense Group. They were formally under the command of the LLDB*—the Vietnamese Special Forces. The LLDB were as arrogant with them as we were with our people, and considered them something less than human.

When the previous "A" team had arrived and established their camp, they had tried recruiting local people into the strike force. We paid them a thousand piastres a month—about ten dollars—and of course they were given rice rations. It wasn't a bad living, not great but not bad. They could buy a considerable amount of beer on ten dollars a month. They lived in the compound, or, if they were married, in a housing development right next to the camp. Some lived in Hiep Hoa.

From what I understood at the time, the government would come along and tell a guy, "You fight for us." If he said no, they took away his rice. So the guy either got out of the area, or he joined the Vietcong. But the Vietcong didn't pay anything. So if the guy happened to be slightly mercenary, he'd say, "Well, I'll go to work for the Americans, and when it comes to a fight, I'll just run away." Which is just what they did. Some of them ran away right after they got to the camp—and took their weapons with them. We figured that they came from the other side of the river, VC territory.

But a lot of our strikers weren't local people at all: they came from the Saigon jails. Saigon would get hold of the "B" team in Can Tho and say, "Well, we've got so many people in the jail. They're not really criminals, you know, they just

* *Luc-Luong Dac-Biet*—Vietnamese Special Forces.

didn't happen to be doing anything, so we arrested them. How would you like to have them in your strike force?" They'd send down thirty or forty to make up a platoon. Of course, these guys were happy to get out of the Saigon jail, but they probably had no intention of fighting.

In a way their cases and mine were similar, but their cases were a little more dramatic. In Vietnam at that time, if you weren't working you were supposed to be in the Army, according to the government. If you didn't want to be in the Army, you ended up in jail by some means or other—you became a political criminal, if nothing else. I considered my situation more a normal chain of events—when I turned seventeen, either I got a job or I went into the Army.

The strikers had no motivation whatever and it was hard to get any of them to do anything. Weber and Camacho were in charge of infantry training—teaching them squad tactics, field operations, how to fire their weapons. They'd take them to the range, where they'd shoot their weapons without hitting anything. It didn't seem to worry them a bit; they laughed, had a big time, and went back to the barracks for dinner.

Besides the local people and the guys from the Saigon jail, we had a platoon of Cambodians. The Cambodians stayed apart from the Vietnamese, who in turn did nothing to hide their dislike for the Cambodians. Sometimes when they were drinking beer down in Hiep Hoa they'd get into fights. The Cambodians certainly were discriminated against, but Weber thought they were better soldiers than the Vietnamese. He singled them out to work with, trying to get them uniforms and equipment at least as good as the rest of the strike force had and maybe a little bit better. "Weber!" we told him. "You're going to get us into a big hassle with the Vietnamese."

But Weber went on with it anyway. He used to like to go down and drink beer with the Cambodians in Hiep Hoa. We cautioned him, "You shouldn't be too friendly with the strike force—familiarity breeds contempt." We had to maintain our arrogance.

The LLDB were supposed to take the strikers out on patrols every day, and at night they were supposed to set up ambushes and perimeter security. With the exception of one platoon, led by an LLDB we called Tennessee Ernie, most of the platoons didn't seem to want to go out. When they did, Camacho seldom went with them, but Weber went along occasionally, and so did Colby, the executive officer. Colby would paint his face all over with camouflage paint. We'd laugh at him—"Where's Colby, where's Colby, anybody seen Colby? Oh, there he is; there's his hat, anyway." Even Horne did it sometimes. Colby'd get madder than hell. Nobody else would put the damned paint on—"Christ, Colby, if they miss you, they ain't going to miss you because of that paint!"

The striker patrols were usually very short; they'd last three or four hours at most. Sometimes Lieutenant Lieu would take them out on patrol in trucks. They seemed to think it was all a big game, and the way they did it, it was. They'd go out and beat the cane fields and run around the rice paddies for a while. Of course, they didn't find anybody, because they went to places where they didn't *expect* to find anybody. They were just putting in their time. It was more like a training session than trying to combat the enemy.

The ambushes never produced anything either, and the night security force would just move out a little distance from the camp and go to sleep. I think Horne asked Lieu why he didn't take them out on some two- or three-day patrols. "That would be very bad for morale," Lieu told him. "The troops would not like that, they like to spend their evenings in camp."

Lieu was another of the things that everybody knew needed to be done—done in. We all figured he was worth at least one VC company in the camp. Horne had no confidence in him whatever and let us all know it. Lieu had thirty-five more people on the payroll than he had in camp, Horne told us, and Horne led us to believe that he knew much more about Lieu—that he was much more corrupt and inefficient than we could see on the surface.

Lieu wasn't interested in any serious military operations; that was obvious. He didn't go over and take Rach Nhum, which was clearly the target he should have been dealing with. Rach Nhum was a village about two miles away across the canal. It was a "known VC village"—nobody could get close to it without getting shot at. Sometimes the ARVN units would shoot at Rach Nhum, and Rach Nhum would shoot back. That's as far as the ARVN would push it; they'd turn around and come home. They'd even start out in armored personnel carriers—really going to war—but in a little while they'd be back. "Well, we couldn't penetrate." They were a bunch of phonies, worse than the strike force.

Sometimes we'd decide to fire some mortar rounds at Rach Nhum, or the guys at the sugar mill would get drunk and say, "Let's go out and shoot up Rach Nhum," and they'd shell it with their 155s—usually over our heads at night while we were playing pinochle. Colby wanted us to attack it by ourselves, but nobody really wanted to go with him except Weber. Once Colby actually radioed Can Tho to ask if we could attack Rach Nhum—"Request permission to attack Rach Nhum and wipe it out." But Can Tho told us no, we weren't allowed to go on any offensives, that was up to the Vietnamese, and besides, our area was pacified.

We never quite figured out why there was no real action against a known VC village so close at hand. Maybe the Vietnamese district chief objected to it for political reasons, or maybe the ARVN were afraid to do the job themselves and equally unwilling to lose face if the strike force did it for them. Whatever the reason, we weren't allowed to attack a known VC village, and that raised a serious question as to just what we *were* supposed to do.

For Morley and me, the two medics, the situation was no better. We could have accomplished a good deal, but we were locked into the whole mess. The previous "A" team had trained a bunch of nurses and set up a dispensary in the camp, mostly for the benefit of the people in and around Hiep Hoa. Before our team took over the camp, there was a grand ceremony relinquishing control of the dispensary to the people of Hiep Hoa. From then on, trained local people would staff the dispensary and would get their medicines and supplies through Vietnamese channels from district headquarters.

But even before the celebration spirits had subsided, the district chief sent down some of his men to the dispensary and stripped it clean of everything of value—medicines, sterilizers, hypodermics, bandages—they didn't even leave a stethoscope. He wasn't *stealing* anything, since the facility had been turned over to him, but that was beside the point. When the Vietnamese dispensary requisitioned stuff through him, they wouldn't get a thing. The nurses trained by us and our predecessors were quite good—certainly better than the area had ever had before—but without medicines or equipment there wasn't much they could do. At least one of them, the wife of our best interpreter, Tex, went back to work at the sugar mill.

I set my own day's work. Basically, I was supposed to assist Morley in training a platoon of striker medics. We made up training schedules and tests and saw that the training was carried out, with the LLDB medic—who was really quite good—in charge.

The most interesting thing I did was go on sick call. Whenever we had enough supplies, I'd get a squad of strikers and an interpreter in a truck and go out to the surrounding villages and hold sick call. Morley would come along sometimes, but he was usually busy seeing to the nurses at the camp dispensary.

There'd be one hundred, two hundred, maybe three hundred people lined up for sick call, and it would usually last all day. The squad went out on a short perimeter around the place as security. If they saw anybody who looked suspicious, they stopped him, searched him, delayed him, arrested him, whatever the case might have been. Anybody who had a machete or a knife, they wouldn't let in line.

The people were very pleased with sick call. They'd call me *bac si*—doctor—because I was the nearest thing to a doctor they'd ever seen. They'd say I did them a lot of good. They were always very complimentary about it.

But the treatment wasn't much. Because of the pick-up nature of the program, I could only treat the symptoms. Once when a woman came up I asked the interpreter what she said was wrong.

"She worried," he said.

"Well, give her some tranquilizers."

"No, no, I don't mean that. She *wearied*."

"Give her some amphetamines, then."

People thought I gave them miraculous, wonderful cures. They'd last about twenty-four hours.

I knew better than to try to treat any chronic disease like tuberculosis. But you can't say, "Well, I'm not going to do anything for you," so I'd give them a shot of streptomycin, which is the treatment for TB. But you have to give it for a year for it to be useful, and I'd probably never see them again. We couldn't set up regular schedules for the vilages or hamlets, or even tell the villagers in advance what day and hour we would return, for fear of getting ambushed.

I couldn't cure TB and I couldn't cure what was wrong with most of them. I could treat cuts and bruises, headaches and boils, dispense antibiotics for infections, hand out medicine for worms. If they were worried, I could give them tranquilizers, and if they were wearied, I could give them amphetamines, both of which I had a good supply of. I dispensed great quantities of methyl salicylate—oil of winter-green—the Vietnamese version of the snake-oil medicines. They used it for everything from warding off motion sickness to relieving stomach disorders.

But all in all, it was frustrating as hell. I was a good medic; during that year of going to school eight hours a day I had learned more than a nurse—almost as much as a doctor. All this training, and they didn't even issue me a surgical instrument set; Horne finally had to get me one in Saigon. I had been taught to use anesthesia, but I had no facilities for it. I didn't even have ether. I didn't have the right kind of sterilizing facilities. They taught me to do all these things and when I reached Vietnam, they gave me a first-aid kit—lots of Band-Aids and a roll of sterile gauze and a vial of merthiolate.

Any damned fool could have given out aspirins, tranquilizers, and wintergreen oil. All my training was just down the drain. It was a great waste, and it was frustrating to realize that. To top it off, I couldn't keep a stock of medicines. We'd set up a program, it would go along great for a few days, and then we'd run out of everything. We'd sit around waiting to get resupplied. They'd say, "It's in short supply, somebody else already unloaded it, there's just so much in the country."

Going out to the surrounding villages and holding sick call was standard practice in Special Forces. It was good public relations, but it wasn't effective. It was like going out and passing out lollipops.

MARAUDING

Our favorite sick-call run was to a village called Ap Chong, a couple of miles from the camp across the canal. Like Hiep Hoa, Ap Chong was a Catholic village. It had a Catholic church, and Horne was having a school built there that would be a Catholic school and, incidentally, named after him. The only other school in the area was Catholic, too. The absence of temples and shrines gave me the impression that the area was primarily Catholic, with the exception of Rach Nhum, where there was some kind of Buddhist altar or shrine.

Ap Chong had a kind of dispensary, and we would take medicines to the priest there, who in turn would bring out the wine, and we'd sit and drink and talk. That's why we liked going to Ap Chong. Whether he was the village chief or not, this priest had the real power in Ap Chong. You could probably compare him to a smalltime warlord, what with the Diem family all being Catholics and one of Diem's brothers being an archbishop.* If he told them to do something, his villagers wouldn't endanger their ass by not doing it. They would become suspected Vietcong very quickly if they opposed the priest.

I didn't really question whether he had any political attitudes other than just kicking the hell out of people if they didn't do what he said. He would have made a good drill

* Actually the *Ngo* family—Ngo Dinh Diem, the president; Ngo Dinh Nhu and Madame Nhu, powers behind the throne; and Ngo Dinh Thuc, archbishop of Hué.

sergeant. He would line the people up for sick call and keep them under control. They seemed either to respect or fear him tremendously. Once, a woman was just milling around— maybe a hundred people would come out for a sick call in Ap Chong and they would all be pushing, shoving, milling around—and *whop!* He just slapped her on the head. She straightened up at once and the line became very orderly. Nobody else seemed to want to get slapped. Of course, I didn't try to obstruct him at all. That would have caused another hassle. We were supposed to be contributors to the situation, not controllers.

Ap Chong was a strategic hamlet. It was the classic strategic hamlet, not like Hiep Hoa, which was called a strategic hamlet but only had some barbed wire strung here and there and some guard posts. Ap Chong had mud walls around it, like our camp. It was set up for defense: to keep people out, or to keep them in.

One night the Vietcong went over and made them tear down about a thousand feet of the wall at Ap Chong. They got everybody out with their spades and shovels and tore down the damned wall. I don't know if the people cheered or not, but it would be pretty hard to remove a thousand feet of mud wall in something like eight hours unless the people wanted the damned wall taken down. From what I've learned about Vietnamese villages, the people would never consent to put walls around them unless they were forced to in some way. They're not the kind of people who can be herded into a concentration camp.

They took down a thousand feet of wall. The place was within a couple of miles of our camp; you could almost see it, but while it was happening, nobody bothered to tell us. They told us the next day: "The Vietcong been there and took down a thousand feet of wall."

Of course, our patrols didn't happen to know about it either. And none of our "reliable informants" knew about it until the next day. The VC came back later and took down some more, as I recall. They were going to take down the whole damned thing.

I never did find out how the priest felt about the wall. About that time our medicine ran out, and we never went back to Ap Chong.

I know there was some sort of Buddhist shrine or altar over towards Rach Nhum, because we burnt it down. It was a little religious shanty, out in the field by itself—they called everything a shrine that had an altar in it.

One morning, there was a goddamned red and blue Vietcong flag flying on the shrine. We woke up and saw the flag flying, and everybody was so pissed off that we decided to go over there and get it. We shelled it for about an hour just to soften it up. Colby got up on the observation tower and called in rounds, trying to hit that flag with a mortar. Then they got the ARVN from the sugar mill and the MAAG advisers and Captain Horne and all our platoons and just about *everybody* mobilized, and about two hundred of us finally went over there and took that damned flag down. Then we burned down the shrine just to spite them.

I think it was Tennessee Ernie's gang that put it to the torch. Ernie was very aggressive. He wore a .45 in his belt with the hammer cocked, and he used more ammunition on patrol than anybody else, so we all assumed he was shooting the hell out of somebody. He only produced one dead person, though—we all went down and took his picture. He was our only real body count.

I assume that Tennessee Ernie and his platoon burned down a lot more things around there. From what I heard, they would go out and raid a certain area. If they suspected Vietcong were there, or if they knew a Vietcong lived there, they'd burn the house down. Or if the people had been giving money to the Vietcong or were suspected of doing so, they'd burn down their houses. Or if they could find anyplace over around Rach Nhum that was undefended enough to go in, they'd burn it down.

Ernie got credit for being the best LLDB around. By reputation, his platoon was very efficient: they killed a lot of Vietcong. Maybe they did kill a lot, but I really doubt it.

Even though most patrols seldom got far enough from camp that they couldn't run back in ten or fifteen minutes, they would invariably shoot off four or five hundred rounds of ammunition. We'd hear it going, of course. When we asked the platoon leader what had happened, he'd report that they had killed two, three, many Vietcong. But Ernie's one dead VC was the only one we saw, and that's using the rule of thumb that anybody killed while running away is a VC.

They brought back prisoners, too, if they happened to catch somebody on one of these patrols. Anyone captured was declared a VC. How's a guy going to deny it? If you say he's one, he's a VC. If he's not on your side, if he's not in the army, he must be on the other side.

All the time I was at the camp we had so-called VC suspects, prisoners of war. The LLDB kept them in two little barbed-wire cages, one about five feet high that people could walk around in at a crouch and a smaller one about three feet high. You couldn't even sit up in the small one: those POWs lay down. They were out in the sun, with no shelter whatever, and they were in there day and night. I don't know how often they fed them. I'm not sure that they even *did* feed them, or give them water for that matter.

We withdrew from that, even though we were paying for the whole shebang. "This is the Vietnamese's project," we said. "They're their prisoners. They caught them, they can take care of them. This is not our concern."

One night I went into the dispensary to give a patient a shot. Lieu and one of our officers were inside with a bunch of other people. One of the LLDB non-coms had a guy in black pajamas on the floor, and he was smashing his knee into the guy's back. Of course the guy would yell like hell, and the NCO would just wham the hell out of him with his fist and beat the guy up. Then they'd ask him some questions, and you could see the guy was refusing to answer them. They were just whaling the hell out of the poor guy, and I asked somebody, "Hey, what's going on here?"

"It's none of your business," he said. "That guy's a . . . a VC. A VC squad leader."

"How d'you know he's a VC squad leader?"

"Oh, you know, they *said* he was."

"Well, *who* said he was?"

"Well, it's none of your business, just pretend you didn't see it."

They had another one in there too that they beat the shit out of. What they did to them later, I don't know. I never saw them again. Very likely they sent them to Saigon, because that's what happened to prisoners generally—the LLDB interrogated them, put them in the barbed-wire cages for a while, and then sent them to Saigon where they got the shit beaten out of them properly because they had professional interrogators in Saigon.

I can't recall anybody saying anything about the treatment of prisoners except maybe McClure. McClure, who was black, was quicker to recognize somebody being taken advantage of than I was. I didn't really pay any attention to it, because I considered that it was out of my line of responsibility and that there was no way that I could change it anyway. And I fully expected to be treated at least that badly if I was captured.

One time an ARVN unit in the area came across an undefended roadblock that they figured was probably booby trapped. That's what made roadblocks effective, the fact that the ARVN were afraid to take them apart. They could have driven a truck through it or used ropes to drag it apart, but instead they just recruited a couple of old farmers who were passing by to take the damned thing apart. Of course, it blew up in their faces.

They brought the wounded farmers to me at the dispensary. One of them had a great gaping hole in his chest from shrapnel, and I didn't have the instruments—or the experience—to go into his chest. I requested Saigon send a helicopter for a med evac, but they refused because he was a civilian. The Americans refused.

"He's going to die," I told them. "He's got a penetrating chest wound. I don't have the stuff to work on him here."

"Well, nothing we can do about it. We can't insult the Saigon government by going in with a helicopter ourselves and taking one of their civilians to our hospital. It has to be handled by them."

The man died, and nobody gave a damn except his family. They were there while he was dying. People say that Asians have no concern about lives, that it's no big deal for them, but they cried just as hard and as pitifully as any family that you can imagine.

The other fellow had a very slight wound, and we repaired him and sent him home after three or four days and never saw him again. I told him to come back in four or five days to have the sutures removed and get another shot of penicillin, but he never came back. I don't know whether he was a Vietcong; maybe he just wasn't coming back around us again. I don't blame him.

The fact that it was the ARVN and not us that got that farmer was an accident. With all his Ranger training and his gung ho spirit, Colby was frustrated as hell. Sometimes he'd climb up the observation tower and play forward observer, calling down fire missions while we manned the tubes. He liked having all the tubes fire illumination rounds timed to light up at the same time, and sometimes we'd go through twenty or thirty rounds—at about eighty-five dollars a round—before he got what he wanted. We shot off about forty rounds one afternoon at two farmers in an open field. "Fire mission! Two people in the open!" We got down there and just blasted them like hell with those mortars. Colby chased those people across the field. Imagine two guys in black pajamas running like hell, and mortar rounds falling, and they're changing direction, and the tubes are changing too. Camacho's down there cranking away. "Another degree to the right, another degree of elevation, drop round." *Bam!* *Bam!* We shot off all the ammunition at hand and had to go back and restock the ammo bunkers in the mortar pits. But we didn't hit the farmers.

Then one day Colby hit a village—accidentally. During one of these fire missions some rounds had fallen short or long or to the right or the left of where he was aiming them. They'd landed in what was supposed to be a friendly village across the river. A couple of houses had been damaged, and I think some children had been wounded. Colby took a squad and went over to apologize to them. He was surprised that it had done so much damage. "That thing cut the grass down for twenty-five yards in either direction," he said when he got back. "I didn't know those things would do that." Weber said, hell, yeah, they have a bursting range of such and such. Colby said, "I didn't know that."

He was playing, like a child with a toy. Imagine a kid who had two 81 mm mortars to fire at will; any time he felt like playing with them he could come out and yell, "Fire mission!" with his megaphone and have two people drop rounds in the tubes and watch them go out and go *boom! boom!* "Fire two more!" *Boom! Boom!*

He was assistant team leader, a lieutenant. That gave him all the authority he needed to tell us what to do.

I began asking some silent questions after I'd been there for a while. It must have been Horne who told me that it was Madame Nhu's sugar cane and sugar mill we were guarding. I considered it—"Madame Nhu's sugar mill? Isn't it for the Vietnamese people that I'm here?" "Well, it's a job," I decided. "We're guarding a sugar mill, somebody else is probably guarding a rubber plantation." Later on, I thought what a prostitution it was of the Special Forces to send them to Vietnam to guard Madame Nhu's goddamn sugar mill.

Tex, our best interpreter, came up one day: "Well, I've got to go vote today, got to have the day off." I said, "Who are you going to vote for?"

"Madame Nhu."

"Yeah? Well, who else could you vote for if you wanted to?"

He was slightly incredulous. "Well, Madame Nhu's *the only one* you can vote for."

While we were at Hiep Hoa, Diem was overthrown. The stories I'd been getting out of Saigon and from the *Army Times* was that Diem was becoming so unpopular in the United States that the U.S. had to do something to get rid of him. They either had to get rid of him or back out of the war, and they weren't about to back out of the war. The CIA admits now that Diem and the Nhus became so unpopular that they had to bounce their ass.

Of course, Madame Nhu left the country before her husband was killed. Just before that happened the black market rate for dollars almost doubled—she had thrown her piastres on the market to get "green" (dollars). She knew they were finished, and she was bailing out.

When the coup came, we didn't know what was going on. Things seemed to be all shook up. We were getting strange reports on the radio, and headquarters seemed excited; they weren't telling us everything that was going on. They did tell us that there had been a coup d'état in Saigon and that we were to stand by in an "emergency situation." Then the coup settled itself. It was apparent that the new president was somebody who favored the U.S. and that nothing had changed. The Buddhists stopped burning themselves, the Nhus were gone, and people seemed to be happier since Diem was gone. That was the only noticeable difference.

Something just wasn't right. I'd come here believing I was helping this government, but Jesus Christ, who *was* the government? It caused me to question my presence, my reason for being there. But I would always end up by saying, "After all, I *am* a professional soldier. This is the reason I am here. Even though this isn't the war of my choosing, or a war that is necessarily to the benefit of my country, I am a professional soldier and this is my job—to go fight wars."

It was one of those things you might think about but you didn't dare mention. I was a Special Forces soldier. I didn't talk politics; it was out of my realm of responsibility.

"PACIFIED"

Frustration and boredom were our worst enemies, and most of our activities were designed to defeat them. Morale was pretty good, nonetheless. The Army was paying our regular pay and allowances into the bank back at Bragg, and we were living on our per diem of nine dollars, which we doubled on the black market. We tried to keep at least two men in Saigon. When they returned, two others would go back on the same plane. Besides blowing it out on Tu Do Street, we picked up the mail and brought back steaks and booze from the PX.

Not that we didn't eat well enough off of local produce. Each of us threw about twenty-five dollars a month into the pot for food, and Mr. Loc, our cook, would go down to Hiep Hoa, the central marketplace for the whole area. The local people brought in their fruits and vegetables, and other things were brought in from Saigon.

It didn't take long before a clique developed that centered on the pinochle players. We always had something going. If it wasn't pinochle it was a horseshoe tournament or maybe just riding up to the sugar mill for a beer. We went down to Hiep Hoa for beer too, but we weren't quite as noisy about it as the previous team had been. From what I heard, they used to go downtown, get drunk in the little shanty-like bar, and have a rowdy time in Hiep Hoa. They were ambushed coming back one night. The Vietcong hid under a little bridge over a ditch and threw a grenade in their jeep, wounding some of the people.

Roraback and McClure weren't in our pinochle clique, and neither was Colby. He thought pinochle was a lot of foolishness, so he busied himself writing a book about bear-hunting with his father.

McClure was an outsider. He was never part of the crowd, nor even a part of the black crowd. And of course O'Neill was as obnoxious as ever. Though he didn't like Jasper or Potter much, he managed to get along with them. But McClure was still a "cotton-patch coon" to O'Neill, who couldn't resist harassing him every chance he got. Even Jasper would laugh sometimes. Naturally, McClure resented it. I didn't think it was quite right, but I chuckled at it. O'Neill was team sergeant, and it was politically good for me to chuckle at whatever the team sergeant thought was funny.

McClure was from Chattanooga, Tennessee. He volunteered for Special Forces out of a regular Airborne unit and became a demolitionist. I don't know whether it was by choice or assignment, because demolitions was considered the dump of the Special Forces. People who couldn't make it anywhere else were assigned to demolitions. McClure wasn't dumb by any stretch of the imagination, but he couldn't get along with people. He was stand-offish and very stingy. He used to go down to Hiep Hoa and buy a case of pop—as we all did—but rather than share it he'd stick it under his bed and drink it all himself.

I never did get along with him. We argued—whenever I could get him engaged in a damn argument. I even had big battles with him while we were prisoners. It was only at the end that I really got to know him, and then I realized that the guy had a lot of fears and emotions the same as anybody else. I tried to understand that maybe he was under more pressure than I was, because of his race and his background.

McClure had just been married before we went to Vietnam. He used to write his wife a letter every night. He'd set her picture beside him when he was writing, and Camacho would torment him about it. "What are you doing, McClure, writing to your mule again?" He'd picked that up in Korea. McClure would just seethe.

McClure was always very popular with the children. He'd go down to Hiep Hoa and buy some gum and candy and pass it around to the little kids. I didn't do that, not because I didn't want to give candy to kids, but because if you gave some to one, you had the whole goddamned village there. They just swarmed all over you, and I didn't want to get involved in that much of a ruckus.

Camacho and I spent a lot of time together at Hiep Hoa. We used to go to Saigon together. We would stand around drinking birch beer at the soda pop stand a couple of little girls had outside the gate at the camp. His background was something like mine. He was from a Mexican-American family in El Paso, and his father had been killed in an automobile accident when he was young. I think his mother used to work in a restaurant, and from what I could gather they had seen some pretty hard times.

Like me, Camacho went into the Army when he was young. I assumed he might have done it for the same reason I did: things just weren't too damned good for him in '55 when he went in. He was in the Eleventh Airborne at about the same time I was, and in Germany too, but in a different unit. We related because of that—the bond of the Eleventh Airborne, the tremendous arrogance that he and I still felt. It was something we had learned in our childhood, and it was almost ingrained in us.

Rather than getting out of the Army, as I had, he'd stayed in and been promoted. He was a sergeant first class when I met him in Special Forces. He was a good Special Forces man. He really lived it. He'd had a couple of missions before he came on our team—one in Vietnam, another in Laos. And he was a career man, a lifer. Hell, I was a potential lifer too.

The days passed effortlessly, if not productively. My medical missions seemed to dwindle. I wasn't getting the supplies that I needed, and I got disenchanted with it besides. We were bored with the whole situation.

Then headquarters decided we would establish a new camp. They sent us a dozen outboard motors. "Where the hell are we going? We don't have any boats!" We got orders to establish a camp about ten miles closer to the Cambodian border. The actual site was secret; they didn't want us getting ambushed as we went in. They told us we'd get boats.

Our new mission was border surveillance. We'd be integrated with a plan to establish a series of camps along known or suspected infiltration routes. We had fulfilled our mission at Hiep Hoa: it was officially pacified. The place had never been attacked and there hadn't been any problems—except for VCs tearing down that thousand feet of wall at Ap Chong. We had control of the area, at least during the daytime, and it could be turned over to the Vietnamese. The camp would still be there, garrisoned by the strike force under LLDB command, but there wouldn't be any need for Americans to train more people. We were doing what Special Forces were supposed to do—establish a camp, train the people so they could be self-sufficient, supply them, and then move on and do the same thing over and over again until they had camps all over the country.

We were even getting rumors at the time that Kennedy thought the war had been won and was getting ready to withdraw everybody. We were worried about our jobs, as the same thing had already happened in Laos. It must have been the padded reports. We were padding *our* reports; everybody was. We were saying that we had accomplished all these missions—when we went out on patrol of course we always killed several dozen Vietcong—and the area was pacified, when actually we weren't doing a damn thing. We padded our reports, and the next echelon padded theirs, and on up the ladder until it got to the Pentagon. "Jesus Christ, the war's over in Vietnam. Got *that* settled right away."

Apparently, Kennedy figured the whole country was pacified. But if he had ever read *Catch-22* he would have known that everybody lies all the way up the line, because it's *demanded* that you lie. If you sent in a true report—"We didn't do anything today"—then they would write back a letter saying, "What the hell you mean, you didn't do anything? What do you think you're doing out there anyway? Please send in a true report." Either that or they'd relieve you, and nobody wanted to get relieved.

Colby or Horne usually wrote the reports. They were going to put me in for a Bronze Star and the Army Commendation Medal, though I hadn't done a goddamn thing except win at pinochle. But they had to give out so many medals because so many medals had been allocated, and we had to divide them up. "You've done a good job around here," Horne said. "Look at all those people you've cured, like the old lady down the road there that you gave those amphetamines to."

Whether or not Special Forces was being phased out, the idea of going into a new area was exciting. Our camp at Hiep Hoa was becoming very dreary. We were really bored with the damn place—even with the pinochle games. The fact that we had a dozen motors meant that there would be a boat for each of us, and we could maybe have motorboat races. We knew about another team, located in a network of canals, that used to race their motorboats. They'd run them to Vietcong territory to a place where they'd get shot at, then turn around fast just to taunt the VC.

I was even getting tired of Saigon. I'd sent for some green from the States—about a hundred dollars in bills that I could exchange on the black market—and somebody had swiped it in the mail. Thanksgiving was on the twenty-sixth that year, and right after Thanksgiving Camacho and I were going to Saigon. It would be our last trip before coming back to the

States. We had something like three weeks left in the country.

Three days before Horne was to take half the team out to the new campsite, one of Jasper's "reliable informants" reported a battalion or so of Vietcong in the area, about four hundred men. He said they were preparing to attack either the camp or the sugar mill or a nearby ARVN detachment. It was night when we got the information, and we all ran out and put our steel helmets on and sat in the mortar pits smoking cigarettes. All was quiet so we went back into the house and started up the pinochle game again.

The next day Colby was assigned to verify the information. Normally, you're supposed to take a probing patrol out and *find* those people, but Colby called Saigon for a liaison airplane and took a ride around the countryside. He didn't find anything—the Vietcong weren't stupid enough to pitch their tents out in the middle of a goddamn cane break. They were hidden somewhere, probably in the villages across the river. Colby came back and said, "Oh, bullshit, there's nobody around." Then he took off for Saigon to pick up the month's supplies, including some steaks for dinner.

Colby probably wouldn't have been able to mount a patrol even if he'd wanted to. That time of year it was pretty wet, and the water was waist-high in places where you had to cross the cane breaks. The strikers didn't want to go out and do *that*. Even if they had gone, they probably wouldn't have found anybody. They would have gone a couple hundred yards and returned empty-handed.

It didn't help any that the same "reliable informant" had reported the previous attack that didn't happen, when Horne had had all the extra ammo dropped in and earned us the "most unprofessional team" award. We figured we had another false alarm on our hands. They had never attacked us; they weren't *going* to attack us. The area was pacified.

The morning after Colby's recon a couple of helicopters arrived to transport half the team to the new camp. Weber was gung ho to go. He took Tennessee Ernie's platoon and left us Lieu. Morley used to ride convoy all the way to Saigon standing behind a mounted machine gun with his beret over his eye, and they wanted him to go. I wasn't going to volunteer for anything.

It took the helicopters about two hours of shuttling to get the detail over, and then the rest of us were left just piddling around—Roraback, Camacho, McClure, and me. Colby came back with the wrong cut of steak. We lazed around and played a little horseshoes. We couldn't play pinochle because the real pinochle gang was gone. Even though Roraback was a terrible player, he, Camacho, and I could have made a game if Tex, the interpreter, had wanted to play. Tex had been in the Vietnamese Air Force, trained in the States, lost a leg in a crash. He lived in the housing compound just outside the camp. He was always ready to play a game of pinochle, and if a game was already in progress he'd stand around and wait for somebody to get tired or mad and quit.

I suggested he join us in some pinochle.

"No," he said. "I think I'll go home and go to bed with my wife." It seemed a bit unusual. Nobody could remember his going home so early before. But I didn't think much about it. Nothing was happening; everything was quiet. The Cambodian platoon was outside the camp on night security, and it wasn't my turn on the guard roster. At eight or nine I gave it up and turned in.

Before morning I would be a POW.

PART TWO: ENEMY TERRITORY

VILLAGE TO VILLAGE

"Guerrillas don't take prisoners," they had told us at Bragg. Guerrillas don't have the facilities, can't afford the men for guard duty, can't handle the logistics of feeding prisoners and guards. Prisoners jeopardize security and impair mobility, they told us—told us when *we* were supposed to be the guerrillas, or at least advisers to the guerrillas. Every time I thought about it, my stomach would tighten up and I'd get the cold shivers.

There could be only one reason for the VC to take us along—interrogation. That thought in itself was enough to make me wonder if it wouldn't have been a lot easier to go down shooting. I had learned a few torture techniques at Bragg too, under the guise of "Countermeasures to Hostile Interrogation." If there were any countermeasures, I wished they'd told us.

While the VC swarmed over the camp, rounding up all our guns and ammo, all kinds of unpleasantness they'd told us about at Bragg passed through my mind. "The enemy will know you are part of an elite organization. As such you will be prized as a prisoner, since it will be known that you will possess valuable tactical and/or strategic information. Try to withhold for twenty-four hours any information that can compromise your group.

"Remember, once you give some information, the enemy will want more. When you can't give any more, or they tire of torturing you, you will be killed."

There had been variations on the theme: "If you are in an enemy-secure area, instead of shooting you when the interrogation is completed, they may try to brainwash you for propaganda purposes. A common practice is to tie a prisoner behind a cart and drag him from village to village, giving him only garbage to eat and foul water to drink. This is done in front of the villagers to show how the mighty have fallen, and the villagers are encouraged to heap abuse, verbal and physical, on the prisoner. In each village a mock trial is held, and the villagers condemn him. Eventually, broken in mind and body, the prisoner is executed in a manner equally demeaning. Because of the elite character of Special Forces, we are often singled out for this treatment."

Over cards at the camp, or drinking beer in Saigon, I'd heard all the stories about Special Forces that had been captured in Laos and kept in caves and had their fingers chopped off. Camacho had told me about a team leader who was caught and cut apart, piece by piece. A month before, Pitzer and Rowe, a couple of guys from Leitz's team, had been caught in a battalion-sized ambush. We'd heard that the VC were taking them from village to village making spectacles of them and that the villagers were beating them with sticks.

As the VC hustled us out over a pile of striker bodies into the cane, being a prisoner was nothing to look forward to.

When they sat us down in the middle of the little hamlet by the river, I asked Camacho if he knew what had happened to the other guys. We were still under guard, but the mood had relaxed. Everybody was laughing and chattering, and it was obvious that the soldiers and the villagers were no strangers to each other. Our curiosity value had diminished some, though it was still difficult to put out one cigarette before someone gave us another one. Nobody seemed to mind our talking.

Camacho shrugged. He didn't know about Roraback. He'd seen him go out of the house, but hadn't seen him after he got outside. McClure was heading for the other end of the camp as fast as his feet would take him. We speculated how McClure had got through the barbed wire that I had had to crawl under.

Camacho thought Colby had escaped, bare-assed and all. "All he had on was his goddamned Ranger harness." Colby and Camacho had covered each other getting out of the camp, when Camacho discovered the rest of us were missing. Colby took off into the high grass; I guess I would have too, under that much fire. But Camacho took a piss behind the little girls' soda-pop stand and decided he couldn't just leave us. Maybe somebody was caught somewhere and couldn't move, or was wounded, he figured. So he went back in and started firing and then got hit in the back of the head with a rifle butt.

That's what he told me. If it's true, he should have had the medal of honor for it. It was suicide coming back into that camp.

Smashing our camp was a major victory for the Vietcong. They hadn't taken a Special Forces camp before—though they did it many times afterwards. As at Can Tho they had made first-round hits; we figured they must have paced it off. Besides someone inside placing the demolition charge, Camacho told me that at least one of the camp's .30-caliber machine guns had been turned in. That might have been the tracers I saw: every fifth round in a machine-gun belt is a tracer. From what we could make out, Camacho and I had been the only two on our side doing any shooting.

"Get any?" he asked.

"Took a few shots at some over by the housing area.

Couldn't tell if I hit any."

"Hell, that wasn't *these* guys. That was the strike force making tracks for town."

Being able to talk with Camacho made me feel a little better, but it didn't really change the situation. They had us sitting on a bench in the middle of the square where the villagers would probably set out and sell their vegetables. It was surrounded by about a dozen small thatched houses. The night sky was clear, and I think the moon was out; we could see pretty well. Most of the Vietcong soldiers who had come back across the cane fields with us had gone aside at the entrance to the village. I figured they probably had boats waiting to take them across the river. Our conversation was interrupted by the others getting to their feet and getting ready to move out.

As I stood up, I reached down and felt something warm and wet on my leg, like blood. I motioned to the guard that there was something wrong with me, and he came over and bent down to look at my leg. He said something to the others and then very carefully used his cigarette to burn off a huge leech. He showed me what it was.

As we started from the village toward the river, I asked Camacho what he thought they were going to do with us. He just shrugged and shook his head.

I'd guessed right about the boats. Our three guards loaded us on a long, narrow boat with seats running down the sides under a low wooden canopy. It had a tiny single-lung motor, and when the boatman started it up, we headed downstream. "Jesus Christ!" I thought. "They're going to take us right by the goddamned sugar mill." There were three other boats with us on the river, carrying maybe twenty VC. As we neared the sugar mill, the boatman cut the motor and the guards put their hands over their mouths to warn us not to talk or shout.

The mill was all lit up as we glided past on the current. But the MAAG and the ARVN were obviously not watching the river—no one shouted or fired a shot—and once we were past, the boatman started up the motor again and we chugged a short distance past the mill on the far side of the river. Then we slid into a small canal and docked at a little hamlet.

I couldn't be sure, but from the position of the mill the hamlet was probably the one Colby had shelled.[2]

In the hamlet, we got a new set of guards. Apparently they had been detailed from the main group to take us to wherever we were supposed to go, or they had been standing by to take up prisoners if there were any. They let us wash ourselves in the canal, and we got rid of all the mud and crud we had picked up while we were slipping and sliding around the cane fields running away from Hiep Hoa.

Unlike the first village, this one was strung out in a line along the canal rather than collected around a square. The guards took us into one of the houses and looked after Camacho's head wound. With the blood washed away, it didn't look serious—a cut perhaps an inch and a half long. They wanted to give him a shot of penicillin but I motioned to them not to bother. They bandaged it up, and then they settled us down to wait for daylight.

At first light the guards started marching us downstream along the river. On the other side we could see the sugar mill and helicopters flying over what was left of the camp. Apparently they didn't see us, even though we were moving over open terrain. The sugar mill's 155s had finally opened up and were firing at Rach Nhum—the opposite direction from the one we had taken when we left the camp.

We passed opposite the village of Hiep Hoa where the canal came into the river, and continued walking down the river. We stopped at a number of hamlets, some very tiny and others bigger than Hiep Hoa, but I didn't recognize any of them. At each stop the people would welcome our guards, and then the guards would tell Camacho and me to sit down.

Somebody would give us cigarettes, and while somebody else brewed tea the rest of the village would gather to stare at us. They'd share the tea with us, and then we'd move on to the next village.

They may have been marching us from village to village to get us somewhere, but they stopped everywhere to display us to the people. But we weren't humiliated—in the first village an old man gave me a pair of pants. We weren't being dragged behind an ox cart with only garbage and foul water to drink. We ate what the guards ate, they weren't holding any trials, and the people weren't spitting on us or beating us with sticks. Sometimes the people were clearly upset and agitated when they saw us, but the guards made it clear that we were prisoners of the Front and they shouldn't hurt us. The closest we came to any abuse was when an old woman in one village couldn't restrain herself and started hitting Camacho with a walking stick. But the guard pushed her back and stopped her before she hurt him.

In one of the villages, someone gave me some old clothes to wear—a net-weave shirt and an old pair of beat-up green cotton pants. They were about four sizes too small, but they were better than no pants at all. The villagers were pretty nice. They really tried to offer me what they had, even though I was a prisoner of war. In another place an old man gave me a pair of old leather shoes. "Here, try these on," he motioned.

"Well, they're too small."

He brought a larger pair. "Try these on."

"Too small, too."

He let me keep the larger pair, and they tried to cut the toes out so I could walk in them. It didn't work; they were too tight, they just turned my feet in worse. Camacho was lucky—he had worn his boots out of the team house.

In some of these houses, the family runs the little village store on the side, and the guards would take us in and give the family some money. They'd get some cigarettes, several packs so they'd have enough for themselves and for us along the way. They'd buy cookies and a bottle of beer for us. We'd sit there, and somebody would bring in some tea. They'd give us rice and fish when they had the opportunity, and these things were just snacks along the way. The people would say something like, "Well, we've had some pastry here for the last week or so, just saving it for a special occasion, we'll give it to these guys."

I had always thought, "Hell, the villagers don't *like* these guys, the villagers are on *our* side." But it was quite the contrary—every place we went the Vietcong were accepted and *we* were the odd people.

At one point, while we were walking along in the open between villages, a helicopter came close overhead. The guards didn't try to hide, and the helicopter passed on. But I had a terrible thought: helicopters invariably shoot at Vietnamese who run. Do the soldiers know this, I wondered. Is it only the peaceful farmers who run—and get shot?

At nightfall we were in yet another village south of Hiep Hoa. They fed us some rice and fish, and the guard changed. Until then the guards had worn the black uniforms and camouflage helmets of a Vietcong regular, but the new guards wore the normal black pajamas that everybody else wore, with perhaps a stray piece of military webbing here or there. They were a mix of older and younger men, probably local irregulars. Through hand signals and half a dozen words that we understood, they conveyed the impression that we would be returned to Hiep Hoa and released.

It didn't sound so impossible. Lying in the dark, Camacho and I talked it over and decided it might explain our good treatment: clean us, feed us, and turn us loose for propaganda purposes.

THROUGH THE CANALS

Whether they ever meant to or not, the VC didn't take us back to Hiep Hoa and turn us loose. Maybe they figured that if we thought we were going back to the camp, we wouldn't try to escape, and their job would be easier. The guard changed from time to time, like relays; they'd take us maybe twenty miles and turn us over to someone else. Later on, another set told us that we were going to be taken to Saigon and released.

The morning after our capture we walked for about three hours along the dikes through the rice fields until we came to another village. There we were turned over to three or four new guards in black pajamas. The damned dikes were as hard as concrete, and by this time my feet seemed like two big throbbing bruises. But our new guards had a little boat, and with a great sense of relief we piled into it and started paddling through the canals. They took us up one canal and down another, switched to a smaller one, back to a larger one, first in one direction, then another, all through the night. Shortly after daybreak we came into a large canal and stopped at a village as big as Hiep Hoa.

After traveling all night, we were happy to get there. The people of the village obviously expected us—they took us to one of the little houses and fed us rice and fish. By that time we were pretty much relaxed. The guards were treating us well and we knew that there was some destination in mind, because we had been traveling and traveling through the canal system all night.

I was taking it easy with a cigarette and a cup of tea when all of a sudden two or three men ran in. "Come on! Let's go!" they said, chattering and waving their arms. They hustled us out of the house and down to a small canal in back, got us into a boat and crossed the canal as fast as possible, then pushed us out into a big swamp covered with high grass. At first we didn't know what the hell was going on, but before we got across the canal we could hear what it was—helicopters. "Jesus Christ, maybe they know we're here. They're trying to rescue us!"

They came in low, firing their rockets into the village. When they had fired off everything they had, a B-26 arrived for bombing and strafing. It had a vulcan cannon which fires five thousand rounds a minute, and the bullets went *dit! dit! dit!* beside us in the water. "Son of a bitch! Why doesn't he shut that thing off after he passes over the village!" The guards told us "Stay down!" and I told them not to worry. My standing up and waving at the B-26 was sure as hell not going to stop that gun.

The air attack went on all day. I didn't hear the village returning any fire. One group of helicopters would finish and another would take over. At one point, what looked like a ten-'copter landing force came over, but then went on. Little spotter planes were flying around, like the one Colby had commandeered to look for the VC. I couldn't understand why the hell they didn't see us—that many people down there hiding in the grass.

I was so worn out that I went to sleep—with water up to my waist, red ants crawling all over me, a B-26 strafing, helicopters buzzing around and around. Camacho just couldn't believe it.

At the end of the day the planes all went away. After that attack, you'd think that the Vietnamese would really have been pissed off at us, but they didn't blame us a bit. They realized that we had been under the gun just as they had been. They brought one of the boats into the swamp and got us into it, and the first thing they did was give us pastry. We hadn't eaten all day, and they realized we were hungry. You'd think that the last thing they'd be concerned about would be feeding the prisoners. Getting the hell out of the area is what I'd have been concerned about.

We never did see where they'd been attacked. We went back up the other side of the canal until we came to a little hut, where they told us to go inside.

There on a table lay McClure, puffing on a great big old cigarette, one of the homemade kind. I had thought he was dead or had escaped. "Damn, McClure! I didn't know you smoked!"

"First time I did, and it sure tastes good!"

For a while it was like a family reunion. "How'd you get through that barbed wire, McClure?" "Hell, I didn't know there *was* any barbed wire there!"

He'd reached the other end of the camp and tried to get some strikers to fire—with about as much luck as I had had. The white-phosphorus round I'd seen land over his bed had spattered over his whole left side and a bigger piece had hit his foot. He couldn't walk very well, so when the attack on the village took place the VC took him to the hut and stayed with him all through the attack. "Roraback is out there someplace, because he was with me up until the attack. They took him somewhere else," McClure added. During the attack at Hiep Hoa McClure and Roraback had crawled out over a bunker and were trying to get through the barbed wire when they tripped one of their own flares, lit the place up, and were captured.

While the guards waited for dark, we tried to piece together what we knew about the attack at Hiep Hoa. The mortar barrage, we decided, had come from over towards Hiep Hoa village, and the troop assault from somewhere between the camp and the first village we were taken to—just about where Weber's Cambodian platoon was supposed to have been. Whether the Cambodians were wiped out, or simply ran, or whether they just hid in the grass and watched the attack, we didn't know. There was one other possibility, we decided: they might even have aided the Vietcong attack. The only thing we were sure about was that they hadn't put up any resistance or fired any warning shots.

We also agreed that the first-round hits and the swiftness of the attack meant that the Vietcong must have had inside help. For the first time, we recalled how Tex the interpreter had broken his routine and gone home early. We wondered if maybe the Americans were the only ones who hadn't known the camp was going to be attacked. We finally figured that Lieu, the LLDB commander, couldn't have known either. He might not have told us if he knew there was going to be an attack, but he wouldn't have been anywhere near the camp when it took place.

The guards let us talk until it got dark, and then they put us back in the boats. Camacho and I were put in one, McClure in another, and we started back along the route we'd traced earlier in the day. It was kind of dusky. I looked over and there was another boat. One of the people in it was wearing an Army fatigue hat—the Beetle Bailey type. I looked a little closer; it was Roraback. "Goggles! For Christ's sake, what are you doing out here?"

"Who is that?" He had lost his glasses and probably couldn't see us.

"It's Smith, who the hell you think it is?"

"What the hell are you doing out here?"

"I got captured, same as you."

Our voices tumbled across the water in conflict with those of the guards, who were also talking to each other. Roraback's boat came around, they transferred McClure to it, and we went on through the maze of canals.

We were hopelessly lost, but they had told us we were being taken to Saigon to be released, and we strained to catch a glimpse of the night glow over the city. Off in the distance we'd see flare ships dropping flares, and we kept thinking that they might be around Saigon someplace. Our camp had been about ten miles from the Cambodian border, and the way the border curves around, to be headed in another direction would have meant that we were headed toward Cambodia. When we noticed that each village we passed seemed smaller than the last one, our Saigon theory started to lose all credence.

We were way out in the country. Things were quiet; the only stirring was people talking or a chicken cackling. Voices drifted across the water. Occasionally we could hear somebody strumming a mandolin, but mostly it was people jibberjabbering, children laughing, a dog barking. We were told to keep quiet. We'd know we were near a village when the mosquitoes got worse and there was the smell of cooking fires, wood or charcoal. It was hot and muggy.

Our escorts paddled through the night and into the following day, stopping finally at a small house alongside a rice field. We were met by an old man and some younger men—if there were any women around, they stayed out of sight—who took us inside. The guards and paddlers disappeared. Our new hosts brought us rice and fish to eat, and tea to wash it down with. Afterwards they gave us the inevitable cigarettes and brought us little things to nibble on. They let us sleep, and we slept through most of the day.

Our guards reappeared when night fell, and we paddled on through the endless canals. The canals all appeared to have been man-made, but some of them may have been widened streams. Some of them seemed to have currents, because the boat would go faster. Others were completely still.

Eventually we ran out of clear canals into some overgrown

with heavy swamp grass, as if they hadn't been used for a long time. There were dikes along the canals, and it looked as if the land could have been rice paddies at one time, but now it was out of use. The fields were overgrown with small bushes, brush, something like scrub oak. The going got very tough for the paddlers but they kept at it hour after hour. When the grass seemed almost a wall, they'd jump out and push, but they never asked us to help or even to lighten the boat by getting out and walking along the dikes. They never even seemed to change paddlers. They were untiring, paddling on and on until we got where we were going. Tough guys, that's why they're so hard to defeat. I could never have done it myself.

Once we saw searchlights a mile or two ahead, and we thought we were coming close to a camp. Whether the lights belonged to a strategic hamlet, an ARVN outpost, or a Special Forces camp, we couldn't guess. Finally, with some hours left until daylight, we paddled up to a dike where we all got out of the boats and settled down to wait.

Those few hours on the dike were about the worst I can remember. The place was a mass of mosquitoes. There was no way to get away from the damned things. They gnawed at us, hour by hour, thousands of them. You opened your mouth to breathe and inhaled a lungful of mosquitoes. They were just *everywhere*—in your ears and your eyes and your nose. I really thought I was going to *die* from mosquitoes.

Our guards sympathized with us and gave us the two mosquito nets that they had, but the damned mosquitoes came right through the net. Nothing stopped them. I finally went to sleep, and when I woke up the next morning they were gone, except for those few that were trapped in the net, which continued to bite me.

When we left the dike in the boats next morning, we didn't seem to be following the canals any longer, but rather a vague trail through some kind of marshland. It was completely inundated—the water stood about three feet deep. The grass was thicker and heavier, and the scrub was higher than our heads, forming a sort of canopy. We could have hidden ourselves in it. Camacho said that maybe we were somewhere in the Plain of Reeds—a vast, virtually trackless area that had been a notorious hiding place for the Vietcong and for the Vietminh before them. If that was right, then we'd been moving away from Saigon, not toward it.

As we went deeper into the swamp, the scrub got higher, finally closing over our heads. There didn't seem to be any particular track through the swamp, but the guards apparently knew where they were going, and about noon, out in the middle of nowhere, we arrived at the first solid ground we had seen for hours, a tiny island not more than a dozen feet across. There our guards made camp.

I'd been keeping track of the days. It was Thanksgiving.

MIDDLE OF NOWHERE

The guards didn't even stop to take a break or smoke a cigarette. They cleared all the brush off the island, then scrounged around for some stout sticks and built us a little thatched hut. It was big enough for the four of us to lie down in, but we couldn't stand up in it. The hut took up most of the space on the little island, and what was left the guards used for a guard post and for the cooking fire; they had to string their hammocks out over the water between some small trees. It was considerate of them; they could have stuck us out in the damned trees and slept on the island themselves.

That afternoon we were joined by a Vietnamese medic. He had come to attend to McClure's foot, and by gestures he asked me to assist him. By this time the foot was infected and swollen and McClure felt very bad. I figured that phosphorus fragments were causing the infection. The medic knew his stuff—he was a lot better trained than our strike force medics were—and he seemed well equipped with penicillin, sulfa powder, and merthiolate. He removed one of the metal fragments from McClure's foot, and together we squeezed out the accumulated pus. Then he bandaged the foot, gave McClure a shot of penicillin, and looked over his other injuries.

McClure had small burns from the splatter of phosphorus he had caught down his side, and was also bleeding a little from the ears. I figured that the concussion of the mortar exploding over his head had probably ruptured his eardrums, but I wasn't sure. From what I could make out, the Vietnamese medic wasn't sure either. But he wanted to do something to help, so he poured penicillin from the bottle directly into each ear. I couldn't imagine how that would do any good, but I didn't think it would do any harm either.

We were on the island for a week, apparently for recuperation. It was the nearest, safest place the Vietcong could hide us and not have to defend us against attack. They were going to let McClure recuperate and let the rest of us recover too. Only Camacho had any boots, and Roraback's and my feet were pretty sore—they weren't torn or injured like McClure's but walking without boots along the damned dikes had really given them a beating. Americans are really vulnerable when you take their shoes away.

They allowed us to rearrange ourselves psychologically, too, to get over the shock of being captured. While we were traveling along the canals, they had instructed us to keep quiet. Camacho and I had talked a little bit when we got to that first village, and when we'd stop at a house to eat or sleep a while we'd have brief conversations, but the guards had wanted us not to talk. They probably didn't want us to be overheard, for one thing, and didn't want us to scheme, for another.

On the island they let us talk, and we speculated busily about what would happen to us, and about the attack, rehashing the whole thing.

They hadn't dragged us through the villages behind an ox cart, or subjected us to any trials. Nor had the villagers beaten us with sticks. In fact the guards had given me one of their large conical hats and had me tie a scarf around my head to disguise the fact that I was an American. They had generally taken care of us. What with the medic coming out to take care of McClure, it didn't seem likely that they were going to kill us.

In fact, it didn't even look like we were going to be

interrogated. The first day on the island, the leader of the guard detail came up to us with a little piece of paper in his hand. He was a friendly, easygoing guy who always wore an old beat-up felt hat like the one Walter Brennan wore in "The Real McCoys." So we called him Walter Brennan. On the piece of paper he handed us somebody had written, "NAMES OF YOUR TEAM."

We got very tense and debated whether we should give them the names or not. Maybe we'd been brought there for interrogation. But that didn't make sense. We weren't being threatened, and it had been four days since they'd captured us; if they'd wanted military information, the first night would have been the time to get it. If we were going to be interrogated, they would have sent along whoever wrote the note to conduct the interrogation. "Walter Brennan" didn't know any English, and neither did any of the other guards. Besides, the names of our team members weren't any secret. We decided it was okay, and Camacho, the senior man, gave Walter Brennan the names.

They weren't going to kill us or interrogate us, but we didn't know what they *were* going to do with us. Still, we relaxed a lot. We were lost in the middle of god-knows-where and prisoners in a war that might last a lifetime, but it didn't seem all that hopeless anymore. I was accepting the situation by then, and I think Camacho was too. Not that I enjoyed being a prisoner of war, but the food was good, there was plenty of it, and I was traveling around strange places— though slightly differently from the way I had expected.

They brought us some cigarette papers and some foul tobacco that Camacho immediately named horseshit because he found a horsehair in it. We learned to roll it and puff on the damned stuff. They gave us toothbrushes and toothpaste too, and insisted that we brush our teeth. Out there in the middle of god-knows-where, up they come with toothbrushes and toothpaste.

We didn't have any work, just sat around in that little hut all day. Every so often one of the guards would disappear into the swamp, and in maybe an hour and a half he'd be back with a boatload of supplies—apparently there was some sort of settlement nearby. They cooked it and gave it to us. I was eating pretty well, Camacho was eating some, and Roraback ate pretty well. They brought us sweet potatoes along with rice, fish, chicken, and a couple of ducks. We didn't have to do anything, not even wash the rice pot. If we'd had a deck of cards, we could have played pinochle.

Of the four of us, Camacho got along best with the Vietnamese. Not that he didn't complain—he did, especially about the food. But he was more familiar with their customs than the rest of us, and he joked with them in sign language and the few words of Vietnamese he knew. He had black hair, and he looked a little bit like them. He also seemed to like them better than I did, or at least he didn't hate them as much.

Despite their treating us fairly and feeding us well, I simply couldn't stand the damned guards. They were my natural enemy, not simply because they were opposed to the United States but because they were holding me prisoner. I didn't like being a prisoner, and therefore they were a bunch of bastards. My arrogance was up. I wasn't going to talk to them. Anybody who would incarcerate me or give me any kind of hard time or deprive me, I was just bound to hate. As soon as they let me go, I might think a little differently.

McClure was hurt, and he felt sorry for himself. I think he really worried about being a prisoner and not being able to walk, maybe not being able to keep up and getting shot because of it. He wasn't going to rock the boat—he did everything the guards asked him to do.

Roraback sat around completely blank. Or if he wasn't doing that, he bitched at the guards or at the rest of us—mostly at McClure, who had lost Roraback's boots. Roraback had loaned them to McClure, but McClure had left them in one of the boats along the way. I couldn't blame Roraback much; it was a dumb thing to do.

Camacho and I amused ourselves with jokes and made-up stories about the guards. We would assume that Walter Brennan actually acted like Walter Brennan when nobody was watching, that he came from the same kind of mountain background, a sort of Vietnamese hillbilly. One of the guys with him had a sporty red hat, and we made up some kind of story about him—that he was one of the cats from Saigon. We just caricatured each of them according to his appearance, made a joke out of it some way—how they happened to get there, what they would rather be doing than babysitting four Americans on this damned island in the middle of a swamp.

We accepted our position as being temporary. Escaping would have been close to impossible in the middle of that swamp, and we still thought that maybe we were going to be released soon. Obviously they couldn't keep us there on that little island for the rest of our lives. "Hell, maybe they *will* release us," Camacho said. He knew of some prisoners who had been released in Laos, and we had heard stories that they had turned prisoners loose in Vietnam. About six months before we'd come, the VC had captured four Special Forces people and had supposedly executed two of them because they were wounded and couldn't keep up. But the other two they had turned loose a couple of weeks later.[3]

Roraback, on the other hand, said they might take us to North Vietnam. Obviously guerrillas didn't have any facilities to keep prisoners of war, he said, so if they were going to keep us they would no doubt take us to North Vietnam.

I hadn't realized, and I don't think any of us had at the time, that the VC were as well organized as they were. They really did have a political organization right there in the jungle. We had thought that they just went from village to village, that they were vagabonds with no bases at all. I had thought that if we stayed with them we would spend the rest of our time traveling.

The vision I had had of the Vietcong before the attack was the vision I had got at Fort Bragg, like the picture they showed us there—a dead, evil-looking old man in black pajamas, a "Vietcong." The word itself seemed to have a special meaning—that this was something like an animal. I connected them with being something strange and remote that was impossible to deal with, people you couldn't reason with, people who would shoot you if you came in contact with them. But here was Walter Brennan giving us toothbrushes and candy and bringing in a medic to take care of McClure.

Each day the medic would come to look at McClure's foot, give him more penicillin, and ask him to try walking on it. At the end of a week he pronounced the foot well enough for McClure to travel, even though it wasn't completely healed. They put us in the boats and we went out the way we had come in, through the scrub and grass to the canals. It was night when we saw the searchlight in the distance once again.

By morning the canals were taking us through different country—wide, open, grassy fields where we could see for miles. In the middle of one field there was a small straw shack. The guards docked the boats and marched us over to it, Roraback howling and yowling every step of the way because of his sore feet. After we got to the shack, some of the guards left, coming back a little later with rice and sugar candy for us. Walter Brennan went off too, and when he returned he brought an armful of black VC uniforms and Bata boots—the green canvas boots with heavy rubber treads that we issued to the strikers.

Rather than giving the boots to us, he dropped them in the shack and took us outside. The first thing we saw was that the guards had fixed their bayonets. That shook me up, but then I saw that Walter Brennan had brought a photographer, complete with still and movie cameras. I figured they probably wouldn't photograph the fact that they were going to gouge us with bayonets.

It was a before-and-after thing. First they put ropes on us and paraded us past the cameras, their bayonets fixed. Except for Roraback, we were a motley crew—and with two weeks' beard, even he was no prize. Then they took us to the little shack and said, "Okay, now you put on these nice uniforms and come back out all sparkling and clean and take the pictures again." There went my beard. They gave us some old "Made in India" razor blades and told us to shave. Christ, those blades were dull—Camacho surmised that they were probably old Budweiser cans that had been honed on the sidewalk in Bombay. Then they pulled us back in front of the cameras. This time the guards stood around smiling and relaxed.

After the ceremonies, they issued each of us a complete personal POW kit that included a pair of pajamas, a mosquito net, a tin cup, an aluminum plate, a spoon, and a hammock which we carried all this gear in.

When the picture-taking was over, everybody stood around talking and smoking. Everything was loose and casual; we were allowed to walk around and talk with each other, and they fed us again and gave us more cigarettes. It was almost as if the Vietnamese were working on a timetable and we were a little ahead of schedule. At noon they walked us back to the boats and we started along the waterways.

Abruptly the terrain changed again. The canal became a wild and spacious expanse of water that brought to mind the Okefenokee swamp in Georgia. There were trees in the water along the edge and swamp grass floating around. Here and there, what looked like big white and blue cranes flew up slowly. The water was deep and very clear, not murky like the canals. The guards were dipping their cups into it and drinking it, so it must have been clean. They were very serious about boiling their drinking water and always told us not to drink any water that wasn't boiled. They used to build a fire every night to boil the water, and they would fill the canteens in the morning; it would have to last us all day, no matter how hot and dry we got. Water had become almost an obsession by this time. I just wanted to sit down and drink all the water I could swallow.

While we were crossing the lake, Camacho nudged me: "Hey, look!" Far ahead and a little to our right was Nuoi Ba Din, the Black Virgin Mountain, the first time we had seen it since we left Hiep Hoa. The Black Virgin Mountain is very unusual because the whole area around it is completely flat. It just springs out of nowhere, a couple of thousand feet high. It was visible from the camp at Hiep Hoa, about fifty miles away. We had traversed an irregular sweeping circuit south and now we were swinging north.

By dusk we were back in the rice paddies and we came to the end of the canals. Walter Brennan and his squad unloaded us on a dike and sank the boats in about two feet of water— to wait there until they got back. Then we started off along the dikes.

We hadn't gone more than a mile before I knew the damned boots and I were going to have to part company. Besides their being too small, I didn't have any socks, and I'd already raised a bunch of blisters on my feet. I took the boots off, but after a few yards walking barefoot I tore one of the damned blisters on a stick and got sand in it.

I was just miserable, complaining all the way, but it was nothing like Roraback's yelling and whining—"Ah, ha, oo, ee, ah!"—every time he stepped on anything that was a little bit more painful than the flat ground. He kept lagging behind and the guards kept trying to hurry him up. They took turns pairing off to help him along, but they grew progressively disgusted with him. They figured, quite rightly, that he wasn't suffering any more than the rest of us. Even I got disgusted with him, as much as I was hurting. Camacho said, "They're going to shoot you, you son of a bitch," and Roraback got scared, thinking they were.

Roraback was smaller than I was, and he didn't belong in the Special Forces any more than I did, maybe even less. One time when we were sitting down taking a break, resting our feet, I asked him, "Why did you come in Special Forces, anyway?" "Well, you know . . . ," he said, and he gave me a big long story.

"You came in here to get *rank*, goddamn it!" I told him. "You couldn't make it in that damned infantry unit you were in so you came in here to make stripes!"

"Yeah, goddamn it!" Camacho agreed.

There was no doubt in my mind that he had been in some outfit where he couldn't make sergeant E6, while in the Special Forces he could become a master sergeant in a matter of months. That attracted a lot of old NCOs—Camacho and I were twenty-four or twenty-five, and to us Roraback was old at something like thirty-three. He *was* old for Special Forces, approaching retirement.

Roraback had been a radio operator in a regular Signal Corps outfit where they have the radios mounted on the backs of trucks. He had really educated himself as far as electronics was concerned—he knew about every damned thing concerning radio you could want to know. He made it through jump school so they figured he was physically fit for Special Forces. Besides, they were short on radio operators. Special Forces was accepting anyone who had a reasonable IQ and was trainable, and Roraback came in to get a stripe. He went to their advanced school and became a high-speed operator, and because of his rank he became the senior radio operator on the team.

Roraback was originally from Brooklyn or the Bronx and

had a typical New York accent. He'd been in Korea. He told us some North Korean nut in a reconnaissance plane used to come by and bomb the barracks with mortar rounds, but as far as I know Roraback was never in any pitched battles. Being in the Signal Corps removed him somewhat from that. Seeing him later, I was convinced that he had never been in any battles: he surely would have been killed because he couldn't keep up with the rest of his unit.

He must have had about fifteen years of service before he came into Special Forces. That's unusual: people don't generally go into Special Forces at that age, because it's too tough, especially for a family man. He had four children. Now that I look back on it, he was probably worried about his family—they lived in Fayetteville, right outside Bragg. I can imagine being in a situation like that and worrying about my family. Roraback had actually purchased a house in Fayetteville, figuring that sooner or later he would return to Fort Bragg.

But here he was, whining about his damned feet. We were all having trouble with our feet. Even though Camacho was wearing his own boots, he had to take them off. Every time we walked through a stream or a flooded rice field, the mud and sand would get inside and start rubbing his skin. We walked on the dikes as much as possible, but water buffalo had made big hoof marks in them when it was wetter and now the hoof marks were as rough and hard as concrete. The Vietnamese must have thought we were babies with all our complaining. They had sandals cut out of rubber tires, but they generally carried them and went barefoot.

When I thought I couldn't put my foot down one more time—we'd been walking about four hours—we came to something like an animal shed where straw and feed were stored. We stopped there for the night and most of the next day. During the day Camacho took a stroll outside in his bare feet and had our first real confrontation with the red ants—they sting like bees, and he ran into three or four hundred of them. For the next five minutes he did a fantastic light-footed dance, jumping up and down and yelling. The guards thought it was hilarious.

Whether they wanted to avoid being spotted or just wanted to take advantage of cooler air, the guards waited until dusk before we moved off again. I assumed that we would walk four or five hours and then rest someplace as we'd done before, but we went right on walking that night. My feet got real sore—a mass of cuts and blisters that throbbed like a toothache every time I took a step. Camacho lent me his boots one time, but they didn't help any. As soon as they got some sand in them the leather would grind it into the cuts and blisters, making the pain worse and starting up new blisters.

To add to everyone's misery, the dew made the narrow dikes as slippery as oil. People were falling down all the time, prisoners and guards alike. It would have been a lot easier to walk in the shallow water of the rice paddies, but Walter Brennan and the guards were adamant about our not stomping over the young rice plants.

By dawn we were in grassland with more and more patches of woods. When I thought I couldn't walk another foot, we were met by a Vietnamese with two oxen and a covered cart. The guards gave us food, water, and cigarettes and loaded us into the cart. They pulled the flaps down so that we couldn't see where we were going and warned us not to look out. Then we started off again.

The track was rutty and bumpy and the cart rolled like it had one square wheel, but still it was better than walking. For the guards, of course, there was no such relief—they still had to walk. Every so often as we traveled through the day we could hear kids talking and laughing or chickens cackling, so we knew we were passing through settlements, but there was none of the bustle of a big village. Every once in a while our caravan would stop to water the oxen and let us relieve ourselves. They didn't take any precautions to stop in an area where we couldn't see where we were, though it was always away from a place where there were people. Each time we stopped we could see the Black Virgin Mountain, and each time it seemed just a little larger. Apparently they hadn't closed us in the cart to keep us from seeing where we were going, but to keep us out of the view of the people we passed along the way. That blew to hell the stories we'd been told about being tied to a cart and dragged from village to village.

Just before dark we caught sight of the mountain once again. This time it was on our left—we'd made a turn to the east. We pulled into a heavily wooded area, strung up our hammocks and nets, and made camp for the night.

The next morning Walter Brennan walked up to us with a Vietnamese we'd never seen before.

"I am a cadre of the National Liberation Front," he told us in English. "I have been sent to talk with you."

It was strange. Boats appear on time in a dozen different places, a medic meets us on a little island in a swamp, a photographer shows up in the middle of nowhere, an ox cart is waiting for us when we most need it, we're meandering all over the map, but never without food. I wasn't happy being a prisoner, and I didn't love the guards much, but I had to marvel at their organization. Somebody at a higher echelon knew where we were all the time, where we were headed, and when we would get there. We'd arrive someplace, and somebody would be waiting for us. He'd bring in somebody who was waiting outside and away we'd go, down the damned road. They never had to put in a requisition or wait for somebody to draw a boat out of the boat pool. They were all there in the boat, ready to go, with a straw bed made up for McClure.

I had felt that the Vietcong probably didn't have much organization, except for cadres, who told them what to do. But their organization—and the communications network that they obviously had—were amazing. Whenever we got someplace they were ready for us. Yet I never saw a radio.

When I got over the surprise of being spoken to in English, I wondered if the cadre was the person who had written us the note in the swamp.

"You will not be harmed if you obey orders," he told us. "Above all you must be . . . polite." Polite, that was the word he wanted. He stared at each of us intently. "Yes, at all times you must be polite."

I couldn't tell whether he meant polite, or courteous, or respectful, or what, but it sounded like Walter Brennan had given him a full report on our attitudes. Camacho, though he would clown with the guards, had been making no effort to hide his disgust with the food, even though it was the same the guards were eating. Roraback didn't have any problems eating the food—he was always taking more than his share— but he whined and complained to the guards about everything else. McClure was sort of resigned and wasn't saying much of anything. But I was continually objecting to carrying those Bata boots they had given me. And it must have been apparent at times that Camacho and I were making jokes about the guards, laughing at them. Knowing that they couldn't understand us, we talked about them as if they weren't there.

The cadre waited until we nodded that we understood we were supposed to be polite to Walter Brennan and the guards. Then he said he'd been told that we were having trouble walking. They'd supplied us with boots, he said, so what was the problem? "They're too small," I told him. "They make blisters." And I showed him my feet so he'd see that we weren't just being nasty. He promised to give us some sandals that would be better.

"And you," he turned to Roraback. "I am told you have lost your glasses. . . ."

"I didn't lose them, they were taken from me." Roraback was always graceful. "And so was my watch and cigarette lighter."

The cadre stiffened. But he asked Roraback what his prescription was—they'd try to get him another pair. Then he turned to all of us. "Now you must rest and eat," he told us. "You are to embark on a journey to a camp very far from here. There you will be able to study—to read books—to think about things."

SLAMMERS

How much further could we go—unless we were going to North Vietnam? I felt like we had traveled over most of Vietnam by this time. Thinking about walking through all those mountains and jungles made me want to give up then and there. On the other hand, I had conjured up a barracks somewhere like you see in the movies—a POW camp with a barbed-wire fence around it, a place where I would have plenty of everything and would be away from the war. POW camps are supposedly in a safe area, not subject to attack. At Fort Bragg they had shown us a sort of comic film: what you're supposed to do in a POW camp and how they're supposed to treat you. You're supposed to ask for more straw for your bunk, and the camp commander replies, "Straw? Give this man more straw."

I started to conjure up this sort of place in my mind: we'd have a yard, and sometimes they'd take us out on roadwork details. "Well, hell, we're going someplace where I can sit down and read books," I said to myself. "That'll be great, to sit around and read some books for a while." With that picture in my mind, I was determined to make it to the end. I felt better having a goal, especially one that pictured us living some place other than the damned jungle.

They loaded us back in the ox cart when they started us off that morning, but that lasted only until nightfall, and then we started walking again. We'd got our sandals okay, but they weren't exactly what I'd had in mind. I thought we were going to get the same Ho Chi Minh sandals with the rubber-tire soles that Walter Brennan and the guards had. I was really looking forward to a good pair of those sandals—they were a prize. But instead they gave us a bunch of rubber shower sandals, "zorries" or "go-aheads." Besides being hard to keep on in the mud, they raised blisters between my toes— probably the only place on my feet where I didn't have any damned blisters already. Now besides the Bata boots I had these damned sandals to carry.

Our column swelled to about thirty people. Along the way we picked up soldiers who were in the area, combat troops apparently, because they had weapons. I don't know whether it had been prearranged that they would escort us; perhaps they just felt it would be convenient to travel with us.

We spent most of the night trying to balance our way along the damned dikes. They were slippery as hell, and at least a dozen times my feet flew out from under me and I went crashing and flailing and yelling into the wet rice paddies. Every time I did, I got a great round of laughter from the Vietnamese. I did a fair amount of cussing that night—they even put their fingers to their mouth and asked me to be quiet. But the Vietnamese weren't selfish with their laughter. When one of their own did the windmill number, they greeted him with giggling and guffaws as he emerged sputtering and yelling. It was a great game.

After a while we ran out of dikes and paddies and came to a large stream. Waiting for us there was a large, broad-beamed open boat, probably the largest hand-driven boat I had seen in Vietnam. It looked like Noah's Ark, except it didn't have a house on it. It was both propelled and steered by one big oar aft which the helmsman could use to pole along the bottom if he wanted to, like a gondola. It must have been designed for hauling some kind of cargo, but it was large enough to hold thirty or forty people sitting around the sides. We jammed on, all thirty of us, until it was difficult to see the boat for the people.

There was a lot of traffic on the water, most of it going the other way—farmers paddling or poling little flat-bottomed sampans. It was obviously Vietcong territory because they made no effort to hide themselves: they were in complete control. But it was more scattered, more sparsely settled, than Hiep Hoa.

Some time in the morning we docked and the guards walked us a short distance to a beautiful glade in the forest—green grass four or five inches high, clumps of small trees. It looked like a planted park, the kind of place where you'd stop and have a picnic if you were driving through the countryside.

We sat down and the guards spread one of their plastic ponchos in front of us. Others proceeded to set a feast before us—a huge bowl of rice, a can of sardines, and a platter of fish. It was picture time again. A photographer took movies and stills of us from every angle while we ate. After we finished, we were put in a line and a medic passed down it and gave each of us an aspirin, while the cameras documented us getting medical care.

Then, with our gear on our backs, we were led back to the barge. I thought we were going to continue our boat ride, but as soon as the photographers had enough pictures, we were ordered back out and told to walk.

Walk we did. "We're going north," Camacho said. "They're going to take us all the way to Hanoi."

"Hell," I said, "that's a long walk."

"About seven hundred miles."

Christ, I thought, this could be a bitch.

Days blurred into nights and nights into days. I lost all track of time. It seemed like we walked for months, but actually it must have been about a week. We traveled trails wide enough for ox carts and others that were overgrown and impassable except by foot. Somewhere along the way my feet began to harden or else my fatigue overcame the pain. Camacho was walking barefoot now, having given his boots to Roraback, mostly to stop his yowling.

Roraback's feet didn't toughen up, they only seemed to get worse. He was getting on everybody's nerves and the guards were just disgusted with him. They were almost carrying him along—a guard on either side of him, an arm on either shoulder. You could read the expressions on their faces, "Oh, Jesus, why did we have to catch *this* guy!" The rest of us would have helped him, I suppose, but I could barely make it myself, and the guards didn't ask us to help. They were interested in getting us where we were going; if they had to carry Roraback in the process, then that was part of it. Camacho just gave Roraback his boots and told him to shut his mouth.

The column grew and grew. We would arrive at a turn in the path, and there would be another squad of Vietcong waiting to join us. Going down the road or around a curve, I couldn't see to the other end of the column. There must have been two hundred people in it, and they appeared to be combat troops. They all had weapons—mostly our M-1 carbines, though some of them had heavier stuff like automatic rifles. They really liked those BARs, heavy as they were (eighteen-pound jobs). They're extremely accurate and dependable weapons, more accurate than a machine gun. I hated them myself, couldn't have stood carrying them all the time the way the VC did.

Those guys were hard workers, the opposite of our strikers, who were a bunch of lazy asses. When the strikers took a BAR—which usually they didn't—there were two people assigned to it who took turns carrying the damned thing. But these Vietcong combat troops would be carrying a BAR all by themselves and ten or twelve magazines around their waists besides. The magazines themselves weigh two or three pounds apiece. A well-trained American unit wouldn't have been able to sustain the pace they did with that much equipment, and they're a hell of a lot smaller than Americans.

These were dedicated soldiers. We were paying the strikers a thousand piastres a month, and these guys weren't making a thousand piastres a *year*. But nothing seemed to deter them. Whatever they had to do, they said, "All right," and they did it. I never heard any complaints about taking orders or saw any dislike of doing what they were doing. The strikers had reminded me of a bunch of children—kids playing games. If they had to go out on patrol, it was a lark; they went because they were mercenaries. They weren't going out to look for Vietcong, they were going out because somebody said, "You have to go out today, but you'll get to come back and have a hot meal and go into town tonight." The only thing the Vietcong could look forward to was getting up the next morning and doing the same thing they had done the day before—traveling, carrying supplies, getting bombed—for forty piastres a month.

"Why are they doing it?" It became a thing with me to ask

myself that. "Why are they so willingly doing this, when the strikers aren't willing to do what they're doing?" The strikers ran away from the camp, they weren't even willing to defend their own country, and that's what we were there to help them do, supposedly. But these guys were willing to do all this, for practically nothing, under the most adverse conditions.

I figured maybe they were really fighting for something. "Maybe they really do believe in what they're doing—they couldn't be *forced* to act like this." They might be under this great power that communism is supposed to have that forces people to become slaves, I thought. But even if you could force people to do things, you couldn't force them to do it gleefully, as these guys were doing. It was obvious that they were doing it because they believed in it. That forty piastres a month had nothing to do with it; it was just something they bought cigarettes with. If they hadn't had the forty piastres a month, they simply wouldn't have bought cigarettes. They were dedicated to doing whatever it was that they were doing. If they were out to liberate their country from whatever force was there, then that's what they were going to do.

We didn't walk all the way to Hanoi. We were still deep in South Vietnam, traveling along a narrow path under a heavy jungle canopy, when our way was blocked by a huge fallen tree, its trunk extending back into the jungle. We turned and traveled along the trunk and suddenly before us was a camp—a permanent camp. There were thatched houses and a mess hall, even a "shower point" consisting of a log floor and a huge tub with a pail for dipping water.

We were met by a young Vietnamese wearing a maroon turtleneck sweater, apparently the officer in charge. He billeted us where the jungle was thickest, away from the main part of the camp. Before we bedded down there the guards took us to the main area to have showers and we stripped down and poured huge amounts of water over each other.

In the morning there was a changing of the guard. With much gesticulating, Walter Brennan told us he was leaving and taking his men back to the Delta. Amazingly, he projected regret at having to part from us, as if our long forced march had been a social affair and he had enjoyed our company.

"This guy didn't do too bad," I conceded to myself. "He made us walk all this way, but I suppose he didn't have any choice."

Compared to Walter Brennan's crew, our new guards seemed young—eighteen or twenty. Where the old guards had worn rag-tag clothing, these wore regular black uniforms and camouflage helmets. Some of them carried French MAT-49 submachine guns—apparently captured ten years earlier in their fight against the French. Others had new-looking bolt-action rifles they claimed were made in North Vietnam. They lavished pantomime praise on it, extolling its virtues over the M-1. They also had a couple of the BARs they liked so much.

Turtleneck, the officer, had a watch that he was constantly referring to. Every hour on the dot he would come over and pass out one Cambodian-made ARA cigarette to each of us. We found his seriousness for this ceremony quite amusing. Finally, of course, he ran out of the ARAs and substituted the usual horseshit. Our hosts were determined to show us any kindness they could with the little they had, and giving us cigarettes was their foremost method. You always had to smoke one with your tea; they were insulted if you turned one down.

We were in that camp for four days. Then a tall, skinny Vietnamese in khaki showed up and spoke for a few minutes to Turtleneck. A few minutes later, he told us to roll up our hammocks and other gear and we moved out.

We walked through the jungle all that day. Late at night

we entered what could only be a large permanent base camp, and an old one at that. The thatched buildings looked a little run-down, and the weather-worn camouflage netting over the pits of *punji* stakes had fallen in and not been replaced.

Then we saw something new—a large cage. Eight feet by fifteen, maybe seven or eight feet high, the cage had a thatched roof and closely set poles pegged together to form the walls—bars. The beds were placed end to end along the sides. At one end was a table, at the other a door made like the walls and hung with split and laced rattan vine. Our guards ordered us inside and then swung the door shut and secured it.

"Well, a slammer, huh!" said Camacho. Somewhere Camacho had been—in the States or in Korea—a jail had been a "slammer." So this cage became a slammer for us, too.

This, I thought, was going to be where we would spend the rest of our time—until the war was over, or we were dead, or they released us. And it didn't seem likely that they would take the trouble to build that slammer if they were going to release us soon.

It wasn't quite what I had imagined our POW compound would look like. I had conjured up in my mind a library and all the water I wanted to drink. I felt a great wave of depression; we had been approaching it for so long, and I finally realized it was not what I had been expecting at all. We'd been walking around the country for a month. And when you walk under those conditions for almost a month, it feels like an eternity. You feel that every day is just like the last one; you're going to get up in the morning and you're going to walk all day long, and you're going to stop. And the next day you're going to get up and walk all day long. . . .

There had been nothing to indicate that it would end anywhere, and then we finally got to the slammer. We end up in this damned slammer in the middle of the jungle, instead of some nice town where we could sit around, visit the public library, walk around, drink coffee, and bullshit. I had to laugh. It wasn't going to be like that at all. That was a foolish, childish idea that I had had. It was a shocking awakening.

PART THREE: INTERROGATION

MAN WITH GLASSES

Our first visitor the next morning was a small Vietnamese in black pajamas who came in carrying a bunch of posters, a hammer, and some tacks and proceeded to decorate the slammer's bamboo walls with propaganda signs, just like you see in the movies: "Stop U.S. Imperialist War of Aggression" and so forth. One was directed at black soldiers: "You are committing the same heinous crimes in Vietnam that the Ku Klux Klan is committing against your people in the United States."

We had been expected—these things couldn't have been done in an hour or so. They were carefully hand-lettered, and there were a number of them. The signs were all in English, but the man spoke French.

When he had finished decorating the slammer he left, and we were visited by a thin, gaunt woman about forty, also in black pajamas. She brought with her a refined-looking man in his thirties. In broken English with a half-Vietnamese, half-French accent she introduced him as the camp commander. I had expected to find some really mean bastard commanding the camp, but this guy was very gentlemanly. He handled himself carefully, dressed neatly in khakis, and spoke in a nice tone of voice. We named him Suave.

Suave passed around the usual ARAs and made a brief welcoming speech, which the woman translated. "In some days men will come and explain to you," he told us. Then he said something else, and the woman asked, "What would you like for Christmas?"

A whole flock of smart replies came to my mind, like, how about a plane ride home? I didn't know what their silly game was, but I wasn't going to play it. But rather than saying anything that would insult them, I just kept quiet. The others must have felt the same way. We just kept our mouths shut and shuffled our feet.

"In two days it will be Christmas. For Christmas you can have a special meal. The camp commander wishes to know if you have a special desire for your meal."

That sounded more like it. Up to this point we'd had plenty of food but not much variety. The main staple was rice, of course, and we were just fed up with the damned stuff. We all wanted the same thing—bread.

When that was translated to him, Suave nodded. "Do you desire to eat at midnight, or do you desire to eat in the day of Christmas?" We settled for midday Christmas dinner.

Toward evening the next day, the small Vietnamese man brought us a three-dimensional star made of small sticks covered with rice paper. He put a little candle in it and lit the candle, then hung it from the top of the cage. Next the Three Wise Men would come riding out of the jungle, I supposed.

"Well, shall we sing Christmas carols, or what?" asked Roraback, but we hooted him down.

The following day a guard we named Moe brought us our Christmas dinner—a whole chicken cooked in a pot, with various herbs and spices and a dozen loaves of fine French bread. We had a regular orgy of bread. They obviously hadn't baked it in the camp, so Suave must have detailed somebody to walk out to the nearest town to get it.

The days passed one after another as we tried to get used to being prisoners of war locked up in a bamboo slammer in the middle of the damned jungle. The guards let us out of the slammer to draw water, wash our plates, and use the latrine. Our main pastime was bullshitting among ourselves while we watched the guards building three more little slammers nearby. McClure passed countless hours brushing his teeth, and I learned how to take a whole hour to wash my plate.

We named Moe after the lead man in *The Three Stooges*. He looked a little like him—same square haircut—and he acted like him, too—the big boss, ordering the other guards around. It was obvious he was in charge of the whole damned outfit, and he made sure that we knew that he was. He had the same way as the Three Stooges' Moe of trying to show somebody how to do something simple and getting exasperated with the dumb clucks when they screwed it up. Most of the time we were the dumb clucks. "C'mon you guys! Don't you know how to do that?! Lemme show you! Out of the way!" We couldn't understand what he was saying, of course, but the way he acted, we knew what he meant.

Moe went to great lengths to show us how to draw water out of the well with a bucket and a length of rattan vine. I really didn't *know* how to draw water out of a well with the damned rattan vine. I didn't know how to get the damned bucket to sink. I'd lower it into the water, and the bucket would just float. Moe would get exasperated, and he'd shake the vine and get the bucket to tip until it would sink and fill. Then he'd motion, "Okay, pull it up."

I'd start pulling, and the vine would be wet and start slipping in my hand. I'd get the bucket halfway up, and it would start slipping back. And he'd get even more exasperated and and disgusted and push me out of the way and pull the damned thing out the proper way, getting it at the joints and twisting it in his hand, and bringing it up, hand over hand.

But he wouldn't leave it at that. Once he'd established that I didn't know how to fill a bucket or pull up a rattan vine, he'd show me how to pour water into the pan. Then he'd give me soap, trying to show me what soap was. I'd try to bend over and wash the pan, "No, no"—he'd show me how. He'd make me squat down to wash the pan, not bend over. I'd squat down and wash it, and he'd tell me when the pan was clean enough and teach me how to pour water in and rinse it.

And then he'd take me back to the slammer and get Roraback out and go through the same thing with Roraback. Roraback acted even dumber than me. I guess he resented the fact that Moe was trying to tell him what to do. Moe would look at Roraback and get mad. Roraback would look at him, then put the bucket down the well. "Okay, get it back out of the well!" Roraback would look at him, then do it.

Cooped up in that tiny space with nothing to do, Roraback really got on our nerves. He wouldn't draw water or wash his plate because he said his feet hurt too much, but his feet didn't keep him from taking trips to the latrine. He even tried to make me take his KP. We had servants at Hiep Hoa, and of course at Fort Bragg the NCOs didn't have to pull KP because we had the lower-ranking people doing it. But Roraback apparently thought he was going to be an NCO in the jungle—he seemed to think McClure and I should cater to him because he was a sergeant first class and outranked us. I should wash his plate, I should go carry water from the well, I should do all these things. "Bullshit, buddy, you wash your own damned plate! I'm not going to be your KP!"

"You better watch out what you're saying. Do you realize who you're talking to? I'm sergeant first class, and I'll have you court-martialed when we get back to a court."

"Go get your damned court and try me right here! Otherwise, you son of a bitch, you keep your mouth shut. I'll punch you in the goddamned nose. You wash your own plate." Camacho would interrupt when I was about ready to burst Roraback wide open. Roraback remembered those POW training films where the NCOs supervised while the lesser men got the picks and shovels and went out to do the work. Maybe if there had been two hundred of us that might be true. But there were only four of us, and everybody would do his own share.

Roraback took it to the extreme. He got to me first, trying to give me orders out there in the jungle, but pretty soon McClure wanted to beat the shit out of him, and then it was Camacho's turn. The only thing that kept Roraback from getting thoroughly stomped was the guards finishing those other slammers. They put one of us in each of them and told us not to talk across the twenty feet that separated them.

The thin woman came by two or three more times to ask us if we wanted anything. Somehow we got around to asking her where she had learned English. She bit her lip and looked away—it was clear that she didn't like thinking about it. "In a Saigon jail," she said bitterly. "When I was released, I joined the Front."

The last time she came by was to say good-bye. She repeated what Suave had said when they had first talked to us: "In some days men will come and explain to you."

We figured we were in for indoctrination.

The third day after we had been put in the new slammers, Suave and a young Vietnamese I had never seen before roused me in the night. "I am interpreter," the new man said. "Camp commander say you must pack equipment. We leave very soon."

They stood there while I rolled up my bedding and put it and my other things in the gunny sack. As usual, Suave gave me a cigarette. I wondered what was up. The camp we were in was obviously a permanent one, and judging from all the traffic in and out of it, it was a supply point too. Since they'd gone to the trouble of building three new slammers, I figured they planned to keep us here a while. Why should we be taking off in the middle of the night?

But Suave wasn't volunteering any information, and in an

hour we were on the trail. The Vietnamese were taking every-thing they could carry on their backs or load on a bicycle, and they gave us things to carry too. Camacho and I both had sacks of rice. We couldn't bullshit along the way about why we were moving. The guards wouldn't let us talk to each other, and they separated us during the breaks.

By morning we were in what seemed to be virgin jungle. While the rest of the column continued on along the trail out of sight, the guards took us off to the side, and with their heavy machetes chopped a trail through the jungle. Then they cleared an area and ordered us to string up our ham-mocks, keeping us out of sight of each other. We weren't in the slammers anymore, so for the first time they put chains on us. They chained my foot to a tree at one end of the hammock and put a rope around my neck and shoulder and tied it to the tree at the other end. I wondered, if I fell out of the hammock would I reach the ground? Moe and the other guards weren't too happy with the arrangement either—they had to do a lot of fetching and carrying of water and the like while we were lying in our hammocks chained hand and foot to the trees.

Eventually the interpreter—I called him Prevaricator because he couldn't seem to give a direct answer to any-thing—came and unchained me and gave me a razor and water. "You must shave. Be neat. Our cadre wishes to speak to you."

I scraped and hacked at my three-week-old beard. Then the interpreter took me to another cleared-out area where the guards had built a small thatched house. In it was a little low bench and a table and a couple of chairs.

Sitting at the table was a frail middle-aged man wearing a pair of rimless glasses. He was clean-shaven, very neat, and though he was wearing the black pajamas, he looked like the kind of guy you'd expect to find in a business suit. Beside him was a man in black uniform wearing a pistol, probably an officer. Prevaricator sat me down on the little bench, and the Man With Glasses and the officer pressed him into service bringing tea and sugar and candy to us. Prevaricator looked pissed—he obviously considered the role menial and didn't like it at all.

It was right out of the movies: the prisoner confronted by his interrogators, who were sitting on a higher level and making him look up at them.

"Look at you," Man With Glasses began, not unkindly. "You are pitiful."

I couldn't argue about that very much. I was shaggy, my clothes were raggedy, snagged by the thorns and brush. I was in a sorry condition, and I felt the way I looked. I was spending a lot of time feeling sorry for myself, and I guess it must have showed.

We had known interrogation was inevitable and had feared it for so long, but it didn't go the way it was supposed to. The guards were off somewhere out of sight. No one shone bright lights in my eyes. In fact, I sat in the shade while Prevaricator served me tea and candy and cigarettes.

Man With Glasses did most of the talking, though he encouraged me to say anything I wanted to. He insisted on giving me their side of the story—why they were there in the jungle and why the NLF had gotten together and was fighting the U.S. and the Saigon regime. "We are fighting for Vietnam," he said. "We do not try to take over your country. This is not in our plans. We are worried about our country. We love it very much. We are a proud people, and we want to keep our country." And he wanted me to tell him why the hell I was there anyway. Didn't I know I was wrong to be a part of the United States effort in Vietnam? And if I did, would I write a statement saying so?

He talked to me for about an hour, and at the end of the session he gave me a pack of the Cambodian cigarettes. "For your enjoyment. Take them with you. When you are resting and smoking, I would like you to think deeply of what we have discussed."

Prevaricator led me back to my hammock, and I did what Man With Glasses had told me to do—smoked and thought.

If sitting in the shade drinking tea while I listened to this old guy talk was "brainwashing," then it didn't fit any description I had ever heard. I recalled the stories I'd heard about Korea—the *Manchurian Candidate* scene where they hypnotize you, or drop water on your head, or put you in complete stillness—something that will drive you out of your mind. Then once they've taken everything from your mind, they start over again. When somebody says "brainwashing," this is what I consider they're talking about—the classic Korean example. Or the stories that came out of there, anyway.

After smoking a few cigarettes, I hadn't gotten any further than figuring out where Man With Glasses fitted into the chain of command. "I represent the Central Committee of the National Liberation Front," he had said—he didn't tell me his name. "I have been sent here to talk to you." He said that he had been a professor at a university in Saigon and that he had been driven out for political reasons. The Diem regime was applying pressure on him, and instead of being thrown in prison he had fled Saigon and joined the NLF. He indicated that Diem's people had wanted to get him on their side, tried to get him to sell out, but his conscience wouldn't allow him to do that. He felt strongly about Vietnam, he said, and his place was with the NLF rather than the Diem regime.

Apparently, he held no command function. As camp commander, Suave was responsible for the prisoners, but primarily as our custodian. Man With Glasses was probably a notch above Suave, not his superior but in some kind of policy-making position. And as he was a representative of the Central Committee, when he said jump, Suave jumped.

The next day, and every day thereafter for a week, Moe or Prevaricator would take me up to the little house for a session with Man With Glasses. Each time, Prevaricator would pass around tea and candy and cigarettes with the same glum look on his face.

I think it was on the second day that Man With Glasses seemed to sense what I was worried about. "We are not interested in military information," he assured me. I felt relieved. I wanted to believe him, but I didn't know if I dared. It must have shown on my face, because he laughed. "We know that you know nothing of value. Besides, there is no point in going to so much trouble. We have better ways to find out what we want to know—our own people. We can tell you what will happen in your headquarters tomorrow."

I could believe that. There were any number of stories about how the VC seemed to know about an attack before the unit that was supposed to be making it did.

"Do you know how your camp was overrun so easily?"

"I heard that it was because of an inside job—that there were traitors."

"Yes, that's true. And how do you think that happened?"

"Well, probably, you know, we didn't have the confidence of the people who were fighting for us."

"Yes, that is why. This is why I tell you these things. The Saigon government would fall immediately if it weren't for the Americans. You are not liked here, you are hated. The Saigon government is hated. By *all* the people."

Rather than interrogating me, Man With Glasses gave me a history lesson on Vietnam, much like a lecture. I suppose you might call it re-education. You could compare it to the area studies we had been given back at Bragg, except at Bragg they had told us zero, and here Man With Glasses even kept urging me to express my own views.

He started with the French occupation, and then he went through the time Vietnam fought the French, and how after they had defeated the French at Dien Bien Phu they had gone to Geneva and gotten the Agreement. He explained the Geneva Agreement in detail: he said that after a two-year interim there were supposed to be elections to decide what government Vietnam would have, that it must be a *free* election supervised by the International Control Commission, and that the boundary between North and South Vietnam—which were never supposed to be separate countries—would be removed after the election.

He explained, of course, that Diem had been installed by Dulles, and that with the connivance of the United States Diem had refused to hold the elections, which he would surely have lost to Ho Chi Minh. While Vietnam was fighting the French, he said, Diem had spent most of his time in New Jersey.

He gave me a general background on Vietnam: the reason they were fighting was to try to gain back what they had won from the French; they wanted to have these elections in Vietnam; they had wanted to have a free country rather than the "neocolonialism" that U.S. involvement was—and I suppose that's a pretty good description of it. The United States wanted to control the economy of South Vietnam, he said. "This is what imperialists do." But he didn't dwell on that.

He explained the whole thing in great detail so that I would have his facts and could apply them to anything else he said. "This is how it is. You can believe it or not believe it. If you believe it, I'd like to know about it." It was their version of things, but many of the facts jibed with what I already knew. They should have told us these things in area studies at Bragg, but they didn't. Of course, if they *had* told us what he told us, we might not have wanted to go. The area studies had turned out to be a hate program that taught you to hate the Vietcong.

The few times I tried to present the version they gave me at Bragg, it sounded ridiculous. Man With Glasses would nod patiently and say, "Yes, we know, you were told such and such." Generally he was right—almost down to the exact words. It didn't sound any more sensible coming from him.

I tried to explain to him what I believed when I came to Vietnam: that they were *invaders* from someplace else.

"Where do you think I'm from?" he asked.

"Well, you're from Vietnam, huh?"

"Yes, this is my country."

It was something we hadn't understood. We didn't even bother to ask *where* the Vietcong were from. We had assumed that they were "Communist aggressors." You don't think of them as being Communists in their own country— they're something like outlaws. These were the things I was trying to tell him, but in the light of what he had said, it sounded silly.

When he got to the abuses of the Diem regime, I didn't have any arguments at all. He didn't tell me anything I didn't know before I got captured, and the only contribution I could have made would have been to add some things he forgot to mention. The Diem regime was not representative of the people, he said. And he talked about how the Buddhists opposed Diem before his overthrow, how he suppressed the Buddhists, how he took advantage of the villagers and how many taxes he had imposed, how he confiscated people's property and threw them into prison for no reason other than that they had followed the Vietminh in their fight against the French, and how of course he wouldn't allow anybody who had been a Vietminh to take part in any election, or to own any property, or to hold any office.

He had a very sound argument, and it was impossible for me to contradict him. Even at Hiep Hoa I had recognized that the Buddhists were being persecuted, and I also recognized that Diem had become so bad that even the U.S.

government couldn't accept him anymore; the people in the U.S. were up in arms about the things he had done and the U.S. had to get rid of the guy.

I couldn't argue with the man as to who represented the people, either. It was impossible. On the way there I had seen that they had the support of the people. Everywhere they went they were accepted; they walked around freely, unchallenged. Even without Man With Glasses telling me, that in itself indicated that the Vietcong were accepted, that they *were* the people. The Saigon government forces had to be armed to the teeth even when they went into their own so-called territory—and they were ambushed, at that. But these guys walked freely wherever they went.

"Now, you are told that you are here to support the Vietnamese people," Man With Glasses told me, "when actually you are here to support an unpopular government headed by Ngo Dinh Diem, who is a Catholic and persecutes the Buddhists."

"Yeah, that's true," I said. And it was.

"Diem would surely fall if your people were not supporting him."

"Yeah, that's true also."

"Of course, you can see that Diem has been overthrown."

"Yeah, that's true."

"And the man who has replaced him is no better."

"Well, I don't suppose he is."

"And do you realize that the man who has replaced Diem has also been replaced, that he has been overthrown?" He got a chuckle out of that.

When he finished with all the excesses of Diem, he started on a patient, logical progression connecting the United States with the Saigon regime. He went through the whole mess. The U.S. had installed Diem. It had helped him prevent the elections and trained his army and secret police. And of course U.S. money was keeping the Saigon government going.

The conclusion was pretty obvious. If the Diem regime was guilty of crimes against the Vietnamese people—and it was—then wasn't the United States at least as guilty?

Field that one in the jungle if you can.

I tried to explain to him what they had told us at Bragg—that Diem was the elected president, the "George Washington" of Vietnam. They'd told us, "This guy is just *great* and they're trying to overthrow him. We've got to help save him, because he's asked us for our help. The poor guys don't have any money or any army." Man With Glasses thought this was rather amusing.

It seemed that supporting this sort of thing put us in the same category as Diem, as far as the world was concerned, as far as I was concerned. "How come you're in my country?" Man With Glasses would ask. "Uh . . . uh . . ." I had no excuse except to support Diem.

I was embarrassed. "Hell, they conned me just like they conned a lot of other people. I really wasn't aware when I came here that Diem was such a bastard." I think Man With Glasses pretty well believed that. It was true. Even before I was captured, people would ask, "What are you doing in Vietnam?" And I'd have to say, "Protecting Madame Nhu's sugar mill"—thinking to myself, "God damn! Kind of embarrassing to say this is my mission in life—to go around flunkying for Madame Nhu." I hated to admit it, and I *had* to admit it to the man there in the jungle. It gave me kind of a shitty feeling. I felt like saying, "Geez, I'm sorry. I didn't realize what the hell I was doing. I thought the situation was greatly different, or I wouldn't have come in the first place. And if it's okay with you, I won't do it anymore."

I was a professional soldier. I was working for a man who paid me to fight wars. I'd get promoted if I did a good job, gain a little power. The fact that we were members of the U.S. Army didn't detract from the fact that we were mercenaries. We wore the tag that said "U.S. ARMY" but we were doing it for the pay, and that was the reason I didn't give a shit about whose politics it was or whose country it was. This was what I did for a living. "Go to Vietnam? Sure! Who's in Vietnam? What does it do?" It was just part of a job—who could really give a damn about the people?

One morning while we were sitting there drinking tea, Man With Glasses pulled out a piece of paper. "You have just received a pay raise."

"Oh, yeah?"

"That's right, you did. How many years have you been in the Army?"

He had a new pay schedule right there that some VC had probably stolen from some sergeant's desk somewhere. He ran the whole thing down, and it turned out I was making something like seven or eight hundred dollars a month. "Very good pay."

"Well," I said. "It's not bad."

"Do you know how much our men make? They get no pay at all." He laughed. "We realize that your government does this to get you to Vietnam."

"We have treated you well," Man With Glasses told me; "we could have killed you. You realize, of course, that our people are treated much worse when they are captured by Americans?"

Of course, I knew this was true. Our bamboo slammers were a hell of a lot more comfortable than the little barbed-wire cages the strikers had kept our prisoners in. And talking with Man With Glasses while we smoked cigarettes and sipped tea was a whole lot different from an LLDB sergeant smashing his knee into the back of the "VC squad leader."

"We have no reason to hurt you. We realize that most of the Americans here are here because they do not know the true situation in South Vietnam. We want to let you know that you have the opportunity to learn that now.

"We do not want to keep you here in the jungle. You are very much trouble for us. But we do not want to release you if you are going to come back and fight us and kill us. That would be foolish. We are not fools."

Of course, the conversations I had with him that week were limited. We would talk for an hour or two, and then he would send me back to my hammock with a pack of cigarettes and tell me to "think deeply of what we have discussed." It was a good background history of Vietnam, what he told me, and the whole point was, according to him, to let me know how they felt about it—why there was an NLF and why they were fighting—and then allow me to decide whether or not the United States was wrong, and whether or not *I* was wrong. And if I felt I was wrong, I should say so—they'd want me to write a statement.

"You can write these things down. And then the Front will look at what you've said. And if they feel that you understand the situation, our situation, perhaps they will let you go home." Even though I pretty much agreed with him about the war, I wasn't at all sure I wanted to write that damned statement, and I kept trying to put him off. I thought maybe we could both just forget the idea.

The routine for the other three was about the same as mine and I assumed that everybody else had about the same response to Man With Glasses that I did: that he seemed to have a pretty reasonable argument about why we should never have come to the damned country, and that we liked the idea of getting released, but that we wished he'd stop talking about writing anything down. As it turned out, Roraback was an exception. Apparently he was trying to do the impossible—trying to indoctrinate Man With Glasses with the same silly reasoning we'd been given at Bragg.

The first hint I had of this was when Man With Glasses asked me quite seriously one morning, "What is wrong with

Ror'back? Does he not understand his situation? That we have no time to play games? That there are many lives at stake? Perhaps his own?" He couldn't figure out why Roraback was persistently obnoxious and rude, and I couldn't blame him much. Knowing Roraback, I figured the way he treated Man With Glasses wasn't motivated by the Code of Conduct,[4] just by his usual nastiness.

When I wasn't talking with Man With Glasses, I didn't have much to do except lie in my hammock and smoke and think. Naturally, I did ponder over my conversations with Man With Glasses and wonder what the outcome of our sessions might be. It didn't take a genius to understand that what the NLF wanted was a written statement from each of us that in some way condemned the U.S. involvement in Vietnam. I imagined they'd probably use it as propaganda. What I had to figure out was what would happen to me if I wrote the statement and what would happen if I didn't.

The more I thought about it, the more I realized how much was involved in my decision, and how complex my situation was. It wasn't going to be as simple as getting captured and going to some POW camp and sitting there until the war was over. I was going to be confronted with many things, and I was going to have to face them and make decisions about what I was going to do. One contributing factor was that I did in fact believe the war was wrong and the U.S. responsibility for it was wrong too. They hadn't started the massive search-and-destroy missions or saturation bombings by the time we were captured, but what *was* apparent was how our support of the Saigon regime had done nothing but harm to the Vietnamese people. What I hadn't seen with my own eyes, I'd heard about in bars in Saigon or Can Tho.

On the other hand, I was a member of the United States Army, a professional soldier, and I kept telling Man With Glasses that I was in Vietnam because I was sent, not because I especially wanted to be there. I wasn't responsible for policy decisions, I told him, I obeyed my orders just as the soldiers of the Front obeyed theirs. And I was forbidden to make any damned statements against my government.

"Yes, I understand this," he told me patiently one day. "I have read your Code of Conduct. I have it here. Would you like to see it? It sounds noble. If we were attacking your country, I would consider you an honorable man.

"But as it is, your government is committing criminal acts against our country and our people on the pretext that our people asked you to commit these acts against us. You and your friends are instruments of these crimes, for which you are highly paid. You have even been given a pay raise. In our eyes it is impossible to see you as honorable soldiers fighting for the freedom of your country. Our people can only see you as men performing criminal acts against us.

"You say you were sent to Vietnam, that you had no choice. But you belong to a volunteer organization, one from which you could have resigned at any time. We have no desire to punish you as a criminal—in the end it serves no useful purpose. But you must realize you are wrong—that you have been tricked by the false propaganda of your government. If you show you are sincere and understand the situation, maybe you can go home. We have no desire to keep you. You make problems for us. It's up to you—it's your life. Think about it."

It was a long speech, and he delivered it with intensity and patience. I thought his hint that my life was in jeopardy was not a threat but an honest evaluation of the circumstances. I had the feeling he didn't want to say anything more about it because he didn't want to insult my intelligence.

He didn't have to explain about how we made problems for them. They'd put a lot of effort into getting us to wherever we were, and now they had to detail at least a squad of men to guard us. They had to build our slammers and keep us supplied with food and cigarettes. They knew that if any one of us escaped it would jeopardize their entire camp. And it must have been difficult for the cadres to explain to their soldiers why we were being treated so well, when Vietcong prisoners were being jailed, tortured, executed. The way some of the people in the villages we had gone through had looked at us, it was pretty clear that if the Front hadn't told them to leave us alone, we would be dead. But even if Roraback was the most obnoxious of the four of us, none of us had shown any gratitude for our treatment or even for being alive. We resented being prisoners, and we showed it. We bitched all the time and openly showed our disdain for our hosts. In short, we were a pain in the ass.

I couldn't see why the Vietcong should keep us around, dragging them down, if we didn't show some positive response. They could release us, but as Man With Glasses said, they weren't fools, and they wouldn't let us loose if they thought we were going to come back shooting. It seemed that if we didn't write something, we couldn't count on staying alive.

But would we survive if we did give them statements? We had no guarantees except that we knew they had turned other American prisoners loose. "If you can show that you have changed your attitude," Man With Glasses told me, "if you can show that you no longer want to wage war with us, then possibly—I can't guarantee, because I am not the final authority—but possibly the Central Committee will decide to allow you to return home." And he cited two or three other people they had released.

I knew that according to the Code of Conduct—the Superman Code Eisenhower had worked up after the Korean War—we weren't supposed to make any statements, written or oral. As prisoners of war we were only supposed to give our name, rank, serial number, and date of birth. But there were a few complications. Officially, the United States was not at war with the National Liberation Front. The NLF did not consider me a prisoner of war, but somebody who had committed crimes against the Vietnamese.

"We realize that most of the people of the United States still have the spirit of 1776—they want to see other people free," Man With Glasses told me. "It is your *government* that is doing this to us. Of course, if you are a reactionary and support that government, then you remain our enemy and we cannot forgive you for what you have done here—the crimes you have committed against our people."

"Wait a minute," I said. "I didn't hurt anybody."

"You are here," he said. "This is a crime. We did not invite you."

All of which put me in the position of being a soldier in an army not at war, captured by an organization that did not exist in the eyes of my government, which was *fighting* that organization. It was straight out of *Catch-22*. Since the NLF was a nongovernment, the U.S. couldn't logically expect it to follow international agreements concerning prisoners, but by the same token the U.S. couldn't negotiate our release without recognizing that the NLF was quite real—something it wasn't about to do.

But on the other hand, the NLF obviously did exist and did hold territory—hell, you could argue that they controlled Hiep Hoa, considering how easily they kicked our ass out of there. By our own government's policy I wasn't at war with them—or with anybody else, for that matter—but by mortaring their farmers and training strikers to go marauding and burn down their houses, by this alone I could be considered a criminal.

Now, according to the Superman Code, the Army wanted me to suffer torture and death rather than give up anything more than name-rank-serial number. I had been captured while guarding Madame Nhu's goddamned sugar mill—while her own soldiers in the mill hadn't fired a shot. Dying for that didn't make any more sense in the jungle than it did when I was crouching in that bunker with the bullets going *dup! dup! dup!* all around my head.

In the end, I decided to write a statement. How much weight could anybody give to a statement written by a POW under god-only-knows what conditions in the middle of the damned jungle? And if the statement *were* released, it would at least tell the Army and my folks that I was still alive.

So at one point when Man With Glasses asked me, "Could you write a statement about what we've been talking about?" I told him, "Yeah, I do agree with you sufficiently. I feel we shouldn't be here. I feel that you're basically right."

"Could you write something explaining your feelings?"

"Yeah, I suppose I could."

I worked on it carefully—it ended up about two and a half pages long and I was careful to make it as ambiguous as possible. "If things are as they say they are, then of course I'm wrong for being here. If what I was doing was a crime, then I'm sorry." Of course, this completely removed me from the situation, and of course that was not what Man With Glasses wanted. He wanted me to say that I felt I was wrong for being there, but I wasn't going to commit myself. But Man With Glasses made no attempt to tell me specifically what to write, and if he read the paper he certainly didn't analyze it, because he seemed satisfied with it. Before he left he told us he would take our statements to the Central Committee and then perhaps we could go home.

Two days after he left, Moe got us packed up and we prepared to move. For the first time since our capture we were blindfolded, but luckily it was only for about ten minutes, just time enough to get us thoroughly confused about what direction we were taking out of the camp. We walked through the jungle for the rest of the day and on into the night until about midnight, when we came to a brand new camp.

I thought I'd call it Auschwitz.

"AUSCHWITZ"

Auschwitz had obviously been built while we were out in the jungle talking with Man With Glasses. The Vietnamese had been working on it for about three weeks, I guess, and they must have had it about half finished. There were four new slammers—bigger than the ones at the first camp—and they were grouped in a square with the guards' house in the center. It was bigger than the slammers, and about a dozen of them slept there; they had their beds in rows side by side.

Suave was still camp commander. He was apparently responsible not only for the prisoners but for finishing the camp and for the fifty or sixty people in the permanent camp company. He also had to keep track of the two or three hundred guerrilla regulars who were constantly coming and going in and out of the camp. The camp company was a ragtag outfit. They wore what appeared to be hand-me-down uniforms, some of them khakis, some of them purple shirts and black pants. But the people coming in and out wore black uniforms and camouflage helmets. We figured they were being resupplied or were on recuperation leave.

Suave must have been in charge of the almost nightly camp meetings, too. They were more or less political rallies, I guess. They all got together around the central fire, down by the mess hall. Somebody would speak—I suppose they were telling about what had happened during the day, after-action reports—"We captured another camp today," or, "We won another battle." They'd bullshit for a while, and then they

sang their anthems. It usually sounded like there were anywhere from fifty to a hundred people there.

With the change in camps, we also had a change in guards.
When we got to Auschwitz, Moe left with most of his squad,
and a bunch of new people showed up. The new squad leader
was older than Moe—at least thirty—and he was husky and
strong. He shouted and carried on—he had the guards scurrying here and there, chewing them out at frequent intervals.
He seemed to be one of those people who are only happy
when they are miserable. We assumed that he was some
sergeant who had been passed over for promotion several
times and then had been assigned to guard us—and that this
was just adding insult to injury, that he felt his place was
leading a platoon on the battlefield, not nursemaiding four
damned prisoners.

He took it out not only on us but on the guards as well. At
first he was rather kind towards the prisoners, but we
managed to irritate him rather quickly. Some of the Vietnamese were very patient, but not him. He acted like he
might have been from the city—from a faster life than most
of the other guards, who were probably peasants.

He would give them orders in the morning. He usually held
a morning formation in the guards' house, where they
gathered around the table, and he'd tell them what they were
going to do that day. They'd all take off in different directions to dig holes or chop wood or carry in bamboo poles.
Sometimes he'd have a meeting with them at night, too, to
find out what happened during the day—and at the same time
tell stories about Sumit and 'Macho and Ror'back and 'Clu.
Later on Man With Glasses told Camacho they nicknamed me
the White Wise Guy.

Every morning he would assign two or three of them to
guard the prisoners, and sometimes he would help supervise
the prisoners, too. He'd get us out and have us do some little
detail like chopping up a tree for firewood. We'd usually

screw it up real good for him, and he'd lose his patience and tell us to get the hell back in our cages. He'd go off mumbling to himself. He talked to himself a lot.

He had black hair, of course, high cheekbones, rather deep-set eyes—more of a monkey face than the round face that is common to a lot of Vietnamese. And he had a stub of a finger on one hand. McClure figured he was such a nasty bastard that he just got so mad he couldn't stand himself and bit off a finger. He seemed to be more knowledgeable at handling people than some of the other guards—perhaps he had been with the Vietminh when they fought the French. He was old enough, and he was more or less a professional-type soldier. In many ways he was the perfect parody of a first sergeant at Fort Bragg. We named him Anus.

They had finished the slammers when we first got there, but they hadn't had time to furnish them the way they wanted. The second day there, Anus took me out of my slammer, handed me a five-pound machete, and showed me a pile of poles lying on the ground. "Here, build yourself a bed." No hammer, no nails. "Great! How the hell am I supposed to do *that*?" I didn't have the slightest idea, of course; I guess he figured I was being ornery or just plain lazy. He looked pretty disgusted. But they showed me how to build a bed. Took a couple of seven-foot bamboo saplings and peeled the bark off. If they left the bark on, termites got under it, they said. Then they put some cross-members on it like rungs, so that the thing looked like a seven-foot ladder. After that, they took some small bamboo about the size of a fishing pole and split it lengthwise three or four times. Finally they cut these strips to seven-foot lengths and laced them along the length of the bed with rattan vines until it formed a table top. Hard as a table top, too—very little give in the bamboo slats. They set it on four legs driven into the ground.

Anus made a project of trying to teach me how to split

rattan vines and make a cord from it. I guess it's a matter of learning the skill from childhood. I'd always get about four or five feet of it and run off the edge and ruin the vine, and then I'd have to start all over again. He used to get so exasperated.

Anus seemed to have about the same attitude toward Prevaricator. Man With Glasses had told me that Prevaricator had been "forced from the school bench" by the Diem regime because of his anti-Diem activities. He was probably from a wealthy family, because usually education in Vietnam is reserved for that class of people. He was a city boy, but he liked to pretend that he wasn't. Most of the guards went barefoot or wore sandals, but he wore shoes sometimes. He didn't seem to know how to do things a whole lot better than we did. He'd be trying to do something that the guards were doing, building something, but he wouldn't be doing it right, and Anus would come over, tell him to get the hell away, and do the job himself. And Prevaricator would just stand there and look at him. By virtue of the fact that he was an interpreter, Prevaricator probably came under the direct command of Suave, but still Anus had to put up with him because he was attached to his squad.

I was the one who named him Prevaricator. I wouldn't let anybody else name him. It seemed to be a fitting and proper name, because whether he meant to or not he told us things that just didn't happen to come true. He would tell us that somebody would be coming to see us, and then they wouldn't come. "I will bring you something," he would tell us—and it would never show up. He would come back later and tell us something had happened—"But nevertheless we'll do *this* for you." And then that wouldn't happen either.

I'd tell him I needed some more tobacco, could he bring me some tobacco. And he'd say yes, and then maybe I wouldn't see him for another week. Then he'd come back with the tobacco like I'd just asked for it a few minutes ago.

I'd ask him some long, involved question, and he'd just answer "yes." Something like—"I need to wash my clothes; is it possible that you can get one of the guards to find me some soap someplace and take me down to the well?" "Yes." And that would be the end of it. Of course, "yes" really did cover the question, it just didn't tell me anything. Having told me "yes," he'd just leave, and I'd never see him again. You could sit there and ask him anything, and he would say "yes." He was very strong on saving face. And if he didn't understand what you said, he'd just say "yes." That took care of the whole thing as far as he was concerned, and he grinned and left.

Naturally, with nothing to do but sit around and learn how to split rattan vines, we got incredibly bored. The slammers were close enough so that we could see each other, and they told us not to talk across the space that separated them, but Camacho and I used to talk quite a bit. They'd let us get away with it for a while, and then they'd tell us to shut our mouths. Then Camacho would start singing, and they wouldn't know what he was singing. Finally they'd tell him to stop, but they weren't all that strict. If we wanted to say something, we'd go ahead and say it, there was no way in hell for them to stop us.

Nonetheless, Prevaricator became our main line of communication with each other and bore the burden of our attempts to pass the time. He'd come up each morning and ask, "How do you take your meal?" This astonished me at first. "How do I *take* my meal?" How do you answer that? I finally associated it with taking castor oil or something, and I could understand it: how did I like my food, was I able to eat it. I told him something different each day, just to throw him off. "How do you take your meal?" "Oh, I couldn't eat it today." He'd come back the next day—"How do you take your meal?" "Wonderful, I think sardines are very good for me"—they gave us sardines for breakfast.

In all fairness, the food was pretty good. At least it was the best they had—we ate the same as the guards.

Sometimes the camp cook would come up to see how we "took" the meal. The cook we had had at Fort Bragg was called Coburn. He was a terrible cook—the worst. He burned everything. This guy being a cook, of course the first thing I called him was Coburn. In our sort of broken language together he'd ask me how I liked my meal. "Christ, Coburn, this is awful shit! Achhh!" And he'd frown, as though to say, "What am I going to do? I don't have anything else to give them. What the hell do they expect out here anyway!" He seemed to take a great interest in pleasing us with his cooking, and if I told him it was very good, he just beamed from ear to ear and ran back to the kitchen. If he had some more, he usually sent it up.

My own nastiness aside, I just couldn't adapt to the rice diet at first, and neither could Camacho or McClure. Roraback was never affected—he went right on eating rice by the barrel full. He thrived on rice while the rest of us were sort of starving, complaining and carrying on about how lousy the rice was and that we weren't going to eat it. McClure got himself to where he couldn't walk. Maybe it was some kind of culture shock. He hadn't been in the Army as long as the rest of us; he hadn't had his brain numbed as much. Maybe that was it. Roraback had been in the Army longer than any of us.

I had more or less become accustomed to the unpolished white rice; I could eat it, anyway. When we got to Auschwitz the first thing they did was bring me a plate of red rice. If it was polished I suppose it would be white, but this had sort of a reddish color to it.

"What the hell have they done to this rice?" I tasted it, and it had a straw flavor to it. I just refused to eat it, and Coburn came and asked me what was wrong with the rice. I told him it tasted like the roof. He looked at me for a long

time and went away. Then somebody else came—I think it
was Prevaricator. "What is wrong? Why do you not eat this
rice?" It was just sitting there in a pile on my plate—the ants
were taking it away. "I can't eat that. It tastes like straw. It's
ridiculous. I want some white rice." He went away shaking
his head, and they brought me some white rice later on.

But after we'd been there two or three months it got so
that I could barely swallow any rice at all. It was psychological. I'd just decided that I wasn't going to go on eating
rice. I looked too many days ahead, and all I saw them bringing me was rice, rice, and more rice, and I just rejected it
mentally, more than physically. Of course, I actually got sick
eating it, since I decided it was unpalatable. If I swallowed it,
it just came right back up. I'm convinced that rather than
there being something wrong with the rice, it was my frame
of mind. It was the same rice they were eating.

The Vietnamese seemed honestly puzzled and concerned.
They brought us other things, but that didn't help much. The
guards would go down to the mess hall in shifts, and they'd
usually send our plates with the first four of them who came
back. Or they'd bring it up all in one big pot, and they'd
serve it on the guards' table. Like one time they brought back
noodles, plain, boiled, rice noodles. "Oh, no, not *noodles*!"—I
just threw a little fit and sent the noodles back to them. They
went back talking to themselves—something like, "This is the
best thing we've got, we give him noodles, and look!" They
ate the noodles themselves.

They were giving me the best they had. Later on they
brought me a nice piece of fish, nice fresh fish, and I told
them I couldn't eat boiled fish. It had *nuoc mam* sauce on it.
I just took the damned thing and threw it out of the cage. It
was a big piece, a nice piece out of the middle—they gave me
the choicest part of the fish. Thought they were doing me a
favor, and I threw it out the damned door.

Nuoc mam is pickled fish. They salt it in layers, and the

stuff that drains off is the best quality sauce. And then they mash up whatever is left and use if for a sort of paste—that's the cheapest quality, which is usually what the Vietcong used. But I suppose it would have a lot of minerals in it. It just stank to high heaven and tasted worse. It would just tear your mouth open. You tried to eat it, and you wanted to spit and hack. But after a while the rice became so bland from eating it all the time that it was kind of nice to get a little something to flavor it. I started taking *mam* in small doses, and I got so I liked the damned stuff. After a while I got so I *demanded* a certain amount of it. Once I got to like *mam*, I didn't have any trouble with the rice.

Camacho went through the same thing with the rice, only worse. He just absolutely quit eating rice. I would eat as much as I could stomach, but Camacho just refused to eat it. He'd eat nothing for days and days. He got so damned skinny I thought he was going to disappear.

Prevaricator knew I was a medic. He was talking to Camacho one day and he came and told me, "Camacho's foot hurts very much." Apparently what was wrong with Camacho was that he had a vitamin deficiency or something—beriberi, vitamin B deficiency—something that makes your legs swell up.

"What do you think is wrong with him?" Prevaricator asked.

"Oh, he has gout—that's what's wrong with him if his foot is sore."

And so Prevaricator went back and told Camacho, "You have gout." Of course, gout comes from eating too much rich food—that's the myth, at least—and Camacho couldn't have had gout by any stretch of the imagination. He just blew his top.

From then on, every time Camacho had a sore foot or his legs got swollen, Prevaricator would tell him, "You have gout," and he would smile very broadly, and Camacho would just seethe. Of course, I always laughed. I thought it was hilarious that Camacho had gout.

But Camacho found a good way to supplement his diet. The guards would come over to his cage and say, " 'Macho! *Giai Phong Mien Nam!*" And he'd start singing this song. I didn't know what the hell was going on at first. Finally, when we got together I said, "What the hell are you doing over there?"

"Well, I sing that song, and they give me a cigarette or sugar or something like that."

Apparently they had taught him this song in the camp where we were separated, when we were out in the woods talking to Man With Glasses. It was one of their campfire songs, perhaps their anthem. It started out, *"Giai phong mien nam, chung quyet tien buoc. Diet de quoc my, pha tan be luc ban nuoc"*—"All together, forward march/To liberate the South!/Death to the Yankee invaders!/Death to the clique of traitors!"

We actually didn't learn what it meant until later, but Camacho said he felt it must be bad, because they liked it. He was sort of an attraction for visitors. The guards would come up and say something like, "You want to see those prisoners sing *Giai Phong Mien Nam*?" "Yeah, let me hear them sing it." " 'Macho! *Giai Phong Mien Nam*!" He'd start singing, and they'd cheer. Then they'd come over to me. "Sumit, *Giai Phong Mien Nam*!" And I'd just look at them. They'd mumble and go away.

Prevaricator took everything literally, and we made a regular project out of getting him to do things that would get his ass chewed. The most spectacular was the time he came up and asked Camacho if he needed anything. "Tell the camp commander I need toilet paper," Camacho told him. "I have much hair on my ass and cannot clean myself with the leaves." Prevaricator looked a little embarrassed, but he trotted off to find Suave. We figured Suave must be some-

thing like a full colonel, and I could just imagine an interpreter going to the camp commander in the United States
Army, some full colonel, and saying, "Prisoner up there
wants some toilet paper, says he has much hair on his ass."

A little while later Prevaricator runs back up the trail looking very unhappy and tells Camacho, "You must use leaves."

But Camacho would send him right back with another
request. It was almost classic, the things he asked for. He
convinced Prevaricator to try to bum one tailor-made ARA
from Suave, "just one." Surely *Suave* didn't smoke the same
horseshit we did. Prevaricator of course assured him that
everybody smoked that tobacco—which was true. But
Camacho insisted. So Prevaricator trotted off to Suave: "The
prisoner wants to bum one cigarette, sir—just one."

Then Camacho asked him if he could have one cup of milk
a month, and Prevaricator went off to Suave with that
request. But this time when he came back he told Camacho,
"Too much milk is not good for you." I laughed at Camacho
that time. I figured Prevaricator was one up on him.

Of all the guards, only one was continually and openly
hostile, a young little guy named Xuan. He always had his
weapon ready, like he would like to shoot you if he got a
chance. He seemed to be just waiting for you to do something so he could scream at you. Camacho suggested that
something must have happened to him to make him hate
Americans so much, and when we got a chance to talk about
it we decided that his house might have been bombed and his
family killed, because he never had a kind word. He tormented us as we tormented them.

By each slammer there was a big earthenware jar full of
water, and if we needed a canteen of water we went out and
dipped it out of the jar. They had a five-gallon kerosene
bucket they'd cut the top out of, and in that we'd carry

water from the well to the jars—about a hundred yards. It took two of us to carry the damned thing when it was full, and one day Xuan had Roraback and me carrying water in it to fill one of the jars. We poured one bucketful into the jar and filled it almost to the top. The jar would hold maybe one more quart of water, but it wasn't full enough for Xuan. He sent us back to the damned well for another bucketful.

When we got back, he said, "Pour it in."

So we poured off a quart or so, and I said, "What do you want us to do with the rest?"

"Pour it out."

I poured it out in the sand and then jumped up in the air and started shaking my fist, yelling and carrying on. *Wham!* he pulled the bolt on his rifle. Roraback almost had a heart attack.

This became almost a ritual. When Xuan was in charge of the work detail he'd make me do something I thought was foolish, and I'd get mad, and he'd get more and more hostile. Then I'd get stubborn, and he'd end up pulling the bolt on his rifle and screaming at me. I usually ended up doing just what he wanted me to do.

I had a major run-in with another of the guards, too, a big dumb guy who seemed to be the company eight-ball. Anus was continually jumping on Big Dumb for doing some stupid thing or other, and the other guards picked on him, made him the butt of their jokes, cheated him at cards—they'd be playing, and he'd start yelling, and they'd all laugh at him.

I tormented Big Dumb too, often for the benefit of the other prisoners. I'd get him really screaming and shouting about something, and Camacho, across the way in another slammer, would laugh. "Well, great," I'd think. "I got Camacho to laugh." And then Camacho would do something completely absurd, and I'd laugh. And McClure would laugh at both of us. But Roraback never found anything to laugh at at all.

I was a real nasty ass. I just didn't want to cooperate at all, and I especially didn't like Big Dumb because I thought he was dumb, for one thing, and because Big Dumb thought he could order me around. The other guards usually didn't bother me, and if Anus told me to do something it was probably pretty substantial, but Big Dumb and Xuan were stuck with guard duty most of the time, and to pass the time Big Dumb would try to get the prisoners to do something, particularly me.

But he'd tell me to do something, and I would just look at him—wouldn't do it, wouldn't make any attempt to do it. He'd tell me to get up in the morning, and I'd just look at him. He'd tell me to comb my hair, and I'd just look at him. He'd tell me to take some exercise, and I'd just look at him.

Nobody was being very cooperative with Big Dumb. We were trying to be as uncooperative as we dared on the occasional work details they put us on. After Man With Glasses left, we deduced that we had some value to the Vietnamese, and we wanted to see just how much we could get away with. I especially perpetrated a lot of these things. I'd say, "Watch this, let's get Big Dumb mad." I'd start walking away from him, and he'd start yelling. I'd turn around and look at him— "Well, what do you want?" And then I'd keep right on walking. "*†%$+!"—he'd start yelling and carrying on.

Of course, none of this was any secret to the other guards, but for one reason or another they refused to come to Big Dumb's aid. I think they figured that if he got himself into it, let him get himself out of it. Big Dumb must have known they felt that way, because it would just make him all the madder that nobody came to help. He was not only getting shit from his peers but he had to put up with it from me, too.

The guards had these little stick brooms; they'd bind a bunch of twigs together and make a broom out of it. We'd sweep our house, and we'd sweep the little yard in front of the houses. I don't know if it was Big Dumb's idea or Suave's, but Big Dumb came over one morning with this damned little stick broom and got me out of my cage and gave me the broom and told me to go sweep *his* house. "Like hell, I will," I said. "Sweep your own house. I don't sweep anybody's house but mine." He started yelling and carrying on.

"Sweep the house!"

He knew exactly what I was saying. He kept telling me to sweep the house. "No! I'm not sweeping your house!" He started yelling and screaming more. "No!" I wouldn't move—I wouldn't go back into my cage, I wouldn't go to his house. I was just standing there on the trail. He was getting red in the face, and his eyes were bugging out. He was screaming for me to sweep the house, and I was screaming back at him, "No, I don't sweep houses for people." Finally, *clak! clak!*—he yanked the bolt on his rifle, and I said to myself, "Well, this guy's just nuts enough to shoot me." And so I swept his house.

Once I was back in the cage I demanded to see Prevaricator and I sent a note to the camp commander. I complained that I was being treated as a servant, and I felt that I didn't need to be a servant for anyone. "I take care of my own house, and I expect the guards to do the same. If you want me to perform labor that contributes to the operation of the camp, this is fine. But I will not be a servant of the guards."

They came up, Prevaricator and Suave's second-in-command. "You must do what the guards say. They do not do this to make a servant of you." I was trying to play back some of their own stuff to them—that people shouldn't be subjugated to work for other people. They realized what I was doing, I think. But nevertheless they said, "You must sweep the guards' house, because they have many other duties to attend to, such as carrying rice for you."

In fact, the guards weren't using us as servants. When they weren't on duty guarding us, they were all working somewhere else in the camp, chopping wood, digging holes, building houses. They never seemed to complain. They worked cheerfully, no goofing off. Even Anus, who was in charge of the whole squad, worked right along with the others digging and chopping. It seemed like the few things they did ask us to do were more to break our boredom and give us some exercise than to save them any work. Half the time they'd spend more time showing us how to do some damned thing than they'd save by having us do it.

One time Anus told me to dig a foxhole in my slammer and then tunnel back and make myself a bomb shelter. They only gave us these little spades they had to dig with, and you had to squat down to do it. It was hard for me to squat for any length of time because of an old knee injury, so Anus jumped in and did most of the job himself—cursing me for being a lazy ass.

We weren't supposed to work, because we were NCOs. They knew we were NCOs, but I guess in their military make-up it didn't make any difference who you were—if the job was there, then everybody pitched in until it was done. That's the way they operate, and that's the way they really get things done, I guess.

But I tried to explain to them, "I'm not required to do this kind of work." Prevaricator would come up and say, "Can you labor today?" I was always frightened to hear the word "labor." Oh my God, I'd think; "No, I can't labor—I'm sick." So he'd go get Camacho. "Can *you* labor?" And Camacho'd say, "Yeah, I'll go out and work." He seemed to be enjoying himself, out running around. They didn't have him do anything difficult. So when Prevaricator came the next day—"Can you labor today?"—I said, "Well, yeah, maybe I can go out for a while today."

If I didn't feel like it, I just told him I was sick and he wouldn't push it. He'd just see if somebody else would go out. "This is exercise for your health," Prevaricator explained. "You must do your part."

Sometimes we'd all go out together, but at least at first this was seldom. Roraback just refused to work generally—bad back, sore feet, headache, whatever. McClure, especially in the beginning, couldn't work.

McClure went through the same thing Camacho and I did about the rice, only more profoundly. He threw up everything he ate, even the canned milk they tried to feed him. He got himself down to where he couldn't walk—he worked himself into that state several times. Nobody had any doubt that he was sick, but beyond that his illness was a mystery. It was as if he had given up all hope of being released and had decided to die. Coburn, who was the assistant medic, fussed over him. They got a nurse who was with them in the jungle somewhere near Auschwitz. She came in wearing one of those long yellowish dresses that Vietnamese women wear and gave him some injections and pills—I presume they were vitamins. McClure swore it made him better, and he did get better.

Prevaricator in his endless search for symptoms came to me one day. "McClure smell leaf," he said. "He say they make him sick. What do you think is wrong with him?"

"I think he's crazy."

He took everything literally. "You think he is crazy?"

It was obvious McClure's problems were primarily psychological. He was even more isolated from anything familiar or friendly than he had been at Hiep Hoa, where O'Neill called him a "cotton-patch coon." One way or another, we were all affected by being prisoners in the middle of the jungle. But Roraback was trying to convince the Vietcong that *they* were wrong, and Camacho and I had the attitude, driven into us in the Eleventh Airborne, that even though we might be prisoners we were still far superior to our guards. "Look at those clods," I'd say to myself, sitting there in the cage. "I'm making seven hundred bucks a month, and they're making sixty cents. Hell, I'm far superior to you bastards, and you don't even know it."

But McClure seemed to associate his situation more with the Vietnamese. We were all prisoners, but he was still black. Of course, he did get better. Maybe it was the obvious concern on the part of the Vietnamese for his health. Maybe it was because they didn't treat him like a "cotton-patch coon." Or maybe it was that Roraback was really the "out" person because of his attitude. Anyway, McClure got better.

V.I.P. FROM BRAGG

I finally fell out with Anus over a digging detail. Camacho was busy digging a big trench from his cage to mine, and Anus kept looking over at me. I was sitting there puffing on my horseshit and enjoying life—I'd learned to cultivate boredom pretty well by that time. He came over and got me, told me to come over and help Camacho. "Well, Anus, you realize that I'm a disabled veteran and everything—I have that bad knee and I can't squat. And I'll have to squat to get in that hole."

He told me to give it a try, so I got in the hole and said, "Oh, ouch, I can't do this, Anus."

He told me to get the hell out of there, then, and get back to my goddamn cage. He was really pissed off at me. Then he changed his mind. He wanted me to stay there and lift a little basket they used to get the dirt out of the hole. I told him this hurt my knee too, and he sent me back to my cage with a lot of shouting and carrying on.

It was really the first time Anus had told me to do anything that didn't relate directly to my own needs. My knee really was sore, but it was pretty clear that he thought I was just being a lazy bastard. It seemed that from that point on he put me in Roraback's category—a fuckoff. He jumped in the hole himself and helped Camacho with the digging.

It was one of their air-raid shelters and they got McClure digging them, too, because McClure was a very conscientious worker. Camacho and I weren't very serious about the chances of our getting bombed out there in the middle of the jungle. It wouldn't be long before I would welcome any work detail they wanted to give me, just to be doing something. But right then I was content to take my meals, smoke my horseshit, and feel sorry for myself and angry at anybody I could think of. It didn't take much to make me angry. The Vietnamese gave each of us a big handful of horseshit each week—more than enough to last through the week. But Roraback puffed his away within two days, and he would send the guards over on countless trips to bum some from me and the others. Consequently, I would run out before the end of the week, and that just burned my ass. It would have been a simple matter to tell him no, he couldn't have any of my horseshit, he would just have to ration his own, but evidently I preferred giving my ration away so I would have some damned thing to gripe about.

At first I thought the guards rationed our tobacco because we were prisoners, but as time passed we learned that everybody in the camp got the same ration, guards and prisoners alike. The same guards who would bring us our tobacco would be back in three or four days asking for enough to roll a cigarette, especially Xuan, as much as he hated us. Either he didn't get a very big ration or he puffed it up right away. He'd come over and say, "I'm out of tobacco—how about bumming one from you?" and I'd usually give him one. He was the only one who ever swiped any tobacco from me. I was awake late one night when he was on guard duty, and he came over and rolled himself one. He didn't say anything; I imagine he thought I was asleep and didn't want to wake me up. The other guards wouldn't touch that tobacco.

The youngest of our guards was about fifteen or sixteen. He was also the smallest. He looked like a little kid, a kind of jolly, roly-poly fellow. He had a little round face with little round eyes and a little round head. He wore bangs, a very common Beatle-type haircut, and he smiled all the time.

He was quite proud of being trusted to guard us. He thought it was a lot of fun to take care of the prisoners. They gave him a big rifle—when he was on duty he used Big Dumb's M-1. There wasn't any doubt about his knowing how to use it, but when he slung it on his shoulder, the butt dragged on the ground—almost a perfect caricature of a little kid playing soldier. He got a big kick out of ordering us around, but he was never mean with us. He'd yell sometimes, but never like Xuan or Big Dumb. He'd give an order very seriously, and I would pretend to comply but just deliberately do something wrong. He'd take it as a joke and he'd laugh. He was sort of a comical character, and I got a big kick out of him. We called him Little King.

After about a month Man With Glasses came to visit us again. This time, he brought two new officers who wore black pajamas and pistols.

The preparation for the meeting was like Fort Bragg when a VIP is expected. We got a special breakfast—some kind of fresh meat that I didn't recognize, along with the regular rice. After breakfast, Anus came up with a razor and comb and told me to neaten myself up. Then I had to straighten up my gear and sweep out my slammer.

As before, they took us to a place set up specially for the meeting, a kind of jungle gazebo, a little house with chairs, and a table for them and benches for us. Prevaricator was there too, glumly serving tea and candy and cigarettes. At first I thought maybe they were going to tell us we would be released, but that hope didn't last long. They were just passing through, Man With Glasses said, and they had stopped by to see the new camp and find out how we were getting along.

Then the new guy spoke to me in almost flawless English. I nearly fell over.

"I understand you come from Fort Bragg," he said. "How do you like Fayetteville?"

I told him I didn't care for it much.

He nodded. "Raleigh is a much better town."

I told him I didn't think much of Raleigh, either, since it was dry. I was just being snotty, but he wouldn't be put off.

"Yes," he said, "there are better places than Raleigh." And he proceeded to name a few.

He made it clear that he had been trained, not only at Fort Bragg, but at the Marine base at Quantico, Virginia. He talked about a Major Hackett who had been in psychological warfare at Bragg. "Major Hackett is a very intelligent man," he told me. "But do not believe everything he said"—Major Hackett might have been smart about psychological warfare, but don't put much faith in what he said about Vietnam.

The three of them also talked to Camacho, McClure, and Roraback. Probably Man With Glasses had brought along this VIP from Fort Bragg just to see what he thought of us—were we on the up and up. I asked Man With Glasses if we would be released and he told me, "Yes, but you must be very patient." He must have seen my disappointment; he told me they would try to provide anything we asked for. They would give us pencil and paper: "Perhaps you can write something about your situation here. Maybe if it is good we can send it to an American newspaper."

That evening Prevaricator came by with a piece of paper. "Write down what you would like to have." I made up a list of practical things I wanted, like bread, sugar, milk, but Camacho told me later that he didn't take it too seriously and had asked for comic books.

The visit from Man With Glasses and the Fort Bragg VIP was our last diversion for a long time. The camp was finished—with a place for the bucket showers, a classroom, even a volleyball court. It was a busy camp, but we could only sit and watch. The guards rarely took us out on work details, and they hardly ever let us work together. Sometimes they'd take us out of the cages to play volleyball with the guards and other people from the camp's company. I guess they thought we needed the exercise. Camacho always went—he'd ask if he could go—and McClure usually went if he wasn't sick. Roraback usually didn't go; he said he couldn't see the ball. I went a few times, but mostly I didn't go. I don't like volleyball. At Fort Bragg all the "in" group played volleyball, and I thought they were a bunch of assholes so I refused to play. Besides, I was a lousy player.

McClure helped pass the time by taking an hour and a half to take a bath. They used to get so mad at him. Big Dumb would scream and yell, "McClure, hurry up and take that bath." And he'd say, "Just one more bucket of water." He'd pour it over himself and then start sinking it back into the well again. Big Dumb—"No, no, no, McClure!"

I developed a way to spend about half an hour brushing my teeth, and I'd spend about an hour washing my spoon and plate with a smoke break in between. I could spend a lot of time watching ants, too. There was a bunch of big beetle bugs that crawled around the slammer, and I would smash one without killing it and then watch the beetle and the ants fight it out. The ants always won, either by carrying the

George Smith displays the National Liberation Front flag which was seized in the Special Forces raid on the Buddhist shrine at Rach Nhum.

Isaac Camacho and Smith at Hiep Hoa, beheading a chicken with a homemade guillotine.

NLF troops use bamboo ladders to penetrate barbed-wire camp perimeter, as they did in the attack on Smith's camp at Hiep Hoa. *(Pacific News Service)*

Smith's "POW kit." The hat and "Ho Chi Minh" sandals were presented to Smith on his release, but the other items were issued early in his stay in the jungle. The "liberation lamp" and metal utensils are hand-manufactured from scrap metal from napalm canisters and downed planes. The items are arranged on his makeshift knapsack—a rice sack from Texas, still bearing the insignia of the U.S. Agency for International Development (AID).

Smith squats in the black pajamas, with his "POW kit" slung behind him.

North Vietnamese news service photo of Smith and Camacho eating in the jungle with their captors, released to the wire services February 11, 1965. *(Wide World)*

The aircraft carrier U.S.S. *Card* floats low at the stern at her berth in Saigon Harbor, May 2, 1964, some ten hours after NLF frogmen blew a gaping hole in the underside. *(Wide World)*

Australian journalist Wilfred Burchett meets the four POWs. *Left to right*: Camacho, Kenneth Roraback, Claude McClure, and Smith. Burchett released the photo to the world press in May 1964. (*UPI*)

Nguyen Van Troi, Saigon electrical worker, executed for allegedly plotting to assassinate U.S. Defense Secretary Robert McNamara.

Cuban journalists meet the POWs. "Anus" is standing at the far right. Those sitting around the table are "Oil Can Harry," Marta Rojas, Raul Valdes Vivo, and the Spanish interpreter. The Vietnamese sitting in front is unindentified. The POWs are sitting with their backs to the camera. Smith and Shumann are in the back row. McClure is immediately in front of Smith, but hidden in the picture. Next to him are Crafts and Cook.

"Prevaricator" (*left*).

Norman Morrison, the Quaker pacifist who immolated himself on the steps of the Pentagon on November 2, 1965. (*UPI*)

Smith, McClure, and NLF cadre Le Van Diep at Phnom Penh press conference November 30, 1965. *(Wide World)*

Smith, McClure, and Australian consul John McNally at Phnom Penh airport, en route to Thailand. *(UPI)*

McClure at home in Chattanooga, Tennessee, with his wife. *(UPI)*

Smith reunited with his mother, April 16, 1966. *(UPI)*

beetle off bodily or eating it on the spot.

Once in a while Anus would treat us to a mandolin recital. He played pretty well, his favorite tune being the "Battle Hymn of the Republic," which he maintained was a Chinese song. Camacho told him that he wanted to learn to play the mandolin, and Anus was willing to teach him, until Camacho broke one of the strings. Anus took the damned thing back with a lot of cursing and muttering—mandolin strings are pretty hard to come by in the jungle. We figured he'd have to wait for the next tobacco run to town to get a replacement.

Prevaricator brought us the notebooks that Man With Glasses had promised. "You may use the book for whatever you wish." Apparently Man With Glasses wanted us to write down our thoughts about the war, but I drew cartoons instead. I caricatured our situation—Roraback in a cloud of smoke, smoking all the cigarettes, Camacho sitting on his bed singing songs, McClure trying to take a bath with a tin can.

One time they told me I had to ask permission to go out to the toilet hole, and when I came back they said, "No, you must ask permission to come back. If you don't ask permission to come back, you stay there." Well, I was very stubborn, so I stayed. But finally they got mad and told me, "You get back to the house." So I went in and drew a cartoon of me on my bed out there at the toilet hole with snakes crawling up the side of my bed and all kinds of birds flying around.

I'd give my notebook to Big Dumb with a new cartoon in it and tell him, "Hey, how about taking that over to Camacho." Big Dumb would look at it and laugh all the way over to Camacho. Most of the guards seemed to enjoy them. They'd come ask for my book so they could see the pictures in it. And Prevaricator went along with it too, at least until Man With Glasses found out what was going on.

Camacho drew them too. We'd try to outdo each other. It became a contest to see who could draw the most ridiculous caricatures. Camacho was more skillful, but I thought mine were funnier. I started a series copied from a *Playboy* feature, "Silverstein's Zoo." I drew facsimiles of Silverstein's ridiculous animals and recorded the verses that went along with them. Prevaricator didn't know quite what to make of any of it, but nothing confused him more than the Gru. It was a fat, vicious-looking quadruped accompanied by an enlightening verse—

> Don't pooh pooh the Gru.
> For if you do, he'll bite you through
> And chomp and chew and swallow you.
> But if you don't, don't think he won't.

That took a little study on Prevaricator's part. After a while he came up to me and asked, "You fear the Gru?"

"Oh, yes, the Gru, he'll bite you."

"Do you have many Grus in the United States?"

"Well, I've never seen one actually, but I've seen pictures of them."

Then he went over to McClure and said, "Have you seen many Grus?" And McClure said, "What are you talking about? No, I never saw any *Gru*."

From time to time they'd bring us a little pamphlet about the NLF activities that somebody had translated into English. They called it an NLF bulletin or flash or whatever they might happen to print on the top of it. It was a little newsletter that came out every week or so. Reading as slowly as possible, you could make them last ten or fifteen minutes. They told about the camps they had captured, the helicopters they had shot down, the battles they had won, and what hard times they had had, but that they would persevere. I was believing a lot of the stuff until a while later when they said something about sinking an American aircraft carrier. "Oh, this is preposterous! You can't *sink* an aircraft carrier.

Especially in a river!" They said they'd sunk it in the Saigon River. What would an aircraft carrier be doing in the Saigon River anyway? After that I decided anything they wrote was questionable. Of course, later on I found out that they actually *had* sunk one, a baby flat-top tied up in Saigon, but the river was so damned shallow it only went down four or five feet. It didn't go underwater, it just dropped down.[5]

Auschwitz wasn't primarily a prison camp. It was a guerrilla base camp, a supply center. I don't think it was a command post, but there could have been a headquarters there that we didn't know about. There could have been almost anything there that we didn't know about, because the place was so spread out.

Base camps supply all the guerrilla units operating in an area. It's a wagon-wheel type of thing: the camp's the hub, the guerrillas operate all around it, and they come in and get resupplied and go back out. And they have a main supply route that they supply the hub with.

It was a more or less permanent camp—they had a rice mill and whatever else they needed to maintain a supply depot. Keeping prisoners there was a sideline. There were all kinds of people coming and going. The camp's company would carry in rice on their backs, poles for building the houses, wood for the fires; they operated the rice mill and supervised the prisoners. Fishermen would go out at night with their tackle and come back the next morning with a mess of fish, and they had a hunting party out most of the time. The jungle is very thick—it's like virgin territory—brambles and twigs and briars and bamboo. It's just impossible to get through unless there's already a path cut. But the hunting parties knew where to go. They'd go out with their rifles over their shoulder and come back with whatever was available— deer, boar, maybe a monkey.

In February traffic through the camp started to pick up and the attendance at the evening camp meeting doubled and tripled. As more and more people came into the camp, they would stop by our barred slammers and look at us and point. I felt like the main attraction at the local zoo. Anus would show them around, and I figured he was telling them about the savage Americans. "Want to see a Sumit?"

"What the hell's that?"

"I got one up here in a cage—just caught him." He'd bring them up to look. "There he is, puffing on horseshit, look at him."

They'd come over and peer through the cage, and I'd sit there and smile at them. "That is one, isn't it. First one I ever saw. How'd you get him, anyway? What are you going to do with him?" It was like they'd caught a rare species. It was funny. They were laughing and playing around. They seemed to be in a party mood.

We speculated on the sudden influx of people. Before, they had come through the camp in small groups, stayed a few hours, and left with their supplies. But now they were staying over and having a big time. And then there was a sudden change of food, too. Coburn started sending up real delicacies—chunks of pork wrapped in a doughy substance, and a similar thing with dates and nuts. They'd bring up these huge rolls of the stuff, four of them on a string, one for each of us. It was not only fine food, there was so much that I couldn't eat it all. After each meal Coburn would come up like the head chef at the Ritz and ask how we'd liked the meal. "Gotta admit it was pretty good, Coburn," and he'd go away beaming, happy with the world.

This went on for three days—good food, laughing and joking, huge song fests at night. "Goddamn!" I thought. "Maybe the war is over." I didn't understand what it was all about until much later when Man With Glasses came again and asked me how I'd enjoyed the holiday. "What holiday?"

"Oh," he said slowly. "It was Tet, the lunar new year, our biggest holiday." It was embarrassing—in our area studies at Fort Bragg they'd forgotten to mention anything about the biggest holiday in Vietnam. And here they were sharing it with us.

THE EUROPEAN

Tet was in February, and it was sometime in March when Anus brought me the razor and comb again and that real luxury, one of the tailor-made Cambodian cigarettes. He told me to neaten up and put my house in order. He looked pretty good himself. He had his whole uniform on—black shirt, black shorts, and the floppy canvas hat he wore all the time. He got his MAT-49, borrowed it from one of the other guards, and took me over to the volleyball court. "Man With Glasses is back," I thought. "Maybe it's release day."

They had built their little gazebo over on one side of the volleyball court, but Man With Glasses wasn't there. It was a real letdown—we weren't going to be released. But I couldn't quite believe who I saw sitting behind the table—a European man, oldish and fattish and grey-haired, dressed in Western clothes.

"Who the hell's *this* son of a bitch!" I thought. "Must be some special interrogator come down to really whip it off me." Without telling me his name, he introduced himself as a journalist. "Sure you are!" I said to myself. "Just freelancing your way through the jungle."

He had two Vietnamese photographers with him, one with a movie camera. He had a camera himself, but when he took pictures of me he remarked, "I don't know if this will come out, there's not much light in the jungle." That didn't help any in convincing me he was a journalist.

My suspicions didn't make for much of an interview. He had what I thought was a British accent, but I figured he was one of their buddies and he was there for an attitude check—that they wanted to see what we'd say to somebody we thought might be on our side. I wasn't going to say a damn thing that would commit me one way or the other. He'd ask a question, and I'd answer "yes" or something else that didn't give him any information—just like Prevaricator.

"Well, how are you adjusting to the jungle?" he asked.

"Well, I suppose as good as could be expected under the circumstances."

"How are you getting along with those shower sandals that you have on?"

"Well, as good as could be expected under the circumstances."

"Tell me something about your house—what is it like?"

"It has a roof, a bed, and a floor."

Anus was standing there too, and nothing he did helped relieve me of my suspicions. Usually on these occasions the guards either went off and left us or sat down under a tree. But this time Anus stood right there guarding me like I was dangerous, a gun over his arm so he could blow me down if I ran. He looked very official and very military.

When the European asked me about my capture and how I'd been treated, I told him pretty much what I'd written for Man With Glasses. I didn't add anything new. When he asked me about the attack at Hiep Hoa I told him it had been a well-planned, well-coordinated, well-executed attack. He said that was true. When he asked me about the food, I conceded it was probably the best they had, but nonetheless I didn't like the rice. "Well, I eat rice myself, there's practically nothing else to eat," he said.

After asking my permission he photographed me and gave me a Cambodian cigarette. He didn't smoke them himself, he said, but maybe I could use one. He said he would notify my parents that he had seen me. "Do you have a message for them?" I guess he thought I might want to write a letter, but I said, "Tell my mother you've seen me, and I'm all right."

And he did. My mother said she heard it on the radio. Though we didn't find out until later when we saw Man With Glasses, he was Wilfred Burchett, a journalist just like he said he was, an Australian who had reported from behind enemy lines in Korea and Vietnam. Later on they gave us a couple of his books. One was *North of the 17th Parallel*, a really great book, a good history of Vietnam right after the French. The other was *Mekong Upstream*, about Cambodia and Laos. It was less political but pretty good nevertheless—in it he told how the CIA picked his pocket in Phnom Penh and stole his passport. I learned a lot about that part of the world in those two books. I wish they'd given me the books *before* he came out there.

Camacho and McClure and Roraback had their turn after me. I found out later they didn't trust Burchett any more than I did, and he didn't get anything out of them, either. Roraback, of all people, seemed to have the most to say. But when Burchett asked Camacho if he wanted to know what had been happening in the world, Camacho asked him who won the Clay-Liston fight. We were all kind of whistling through the graveyard, trying to show that they weren't getting to us.

Small miracles! Next morning up comes Coburn with fresh loaves of French bread. They had gone out the previous afternoon and got the bread, bringing it back in time for breakfast. Suave probably sent some poor bastard after it on a bicycle.

Coburn brought along a can of sardines for each of us too. It wasn't enough that Moe had shown us how to open a pack of cigarettes—now Coburn was going to show me how to eat bread and sardines. I was trying to eat a bite of sardines and then a bite of bread. "No, no, no!" he pantomimed. "Pour the sardines on the bread." And I said, "No, Coburn, damn it, I want to enjoy this bread. Now leave me alone."

After breakfast, the guards lined us up, told us not to talk, and marched us to the volleyball court. It was "Fort Bragg Day"—dress review. The whole camp company was assembled on the court in ranks with Suave at the head. It was the first and last time I ever saw them in anything like a conventional military formation. They were wearing their best clothes and carrying their weapons. Along with the guards were Coburn and his assistant cook, a big fat Vietnamese woman we nicknamed Charlie's Mother.

Suave gave an order to his second-in-command, who called the contingent to attention, and then they went through a salute-and-report routine. All the while the photographers were taking pictures. Then Suave made a speech in Vietnamese which wasn't translated to us. I assumed that he was formally presenting Burchett to the camp—formally, because we had already heard him addressing the rally the night before, in French.

Burchett had taken off his black pajamas and was wearing a short-sleeved sport shirt and slacks. While the cameras clicked away he came over and told us he had asked Suave to get us together to say good-bye. He said he hoped we would meet again under friendlier circumstances. Then, remembering what I'd said about the rice the day before, he told me, "Try to eat the rice—they can't come up with a bread factory in the jungle overnight, you know."

With that, he was gone. There had been no special inter-rogation, no indoctrination. I thought, maybe this guy is just what he claimed to be, and I began to regret that I'd been so close-mouthed and had missed a chance to find out what was going on in the world.

Then I remembered what he had said about their not being able to build a bread factory overnight. I smiled a serene smile—telling a prisoner of war out in the middle of the jungle that they can't build a bread factory overnight! I just enjoyed it. I felt quite a bit better. Maybe we weren't so far out in the jungle that people couldn't come trotting by. We had been feeling like we were someplace in a far corner of the world and no one would ever find us again, and then this guy showed up. People were thinking about us.[6]

I don't know what Burchett told the Vietnamese about his interviews but it must have been favorable. The guards seemed to loosen up considerably—there was a friendlier at-mosphere generally, and they began to let us go out on work details together and sit around and bullshit with each other on smoke breaks. The food seemed to improve, too. There was a greater variety, more meat—some venison—and some kind of edible leaf that Coburn was damned proud of. They were something like turnip greens and they really weren't bad at all.

Some of the work details were hard, but the guards never pushed it. At first I didn't want to work because they wanted me to do it by myself. But when they started letting us out together, so that we could sit down and have a smoke break and bullshit, it became a diversion. The detail they put us on most frequently was collecting and cutting up firewood, so I got a chance to see how their ovens operated. Coburn cooked at all hours without worrying about the smoke giving away the camp's location.

He had a sort of jungle cooking range. The tops of the stoves were about eight feet long and three feet wide, with usually four cooking holes. The thing was about waist high, set into the ground deep enough for the chimney pipe in the rear to be underground. They fired it from the front; there was one tunnel hole to the pit for each cooking hole on top. They fed the fires through these holes, which provided a draft for burning also. The chimney pipe in the back led to an underground maze and then, after a few feet, to an opening in the ground. By the time the smoke had traveled all the way down the chimney maze, it was cool enough so that it didn't rise but just hung there in a big, thick cloud. I never did understand how they figured just how long the tunnel had to be to cool the smoke but still provide sufficient draft.

Cutting wood was hard work, harder than it should have been. We weren't used to it, and we were all in different states of health. I wasn't used to cutting wood with the crude tools they had. They gave us an old crosscut saw and a hand-forged ax that we used to split up the logs. We called it a Donald Duck ax because it looked like something in a Donald Duck cartoon. If we felt like working and they didn't push us, then we did a pretty nice job; but if they came and ordered us around, then we immediately set out to screw up the whole works. Since the Donald Duck ax was completely unbalanced and the handles were homemade, we could break the damned thing about every swing. McClure was especially good at this once he got the hang of it, and he'd keep an ax-handle maker going full time.

It was usually Big Dumb who got stuck with taking us out to chop wood. He'd take us into the forest, and we'd cut down dead trees and lay them on a couple of sawhorses, cut them into lengths, and split them with the ax. They only let us cut dead trees because they burned better and smoked less, and I suppose they thought that smoke would show up on aerial reconnaissance photos. But the saw probably wouldn't have been able to cut green wood anyway.

These dead trees had about a million ants living in them, and Big Dumb had a real talent for finding the trees with the biggest ant colonies. When we cut the damned things down, we'd have to put them on our shoulders to carry them to the sawhorses. The ants would swarm out and climb all over us—we'd be dancing and cursing and carrying on. Big Dumb got a real chuckle out of that.

The meanest ants of all were the army ants. They usually traveled in really large groups, single file. At night you could hear them rattling in the leaves, and until I found out what the sound was, I thought it was rattlesnakes all over the place, hundreds of them. I was afraid to get out of bed. We usually found them on the jungle trails at night. They'd be crossing the trail and we'd step on them. They swarmed all over our feet and they had a bite like a bee sting—the pain lasted two or three days.

They were the really organized ants and apparently they were very strong. Once we killed a three-foot snake, and the ants came and carried the damned thing away all in one piece. A couple of hundred came to investigate, and they sent back for reinforcements. They just kept calling up reserves until they had enough to carry it away. McClure was convinced that they were going to come after him next.

But the ants were really mainly a nuisance. The centipedes and scorpions were more fearsome. The centipedes were about eight to ten inches long, and they had big yellow legs. They were not only scary, they were poisonous. When a centipede came along, the guards really jumped. They picked up scorpions and ate the bastards, so I figured a centipede must be a terrible son of a bitch. One day Anus caught one and took its stinger off and tormented the thing, but it was still very frightening. They move fast and turn quickly. You never know what direction they're going to go in—*whoops!* up an unwary leg.

The centipedes didn't seem to be such great climbers so they didn't bother us in bed, but the scorpions just delighted in getting into bed with us. The average scorpion was almost as big as the palm of a man's hand, and I saw some that were a lot bigger. Coburn caught one the size of a young lobster one day and ate it. He built a little fire, and he toasted the scorpion and ate the claw—"Hey, you want one of these scorpion claws?"

The scorpion's sting was vicious and could paralyze you like an electric shock. I was bitten several times, usually on the hand, but once I sat on one. I made it to the other side of the cage with a single leap, and for a day I could barely walk.

Surprisingly, there weren't many snakes. I saw a lot more snakes at Fort Bragg than I did in the jungles of Vietnam. That was a good thing for the guards; they didn't like snakes any more than centipedes, though they did *eat* snakes.

The most common snake was a large green bamboo snake. I think it's supposed to be about as poisonous as a copperhead, but I'm not sure—one of the things they didn't teach us about at Bragg was the flora and fauna of Vietnam. One of these things, about five feet long, got up onto the roof of my house and was slithering in and out of the thatch and around the pole supports. I got all excited and started jumping up and down, yelling and screaming at Big Dumb to let me out of my cage. He apparently didn't see the snake and thought all my carrying on was just a big joke. But I was making such a fuss that Anus came running up. When he saw what it was I was yelling about, he let me out. He gave Big Dumb a terrible ass-chewing and told him to go in and kill the snake. Big Dumb nearly fainted, but eventually he did get a big stick and kill the damned snake.

The night sounds in the jungle usually started off with a high-pitched insect noise like cicadas make. It would start early in the evening and quit right after dark. There was quite a bit of insect noise in the early evening, and then later at night it would quiet down, and you would maybe hear some kind of cat screeching in the distance, or the fuck-you lizard.

This lizard would stay in one place for two or three days and then it would move. You could hear it taking in air, *buk-ou, buk-ou, buk-ou.* One night one of the guards was repeating what it seemed to be saying in Vietnamese, and I said, "No, no, it says *fuck-you, fuck-you, fuck-you.*" And he went away, *"fuck-you, fuck-you, fuck-you,"* very pleased. Camacho cracked up.

Because of the jungle canopy we very seldom saw the sun. If we did, it was where it filtered down between the leaves. The canopy ranged from eighty to a hundred feet high. There were some places where it was sparse—where you could see the sky—but the Vietnamese usually tried to set up camp where there was a complete canopy that no light could penetrate. When they did take us out in the open field, the brightness bothered our eyes a great deal. Even in the evenings after the sun went down, an open field was bright compared with the darkness of the jungle.

It got light at about six in the morning and dark at about six in the evening. In winter it got cooler at nights, but the days were just as hot as usual—between ninety and a hundred degrees and humid, like the South. I would sweat just sitting around. When we dug a hole we'd get so sweaty that the dirt on us would turn to mud. Roraback seemed to sweat more than anybody, but the Vietnamese didn't seem to sweat much at all.

What with the strange animals and the jungle foliage, it was something like being thrown back in time. It was difficult for us to adapt; everything was different. Being without shoes, eating rice, sleeping on a hard bed, taking a shower at a well with cold water, dipping it out and finding frogs floating in it. I used to envy the guards—they seemed so at home in the jungle.

Of course, it wasn't their home. They had probably come

from villages and cities and farms some distance from where we were. And they had families and friends they were separated from, the same as we did. They got along better in the jungle than we did. They adapted quicker—they were more determined. But it wasn't really their lifestyle.

I'd never seen the ARVN try to adapt to anything except the American lifestyle—they wanted to take it easy and lay on their ass and drink beer every night. The Vietcong were just the opposite—they adapted to the most strenuous type of life and didn't seem to object to any of the trouble they had. On top of that, they weren't being paid anything. The ARVN were doing it simply because they were being paid. The Vietcong were really fighting for something. That's why they were winning.

We didn't go out of our way to show it, but the three months after Burchett's visit were relatively pleasant. We were still POWs and the Vietnamese were our captors, so we kept up our hard-assed attitude. We did as much as we could get away with, and we continued to torment Prevaricator and Big Dumb and whoever else we could.

One reason for this was that I, for one, had figured out from what Burchett had said that Man With Glasses had lied to us and we weren't going to be released. If we were going to be released in the near future, he would probably have said something about it. Instead, he told me to try to eat the rice—which sounded like, "You better eat the rice or you're going to starve here."

Despite his limited vocabulary, Prevaricator interpreted so faithfully that he even failed to filter out sarcasm and rudeness. One day the second in command came by to ask us about the food. It had been getting better for some time. But when they asked me, I answered with my usual arrogance, "It's probably good enough for *you*, but *I* don't like it."

When it was Camacho's turn, he told Prevaricator, "It's not too bad except I don't much like the taste of the rat turds in the rice." When Prevaricator translated that, the second in command almost had a fit. "He says for you to use polite language," Prevaricator told Camacho.

There actually *were* rat turds in the rice. They were about the size of a grain of rice, but they were black. Prevaricator had told us, "You must be very careful when you eat the rice—sometimes there is rat excrement in it." Consequently, I had my lamp by me when I ate my evening meal.

Roraback told them the food was good—the way he wolfed it down, there wouldn't have been any point in denying it. But I constantly bitched about the food. I bitched about the food at Fort Bragg, and I bitched about it in the jungle. McClure said, "Well, I consider it to be very good, under the circumstances." But I said, "Bullshit! What circumstances?"

We were getting sardines for breakfast, and I had it in my mind that the guards were eating something nice like venison. I couldn't think of anything more unappetizing than sardines for breakfast. "Do *you* have sardines for breakfast?" I asked once—the implication being that they wouldn't eat such a thing for breakfast, so why should they expect us to. Prevaricator told me he did eat them for breakfast, but I found out later he was just being kind. The Vietnamese consider sardines a great delicacy and would have loved them for breakfast, but they were just for us.

The rice was going down easier now. We learned to like it. Perverse as always, I had changed my mind and decided I liked red rice better than white. I *demanded* it. They were very confused—they were convinced I was crazy, and Man With Glasses said so once. They considered red rice inferior— you had to eat about twice as much of it to get the same general nutritional value as white rice—but they said it had more vitamins in it, and maybe that's what I needed.

One day we had been sawing wood and carrying logs to the mess hall for firewood. We sawed and chopped all morning. I was really working hard, and I said to myself, "Damn, I did a good day's work. Hell, they'll probably give us something good for dinner." We'd been having deer meat along with our red rice—small portions, of course. We had all told them we liked the red rice, and they were pretty much going along with it.

But for some damned reason that day, here they come with a goddamned plate of white rice and two lumps of sugar. I just stood there and looked at the rice. "Fuck . . . Fuck! . . . *FUCK!*" as loud as I could. Husky, a good-natured guard who looked like a weight lifter, jumped about a foot out of his chair and ran over to find out what was going on. "Look at this shit!" I told him. "I've worked out there all damn day and you give me shit like this!" He was taken aback. He looked at me like, "Well, what do you expect?"

The guards weren't locking our slammers any more during the day, and if Big Dumb or whoever was on guard duty was in a reasonably good mood he would let us visit back and forth. They had a set of Chinese checkers they'd lend us and I'd go over to Camacho's slammer to play, or he would come over to mine, or I would go play with McClure.

Sometimes we'd talk over our situation: what the chances were that Man With Glasses was telling the truth and they might release us, whether or not we should write him any more statements. We'd be sitting on a log smoking on a work break. It would be just casual conversation, not really a discussion. "Hell, these guys have got the support," I'd say. "What do you think, Camacho?" And he'd say, "Yeah, I think these guys are all right."

"Yeah," McClure would say. "These guys aren't bad guys at all." And he'd cite the incident in the village where they were under attack, actually under attack by Americans, when they took me across the canal and kept him in a house all day because he couldn't walk.

That had made a very deep impression on McClure—they were getting their asses busted, yet they took care of him, looked after his wound, gave him cigarettes, didn't rough him up or force him out in the damned swamp or anything. Kind of impressed me, too.

McClure was very agreeable with what the Vietnamese said, as far as I could tell. He didn't volunteer a whole lot of information, but anything they asked him to do, he did. In fact, he was always the first one to do it, very cooperative. I was less cooperative than McClure, and more cooperative than Camacho, probably, except in my arguments with them. Roraback, of course, dragged his feet at everything and tried to convince Man With Glasses that *he* was wrong, not us.

Camacho gave me the impression that he agreed with basically everything Man With Glasses had told us. He told me several times he agreed that what we were doing in Vietnam was not quite right. "Nevertheless, these bastards are Communists," he said. "They've got to be stopped."

But basically he and I seemed to think similarly about the situation, except that Camacho balked at writing anything. He had a fear of being prosecuted when he came back to the States. Nevertheless, he had written a statement—we all had, even Roraback. I shared his fears, but I applied them to the situation we were in. "Who gives a shit, really? What can they do to me—throw me in jail?" I figured I'd rather spend time in the Army's jails than I would in the damned jungle. I'd call Camacho to come over to play Chinese checkers with me. "Camacho, you think we ought to write any more of these papers?"

"Well, hell," Camacho would say, "I don't see anything wrong with saying what we think, what we can see. Obviously, they do have the support of the people."

Then we'd drop it and talk about something foolish, like, "What kind of car do you want when we get back?" or "How much you got stacked up in your back pay now?"

"You suppose these guys will release us?"

"Well, they might."

One day Camacho, up to his usual tricks, persuaded Prevaricator to ask Suave to give me a birthday party.

We'd have the Christmas meal and Tet, and I was talking about my birthday coming up. Camacho said, "I'm going to tell Prevaricator we're supposed to have a party." He called Prevaricator over and told him in great detail that birthdays in the States were very important days, and they were usually celebrated in great style with presents and a cake—he gave him the whole story.

We had a good laugh anticipating the chewing-out that Prevaricator was going to get from Suave, but apparently Suave was impressed enough to give us a party, and after that our birthdays were holidays. Birthdays were the last obstacle—we figured that if you could celebrate birthdays as a POW, then surely everything else went, too. What with our holidays and their holidays, we averaged about one celebration a month.

The guards would let us out of our cages, and they'd move their stuff off the table in their house, and we'd eat there, all four of us together. They'd leave us pretty much alone—this was *our* celebration—but I think it was the Fourth of July when Suave made a speech and Prevaricator interpreted. They gave us the Fourth without our asking for it. Suave told us they were giving us the Fourth of July, not because of the Johnson administration but because it was the celebration of our own revolution. They wanted us to realize that they were engaged in the same sort of struggle the American people had had back in 1776.

They gave us chicken in small pieces with our meals all the time, but for a celebration they'd give us a whole chicken, and if they could get hold of some bread they usually gave us that. At Hiep Hoa I had thought Tiger Brand beer was the worst in the world, but in the jungle it tasted as good as vintage wine. If they could they'd give us a pack of ARAs, sometimes a pack for each of us.

Every so often Anus would get hold of a bottle of what must be the Vietnamese version of white lightning, and he'd give us some of that. It was a rice liquor—fiery and strong as hell. He'd give us a quarter of a cup apiece. But McClure and Roraback wouldn't drink it, and Camacho would only drink about two swallows of his. So I'd end up with damn near a whole cup. It'd just about choke me, but I'd drink the whole damned cup. I'd get such a fierce headache afterwards, I almost swore off it once. But Anus was very proud of me.

At Easter they made a cross for us. I presume Coburn made it, because among other things he was sort of the camp craftsman. It had been made very carefully, sandpapered very smooth, set in a little pedestal. Probably took him a couple of days. They got a rosary from somewhere and draped the rosary around it and put little canvas pictures of saints around it. They brought a candle to burn while we ate. To the best of my knowledge, the guards were all Buddhists.

"40 MILES OF BAD ROAD"

Sometime in late spring we started cutting and hauling poles for a new cage, big enough for at least four men. It was to be between us and the volleyball court, not too far from our little clearing. The guards carried in the straw and put on the roof but they never put a door on it. It stood that way for more than a month. We speculated and speculated as to what the hell they were going to do with it. Were they going to bring in more prisoners, or were they going to put us in it?

But when we did move, it wasn't to that big slammer. Prevaricator came one evening and told us to pack up— clothes, mess gear, hammocks, the works. We moved out first thing next morning and walked about three miles into another area of virgin jungle. Only the guard squad and Prevaricator came along.

On our way we passed some small clearings. They were covered waist-high with elephant grass. Around the edges of the fields, close to the woods at one end or the other, they would have a vegetable plot—hot peppers, eggplant. One time we saw a farmer hoeing.

The guards stopped in an uncleared area of jungle and told us to set up camp. That was pretty simple; we cleared out some underbrush and strung up our hammocks. This time we weren't chained to the trees. Everything was very loose and we didn't have much to do except eat and speculate as to why we were there. Whenever we'd discuss whether we might be released, we'd figure they'd move us off someplace while they made preparations. We speculated that maybe this was the place.

Then for the first time since we came into the jungle, we heard the sounds of battle, a firefight only about a mile away. It sounded like an ambush—there were small arms being fired, automatic weapons. It lasted only three or four minutes, but it was definitely a firefight, because the Vietcong don't waste ammunition. Later they told us that an ARVN unit had tried to penetrate and was ambushed and wiped out. We thought maybe the camp had got word of an attack and moved us out as a precaution. We also wondered how big the camp's security perimeter was and how many people were assigned to it. I had thought the camp company numbered about fifty people, but there could have been hundreds or even thousands of them camped in circles around the camp. Then all they'd have to do to ambush attackers would be to let them through the first circle and chew them up between it and the second.

The third day in the woods we no longer had to speculate about why we were there. We saw Man With Glasses eating in a little shack about two hundred yards from where we'd strung our hammocks. So we weren't going to be released; this was going to be more shit about writing statements.

Camacho and I decided, to hell with Man With Glasses—we wouldn't tell him a damned thing. He hadn't delivered on his last promise—he was full of shit. We were going to show him that we could be stubborn. Camacho was the senior man, and we were supposed to follow his lead. He passed the word to McClure and Roraback but I couldn't see how they reacted because at that point the guards separated us again.

Camacho was the first to be interviewed. When he came back past my hammock, he was smoking the usual ARA. He gave me the thumbs-down signal: same old stuff, don't tell him anything. Then the guards took me down to the shack.

Man With Glasses told Prevaricator to give me tea, and he offered me a cigarette and made some pleasantry. I told him he was full of shit—I had written him his papers, and I hadn't

173

been released. I was just being flippant about the whole thing, a real smart-ass. I told him I didn't give a shit if I did stay there. Man With Glasses cut me off. He was really mad.

"The guards report that your attitude is terrible—in fact, the worst," he said. "You think it is very amusing that you draw funny pictures in your notebook and write funny stories. Are you not concerned about the war? This is a serious situation. There is nothing to laugh about. You complain that the guards make you sweep their house." He was reading out of my status report. "This is very bad. You have been in the jungle all these months, and you do not even want to sweep the guards' house! In your situation, how dare you refuse *anything*? We do not have to cater to your wants! We can make you sweep the *entire jungle*!" He was ranting and raving, but the words seemed to be coming from further and further away. I could barely hear them—I felt like there was some kind of a haze developing between us.

"When I told you to write the paper the first time, you wrote words that say nothing! You have wasted much time! You could be home by now!" I couldn't hear anymore. My head whirled, and I fell off the bench. I almost blacked out completely.

Man With Glasses was on his feet immediately. "Oh," he said. "I didn't realize you were ill." He helped me to his hammock, and I lay there for ten or fifteen minutes while he went and got Anus to help me back to my own hammock.

I was sick, obviously, but because I didn't go through the normal eight hours of sweats and chills it took a little time for us to realize that I had malaria, the falciparum variety.* I could barely eat, but the guards added sweet baby-formula canned milk to my rice and that helped some. I stayed in my hammock for three days while Man With Glasses continued

* This form of malaria is prevalent in the tropics. Although its symptoms are more severe than in other types, it runs a shorter course, usually without relapses.

to interview the others. After every interview Camacho would come back by my slammer and give me the thumbs-down sign. Then one time he came back smiling very broadly and gave me thumbs-up—go ahead and write. Some way or other Man With Glasses had convinced him that if we wrote something, this time we would really be released. But Man With Glasses apparently realized that I was in no condition to stay where we were, and we moved back to Auschwitz.

The day we were preparing to move camp, a big battle took place somewhere nearby. We couldn't hear it, but waves and waves of helicopters went by. It was a helicopter attack. Before we'd only heard an occasional spotter plane. Something was happening; maybe somebody was trying to penetrate the area. There were Americans up there piloting those helicopters, but I didn't have any hope of being rescued. The only hope we had was of the war somehow ending.

I made it back to Auschwitz on my own feet. It wasn't far, maybe an hour's walk. Usually they divided up the rice, and we'd carry some of it, but they didn't make me carry anything. I was pretty weak, but I made it well enough.

Man With Glasses came back with us and continued the sessions in camp. He gave Camacho a kind of outline of what they hoped we would write, and Camacho briefed me on what Man With Glasses was really interested in. If we wrote a paper along those lines, we might be released. We didn't have to if we didn't want to, but he wasn't guaranteeing anything if we didn't.

Generally, what they wanted was an assessment of the political situation in Vietnam: the crimes of the Saigon regime, the goals of the NLF, why the Americans had no business being there. I was in agreement with most of it but I was afraid that if I showed it too much it would be a step toward demands that I couldn't agree with—that they might ask me to join their forces or write propaganda for the Front. We were taught at Bragg that when you sign the first paper, it's just a progression from there on. I wanted to avoid anything that would implicate me further than just stating my own position. This I felt no qualms about doing—even though the United States would probably be after my ass for doing it. I said, "Well, this is the way I feel, and they can't take that away from me."

If anything, my malaria was getting worse. but Man With Glasses asked me if I felt well enough to speak with him, and I told him I would speak to him for a little while.

I had lost my wise attitude. I was calm and more or less told him what I really felt about things. He mostly repeated what he had told us the first time—explaining the war situation as the NLF saw it—but he added what had happened recently. There had been three or four more coups in Saigon.[7] "You can see there is obviously something very wrong with the Saigon regime," he said. "If the United States were not here, the regime would not stand one more day."

What he was saying carried a little more weight than the first time we met with him, when anything he said was very questionable. But after months of sitting around thinking about it, things had begun to fall into place. The U.S. had said this and he had said that, and what happened was much closer to what he had said than what the U.S. had said. We talked quite frankly about the situation, and about that time I decided that I had had it with war. I really hadn't been aware of the political situation when I came, and I felt that the NLF had a very good gripe. I sympathized with them, and I very much wanted to get out of the war myself. I didn't want to fight on either side. I wanted to go home.

To be able to rap with Man With Glasses was sort of an outlet. I actually enjoyed the conversation, and he seemed very surprised. "It seems very strange that you should change your position this quickly," he told me. "Well," I said, "I like to consider that I have an open mind. It's never been explained to me before, really." He seemed to buy that, and from my point of view, it was honest. Hell, you can't resist the truth.

"You have wasted much time," Man With Glasses said. "You have written much, but you say nothing." Of course, he was right. My first statement had more or less said that if what he told me was true, then I was wrong to be there. It really left me entirely out of the whole thing. "I want to hear what you say, not what I say," he told me. "I know what I say." If I would write something more concrete, Man With Glasses said, my chances for release would be very good.

Then he picked up from our last conversation, but without the anger. "The Central Committee is very unhappy with me." When he'd come back with my last letter and the Central Committee had seen that I'd given them a bunch of bullshit, they were very angry with him. "And so I must come back to talk again, and much time is wasted. I am an old man, and it is difficult for me to come and see you. I must travel forty miles. The roads are bad. The planes bomb me, the artillery shells me."

He was almost pleading with me. It was extremely difficult to keep from laughing at Man With Glasses when he went through something like that. He was a funny little guy, not at all the interrogator they had shown us in the movies at Fort Bragg. Instead of living in a nice big building like they did in the films, he walked forty miles of bad road. Later on, Camacho and I fantasied about Man With Glasses running that forty miles of bad road. He's been running that forty miles since he was a young fellow, and every day it gets worse and worse, more planes come in and the artillery is banging away. He goes scurrying frantically from bomb crater to shell hole, pajamas flapping as he puffs down forty miles of rocky road. The forward observers are sitting around just waiting for Man With Glasses, and when they see him coming they jump up—"Man With Glasses in the open!" And the rounds start coming in, the planes start diving.

Typically, Roraback couldn't find anything in it to laugh at and called us damn fools. Roraback was trying to indoctrinate Man With Glasses again. I never heard what he told Man With Glasses, but it must have been pretty sad, because Roraback didn't know anything more about Vietnam and communism than I did, probably less. Man With Glasses would tell him their side of the story, and Roraback would tell him something like, "Well, the way things are back in the States—the democratic concept of government and all that— we just couldn't accept anything you say as being true." Of course, Man With Glasses would blow his cool then. He hadn't run forty miles of bad road just for Roraback to tell him how bad he was. "Roraback is a reactionary," he told me. "He cannot see." I guess he had revised his opinion about my attitude being the worst.

Shortly after talking with Man With Glasses, I got so bad I almost couldn't get out of bed. One day I went out to the toilet and on the way back Camacho asked me, "How are you feeling?"

"Ooooh, I think I'm going to die." I was sort of joking. I felt terrible, but I really wasn't going to die as far as I knew.

But Camacho believed me. He sent a note to Man With Glasses that I was dying, and Man With Glasses canceled the session he was having and in about twenty minutes he arrived with the nurse who had ministered to McClure. After Camacho told them I was dying, I tried to look pretty dead. She gave me injections of quinine serum and some quinine tablets. They added vitamins, mild tea, and special foods to this treatment.

Man With Glasses produced a lemon—he had brought it down the forty miles of bad road in his sack. "Lemon is very good for you," he told me, and he gave me a lecture about lemons, that I must eat the peel because most of the vitamins were in the peel, rather than in the lemon itself. I didn't have much appetite, and Camacho gobbled up whatever I had left over from my meals. "Man With Glasses is funny as hell," Camacho told me after one interview. He had told Camacho, "The guards report that you have a very good appetite. This is good—but do not eat Smith's lemon!"

I took his word for it about the vitamins and ate the whole damn thing. And I got better, so I guess he was right.

Man With Glasses stayed about a week in Auschwitz. Before he left he came by to say he would have to be leaving, and that when I felt better I should write. They would reconsider my case, he said. "We do not wish to keep you here. Very possibly you can go home—perhaps sooner than you think."

NGUYEN VAN TROI

In the third week I started to respond to the medication. Now it became a matter of trying to regain my strength. Camacho told me that he and McClure and Roraback had already written their statements, so I wrote mine. I generally followed the outline he'd given me, which I pretty much agreed with.

After we got together later on, we compared notes on what we'd written. Roraback was resisting, but he still wrote a statement. He said it was something like the first one, taking no position. He hadn't said anything concrete; it was just words.

Mine wasn't as strong as McClure's but it was stronger than Roraback's—I think I criticized "U.S. imperialist aggression." Stronger than Camacho's, too. Either I felt more strongly about it or didn't worry as much about the military. Camacho was always worried about what was going to happen when he got back.

I felt that the fact that we wrote any statement at all put us all in the same category—the content was irrelevant. But everybody agreed that we didn't want any more of the war. It wasn't a good war, and we didn't believe in it. Even Roraback. He didn't believe that communism was good, and he still regarded our guards as Communists, but he agreed that our position in Vietnam was something more than questionable.

While I was convalescing the other three were told to pack their things and they left camp. I began to feel lonesome. But they were only gone a few days. They came back as quietly as they had left. Camacho told me that they had gone out about a mile and camped in the woods. The guards had taken them fishing. It was strange, something like a vacation.

A few days after they came back, Prevaricator asked me if I thought I could walk. I told him I thought I could, and we packed up our things and moved out—prisoners, guard squad, and Prevaricator.

We started early in the morning and walked through the jungle most of the day. On the march we came to some large open fields of elephant grass with little vegetable gardens in the corners. They told us to break off large, leafy branches from the bushes to use for camouflage, and then we walked straight across the fields carrying them with us. When we heard airplanes, they told us to squat down and put the branches over our heads. Every chance we got we'd try to spot the Black Virgin Mountain, but we never saw it.

"They're hard workers," McClure said. "They could have moved it."

Late in the afternoon we arrived at another camp that seemed to have been abandoned for quite some time. It was a smaller version of Auschwitz, with little buildings all over the place. There was nobody there. There was dust on everything, and the termites had left their trails everywhere. Most of the roofs had been eaten away in some places, and all the supporting structures were riddled with termites. The thatch had fallen through on many of the houses, but the largest of the buildings still had thatch on it. We strung up our hammocks and shared the shelter with some of the guards. The rest strung their hammocks under smaller houses nearby. There was a little stream that ran through the camp. So we called it Camp Little Stream.

One of the guards, a newcomer to the squad, built a little footbridge out of sticks across the stream and put his hammock by it. He was a tall, thin Vietnamese with a pointed chin, and I decided he must be a troll, living by a bridge like that. The Troll was a great trapper. He snared all kinds of birds and then popped them into a little cooking pot and asked us if we wanted to share them.

There was another new guard along with us who had fairly long hair and a sort of pretty little Vietnamese face. Camacho said, "Christ, man, they've got a girl." But we caught her in the shower one day and found out that she wasn't a girl after all. That's why we named him Gidget, after the Debbie Reynolds movie in the fifties.

The thatch that we slept under wasn't much help. It was the rainy season and the roof leaked like hell. It would start in the afternoon, rain for an hour or so, and then quit. Sometimes it would start very suddenly with a lot of thunder and lightning; and then it would just pour and drown out all the noise.

We thought we had moved to Little Stream for the period

before being released. Camacho said Man With Glasses had told him that we would be moved to another camp to wait while arrangements were made for our release. Here at Little Stream the guards relaxed their security completely. They were friendly with us and let us get together all the time and carry on long conversations. We slept and ate alongside the guards, and we didn't have any work to do. The only thing Anus had us do was dig an air-raid shelter, but he let us do it in a very lackadaisical manner. We just lay around and more or less enjoyed ourselves. We thought that this was it—we were just waiting for the approval of the Central Committee. "Perhaps sooner than you think," Man With Glasses had said, and three or four weeks had elapsed since then.

Prevaricator even set up a class to teach us Vietnamese, but our response was so poor that he got discouraged and quit. He had a blackboard and everything. He tried to teach us the kind of Vietnamese you learn in language school—what was the correct word and what was the word the guards used. It was all very confusing. Besides, Camacho and I had already picked up quite a bit of the language—enough to make out more or less what the guards were saying to each other—and we didn't want the Vietnamese to know how much we could understand.

We ate very well, too. There was plenty of food, with more meat and fish than usual. Some of the guards would go out hunting every day, and they never came back empty handed. Once a hunting party from another camp passed through and gave us the head of a wild boar, and they cooked the whole head—Roraback got the roof of the mouth and Camacho got a jaw bone. We celebrated one of their holidays, too, with a feast; lacking beer, they gave us some white lightning.

We were waiting for our release, but we didn't get too impatient about it. Man With Glasses would have to run this forty miles of bad road back to the Central Committee. They would have to work out all the logistics—what route we'd take, where we'd be released. It would all take time. It was good enough to know that they were making the arrangements. We could have escaped—they stopped watching us closely and at night we were no longer locked up in cages. It was possible to get out of their sight, though escaping from the jungle was another thing. But there didn't seem any point in it. Things were looking better rather than worse, so it would be stupid to try to escape.

It was sometime in October—we'd been in the camp about three weeks—when a messenger arrived from the Central Committee. It was about nine in the morning and we were all sitting around in our hammocks, speculating about whether we'd be released and what we were going to do when we got home. We were quite excited to see him.

He spoke to Anus and some of the others, and they seemed taken aback. We didn't know what was going on; rather than looking over and smiling with us, they gave us an "I'll-be-goddamned" look.

Anus came over and told us, "Roll up the shit. Let's go." The guards tightened up their security a bit, and they seemed less happy than they'd been before, and less friendly. They didn't tell us what was happening, why the change in attitude, or where we were going. It was a sustained march straight back to Auschwitz. When we had come to Little Stream, I was just recovering from malaria, and piddled along. We'd sit down and have a drink of water and smoke a cigarette. But going back we didn't take breaks and waste time, we moved out.

Auschwitz had been abandoned. They'd torn the bars off our slammer and thrown them in the grass. Coburn was still there with a few of the camp's company, and he gave us lunch. We sat around long enough to have a horseshit, and then they told us to roll it up and we moved out.

But when we got on the trail we started catching up with the convoy loaded down with everything they could carry—

pots and pans and rice and all their belongings. And by late afternoon we came out by the side of a big wide stream into a new camp. There were already some buildings. Anus had us string up our hammocks and start digging a shelter. We weren't on our way to being released; we were there to stay. We couldn't figure out why they had changed their minds. It was a crushing disappointment.

One day a few weeks later Prevaricator brought some tobacco and dropped off one of the NLF news flashes. We hadn't had any for a while, and this one was two or three weeks old, as usual.

I read in it that the Saigon government had executed a seventeen-year-old NLF cadre, Nguyen Van Troi, just about the time they decided not to release us. They had caught him about six weeks earlier trying to set some charges under a bridge that McNamara was supposed to cross over.[8] The NLF had been warning the U.S. and Saigon that if they executed him they would jeopardize the American prisoners the NLF was holding captive.

"God damn!" I read that and it really pissed me off. "They were going to release us! I'm sure they were going to release us. And then those guys did *this* shit!" Camacho and McClure read the thing too. I don't know if Roraback did—he always said he couldn't see to read. I said, "They've executed that guy, and this has really blown our chances right down the damned drain."

We were that close to being released, and we had to admit that this was why we hadn't been. It was so frustrating, so maddening. The U.S. knows we're prisoners and knows there's no way they can help us, and they go and pull that bullshit in Saigon. We figured they really didn't give a good rat's ass for us if they could carry on like that.

If nothing else ever caused me to lose faith in the United

States government, that execution very definitely did. I certainly didn't owe any allegiance to anyone who would be that inconsiderate of our welfare, who would jeopardize us by executing some guy for *attempting* to blow up McNamara. They could have jailed the guy or used him in a prisoner exchange. They knew that the NLF had us and a lot of others, and that the NLF was saying they would retaliate if the guy was executed. They caused us to stay another year, at least, and they caused Roraback's eventual death.

I stopped blaming my captors so much at that point. I wasn't mad at the Vietnamese for not releasing us. They weren't going to have a man executed and then go ahead and release Americans. The United States would go around executing the hell out of everybody if they thought it would persuade the NLF to *release* its prisoners. They had to keep us—they had no choice.

As far as I was concerned the United States and the Saigon government became directly responsible for our captivity from that point on.

PART FOUR:
HARD
TIMES

BIG STREAM

Camp Big Stream was at the largest stream we had seen in the jungle—very wide and four or five feet deep. But the cover was very light. It was almost open country—there were just small brush-like trees, ten or fifteen feet high. The camp was temporary. The Vietnamese didn't make any real attempt to build it up.

For a while we were "the enemy" again to the guards, but then their animosity wore off and we got back on the footing we had been on before Nguyen Van Troi's execution. We marked our first anniversary as prisoners. On the one hand, it seemed incredible that we had been prisoners for so long, but on the other it seemed like it had been forever. We were so engrossed with day-to-day happenings and the daily routine that it was getting difficult to think of another way of life.

The stream was full of fish. We had all the fish we could eat. There were some carp, but they were mostly something like catfish. From time to time the guards let us take a bath and flop around in the stream. It had a good current and it was nice and cool. After taking out baths with buckets out of a well for so long, it was relaxing to go for a swim.

There were lots of people camped up and down the stream. We could hear them talking and could smell smoke from different directions. People would pass through carrying sacks of fish. I saw some of the guards training with little sticks and hoops simulating firing a mortar. They'd make a hoop with a rattan vine and set the stick in the circle to simulate serving a mortar. Some of the people passing through were going to their training area carrying these rattan mortars and sticks for rifle practice.

They didn't make us do much work and we spent most of our time playing cards. They'd given us a deck of cards and let us build a rattan table to play on. We played hearts. It was a good way to pass the time, but we got into fights, mostly because Roraback would accuse us of cheating. Roraback had never learned how to play pinochle. If you played pinochle like the rest of us, then hearts is a very simple game, because you only have to deal with fifty-two cards and four suits, not eighty cards and two sets of mostly face cards. I could play three or four cards in order to produce the other cards in the suit; and if there was one card left, I'd know who had it.

Roraback couldn't figure out how you did that. If we were playing together, I'd try to tell him. Sometimes he'd just play off the wrong suit, renege, and come out with the card later. "Oh, was that played before?" Once in a while our arguments would get so violent the guards would have to break up the game.

Our only real work at the camp was cutting enough firewood for the guards and ourselves. Big Stream didn't have the fancy oven system they'd had at Auschwitz, so we'd have to wait until after it got dark for Coburn to cook our rice and fish. In the mornings we usually had cold rice from the night before, with maybe some cold fish.

We dug ourselves air-raid shelters, too, and every time a plane would come over they'd have us head for the shelters. They'd try to see who'd get to the air-raid shelter fastest. I was usually one of the first. A B-26 came after us one day and I thought he had us. He was going over and then all of a sudden he dived. We thought he'd seen the camp and was going to let us have it. He had that vulcan cannon, and he could strafe like hell with it. We thought he was just going to level the vegetation.

I didn't waste any time that day. I don't believe I ever ran so fast. I passed Anus on the way and more or less leaped the last ten feet to the hole. The B-26 came right down the trail behind me and made a pass right over our heads.

Release seemed further away than ever and Camacho relapsed into the gout again. He also began taking his day-dreaming breaks. He used to withdraw into himself. I wanted him to play cards one day. He said, "No, I want to day-dream."

"Camacho, you can't do that, you know," I said. "That's a very sick attitude."

"Well, I'm going to—I just want to do it."

He'd go over and lie in his hammock and daydream. He'd dream about cars—what car he was going to buy when he got back to the States. Sometimes I did that myself, but I didn't take time out to daydream.

The guards made regular PX runs from Big Stream. They rotated the job. They were going to town and coming back with supplies, and we equated it with when we used to go on R&R leaves to Saigon. We'd go into town and cat around Tu Do Street and get drunk and carry on. Just to have something to laugh about, we'd imagine them doing the same things: Anus and Troll down on Tu Do Street getting drunk and playing dice with the bar girls.

I had the impression that they had a small slush fund to take care of our essentials—new toothbrushes, soap, what-ever—and if anything was left over they could buy us some-thing special. One time it was Prevaricator's turn to make the run. When Anus gave him the shopping list, he told him to buy us something special we might like.

In a couple of days Prevaricator was back, and he handed Anus the usual supply of kerosene, tobacco, cigarette papers, ball-point pen fillers, and so forth. Then he gave him a strange-looking can. They talked back and forth, and Anus was getting madder by the moment. Finally he just blew up and threw down the can, and it rolled down a little hill. From what we could pick up, it seemed the scene went something like this.

> Anus: What is this?
> Prevaricator: Butter.
> Anus: Butter? What is butter?
> Prevaricator: It is eaten on bread. Americans like it.
> Anus: Bread? Where is the bread?
> Prevaricator: There was no money left for bread.
> Anus: You mean you spent all the money on butter which is to be put on bread that you could not buy?
> Prevaricator (shuffling feet): Yes.
> Anus: How much did you spend for this thing called butter for which there is no use?

Whatever Prevaricator told him, Anus just completely blew up and threw down the can. Prevaricator sidled away, and Anus was left there muttering to himself. He picked up the can and put it on a little shelf he had built beside his hammock for his toilet articles. He'd see it there when he got up, and it would put him in his bad mood for the day. He'd get up—"Some day I'll kill that bastard"—and go off to work.

Prevaricator tried to salvage some praise for his gesture by coming over to tell us he had bought us some butter. Good, we told him. We like butter. When can we have it? Well, soon maybe. Great, how about some bread?—that's how we eat butter. "Yes." And he turned and walked away, thoroughly defeated.

We had come to Big Stream in the early part of the rainy season, and when it got into the really heavy part, the stream began to rise and rise. The houses started looking like little islands in a lake. If we had stayed there we probably would have been completely inundated. Nobody could remember having seen so much rain. So we moved again. And Anus carefully brought the can of butter along.

The new camp looked familiar, but they were all built on much the same pattern. They put us into slammers whose bars had been removed—McClure and Roraback in one with three beds, Camacho and me in another with two. After a while we realized we were back at Auschwitz, on the far side of the camp from where we had been before.

On the way back to Auschwitz we noticed what looked like five-hundred-pound-bomb craters in the fields. They were about fifteen feet across and six feet deep. The dirt was heaped up around the outside of them, and they were full of water. In the open fields there would be about two close together and then none for some distance. In the wooded areas there were no craters because the bombs exploded in the trees. Napalm canisters would be caught in the tree limbs or else on the ground where they had fallen among the trees. They were burst open and had obviously burned. But napalm doesn't do much in the jungle. It burns a little bit in the treetops, but it doesn't really damage the trees that much. It was a waste for the Americans—but not for the Vietnamese. They were overjoyed to find a napalm canister—it meant a fresh supply of metal. They all had hobbies building things, usually in the evenings, or in the daytime when they were guarding us.

They built a lot of Chinese-style spoons out of the aluminum napalm canisters. They'd flatten a piece of the metal and outline the shape of the spoon, then cut it out with a machete. Then they'd hollow out a hole in the piece of wood, put the spoon over it, and pound on the spoon until it was as rounded as the hole in the wood. They'd hammer out a spoon in three or four hours and then file down the rough edges.

They'd work like hell for a couple of days making the little lamps they used instead of flashlights. They'd take a three-ounce medicine bottle and make a wick for it out of mosquito-net threads that they twisted together and then fed through an empty ball-point pen filler. They'd take this and put it with the filler spring in a .30-caliber carbine shell casing with a hole drilled in the end. Then they'd fit the whole assembly into the neck of the medicine bottle—the shell casing was a perfect fit for the neck of the bottle. A little bit of the pen filler with the wick coming out of it would stick out, and they'd push it down into the spring and screw the bottle cap on when they weren't using the lamp. When they were using it, they'd pour some kerosene in the bottle, light the wick, and put a leaf behind it for a reflector.

The Vietnamese made use of everything. There was no such thing as garbage lying around—whatever people couldn't eat they fed to the camp dogs, or the chickens, or the half dozen little pigs that Coburn kept and which used to come up and wander around in my slammer. In one of the papers there was a cartoon that showed two grinning Vietnamese carrying a U.S. helicopter off on a pole, like they carried game. We figured that they broke it down and used all the parts. McClure speculated that they made spoons and plates out of the armor, and Camacho figured that they used the motor to run a rice mill. They could have used the wheel bearings in homemade claymores and made underground chimneys from the exhaust stacks, sandals from the tires, knapsacks from the troop seats. And when the motor wore out from running the rice mill, I'm sure they took it apart and found something to use all the pieces for. They wasted nothing.

Auschwitz itself had been bombed while we were away.

We couldn't see the entire camp, just the places we frequented. On the way to the mess hall there was a bomb crater close to an out-of-use well, and around that area an air burst had taken several small trees out. By another well there was another small crater.

Auschwitz was in a free bomb zone. The pilot would fly over and say, "Well, why not?" and drop his bombs, and then fly back to Saigon. He doesn't care whether there's anything down there or not. He's over the jungle: it's a free bomb zone. The Vietnamese understand this. If they drop bombs where there's nothing, they're just dropping bombs. If they drop bombs on a target repeatedly, the NLF would suspect that they knew a camp was there.

We got a new camp commander. Suave didn't make any departing speech; he just left. But we had seen him and the new camp commander together a couple of times, and by the time Prevaricator brought him up and introduced him, we had already given him a name. Even before Suave left, he was nosing around. "Who's this character coming up here, looking around?" Camacho asked. "He acts like Oil Can Harry."

Oil Can Harry is from the Mighty Mouse cartoon—a big tall cat that wears a black suit, a long black coat, and a black hat. He prowls around making trouble. In his black pajamas, we figured he looked like Oil Can Harry; but after he became camp commander the name fitted him even better. He was a real no-nonsense type, and he seemed to lack the polish and diplomacy that had made Suave suave. Suave didn't care if we were there or not, but Oil Can was always coming around bitching about some damn thing.

Oil Can told us, "You must work to eat"—no work, no food. I don't know if he ever enforced it or not—we worked like we had worked before, and we ate. But we had a new work detail at Auschwitz, milling rice, and no helicopter motor to run the damned rice mill, either. The rice mill consisted of two concrete slabs, one on top of the other, with a hole through the top one. The rest of the thing looked like a keg of nails—half the keg was on the bottom supporting one concrete slab, and the other half of the keg was on the top. It had a lid which had a small bar sticking out from it parallel to the ground, and attached to this was one end of a long lever. We'd push the lever back and forth, and once we'd got the thing turning we just kept the pressure on it and the momentum of the turning concrete slab kept it rotating. It's the principle that a piston works on in a car or a train. The piston comes down and turns the crankshaft just as our lever was turning the bar—only *we* were creating the power, instead of the explosion on the piston.

It was really very primitive. If the two people didn't push and pull together, the thing wouldn't operate. It would just get to the other side and stop, and you'd have to wiggle the lever around to get it off dead center again. You poured the paddy into the center hole, and pushed and pulled on the lever to get the thing going. As the rice was husked, it worked its way out to pile up around the sides.

Then we'd put it on a screen and, while one man waved the "wind machine"—a piece of burlap stretched between two sticks—another would throw the rice in the air and catch it. Then we sifted the rice to eliminate the mash, which they fed to the pigs, and poured the rice into a bin. We averaged about a hundred pounds of finished rice a day.

We had to use the wind machine because there wasn't any breeze in the jungle to blow away the chaff. McClure was the best at throwing and catching the rice. It looked simple, but it turned out the rest of us were more useful pushing the lever. If I threw the rice up so that I could catch it, the chaff didn't blow away; and if I threw it up to lose the chaff, I lost half the rice along with it. The rice we milled was for the guards and ourselves. If we'd been left to our own devices we would probably have starved, but the guards did most of the tricky work.

The guards never took us back to where we'd lived before, but they did take us back to the volleyball court to play once in a while. They were friendly and their security had loosened up. We thought maybe they were again cranking up to release us. We decided that if they were going to let us go, Christmas would be an ideal time. What better propaganda—POWs home for Christmas.

One day Camacho and I were lying on our beds just bull-shitting, when *tat-a-tat-tat* three or four rounds spewed across my bed and I was hit in the leg. Camacho and I rolled off our beds and hit the ground. I thought maybe an ARVN force had overrun the camp. I was about to jump in the hole, but there weren't any more shots. Camacho and I realized at the same time that the guard who was watching us, Gidget, had fired his damned weapon. He'd been playing with his MAT-49, pulling the bolt back and forth, and now he was sitting there with the damned thing in his hand and a stupid-ass look on his face.

My leg was beginning to bleed and it hurt like hell. I really did some hopping around and I cussed some, too. I really didn't get all that shook up, but Camacho got very excited about it. "Oh my God, he's been shot!" He was yelling at Gidget to go get a doctor, and I was trying to tell him, "Put a pressure bandage on it, stop the bleeding, and then we'll figure out whether a bone is broken or what else."

More Vietnamese than I knew were in the camp came running from every direction. As soon as they figured out what had happened, they apologized very profusely. Gidget just kept looking at his damned rifle as if it had gone off deliberately. Finally he put the thing down, took his repri-mand, and walked away. They took him off guard duty for a month.

When they finally got things organized, I got a compress on the wound. The bleeding stopped and I got a chance to inspect the damage. It was a clean hole. It had gone under the skin and come out again, but it had hit a nerve that to this day causes a numbness in my toes. I was worried that it might get infected—nearly any wound can be serious in the jungle. It did, finally, but we managed to control the infection with sulfa powder.

Some of the other side-effects were more pleasant. I didn't have to work, and Oil Can began sending me hot milk every morning. Prevaricator would come up with a thermos—it must have belonged to Oil Can, because I didn't see any of the others with one—and he'd pour the milk out for me. The others went to the rice mill, and I just lay there and puffed horseshit until they came back. They brought me special food. I wasn't really that bad off. I even gave Camacho some of the milk.

The only real tragedy of my wound was what it did to our hopes for release. We'd thought things were beginning to look pretty good again—and then they shot me. Camacho said, "Well, Jesus Christ, they're not going to release you with a hole in your leg." Not much propaganda value in that. That blew it again, we figured. But I really don't believe they ever intended to release us at that time. We were just dreaming.

One day Camacho and I were lying around in our slammer, doing nothing, when he said he heard something moving around in our foxhole. We decided we'd better find out what it was: it could be a snake, and we might have to jump into the damned thing sometime.

Camacho got a big stick. The foxhole was about six feet deep and of course we had a tunnel where we'd go in case of an air raid. He probed around with the stick, and something goes "hrrrrrah!"

"Christ, there's a goddamn dinosaur in there!"

We could just see its head sticking out. Its mouth was open and a forked tongue was coming out and hissing. "Son of a bitch, that's a big snake!" Camacho poked at it, and the thing comes running out. "Jesus Christ, son of a bitch *is* a dinosaur." It was something like a gila monster, only bigger, about three feet long, green and red and orange, with spines.

Husky came running over and asked us what the hell we were doing.

"Goddamn dinosaur in there!"

He saw it. "Damn!" He went and sharpened the stick and impaled the thing on it and took it away in the direction of the mess hall. We figured Oil Can Harry ate it.

We were a little leery of jumping down in that foxhole after that, but pretty soon we had no choice.

There were no bars on our slammers, so at night they'd tie our ankles to a post with a chain. This wouldn't have been so bad if it hadn't been for the "Mad Bomber." There wasn't any other military activity happening in the area that we could hear, but a B-26 started making regular bomb runs every night. He'd be flying at full speed, and when he happened to get a twitch he'd pull the salvo button and drop everything he had. It's possible that some damned guy had gridded a map and was working his way across it, night by night, square by square.

Every time we'd hear the Mad Bomber we'd douse the lights and jump in our holes. But when we were chained to the posts, that meant Anus had to come unlock us. One night the guards had a tremendous fire—maybe they were celebrating. They kept heaping more and more huge logs on the damned thing. Around midnight, the Mad Bomber appeared and the guards started yelling. Anus and the others tried to scatter the sticks but that just made more sparks. The damned thing must have been visible for at least a couple of miles—not to mention the column of smoke that must have been rising through the treetops.

We were yelling, too, shouting at them to come unchain us so we could jump in our holes. Anus jumped in his hole and left us chained to the post. "Goddamn it, throw us the key if you won't get out of your hole!" He just wouldn't move. But it was too late anyway. The plane was overhead, and everybody except us was in the foxholes.

He let it all go, and it made the whole jungle rock. The thing was probably traveling at about four hundred miles an hour and he dropped it about a second late. Just missed us—it wasn't a mile away.

That really shook us up, and we complained very vigorously to Prevaricator about being chained to that post. After that they chained us together instead of to the post, so that we could jump in the hole without someone coming to unlock us. And whoever jumped in the hole first would get the whole chain down on top of him.

The Mad Bomber kept making runs every night after that, but he would drop the bombs somewhere else. In the jungle it's quiet at night. We could hear him coming miles away, full throttle, roaring, and then he'd drop and turn and go back to wherever he came from. Some nights he came twice.

Every time we heard him coming after that night he'd missed us, we'd jump in the hole, because we figured he was out to get us. One night when he came back we jumped in the hole as he came right over the camp. We heard the swish of the bombs coming down—they were exploding in the trees right above us. He was knocking down trees right around us. He dropped some napalm, too—we could see the napalm burning in a treetop down near the well. There wasn't any real damage, but one very large piece landed in McClure and Roraback's house.

Prevaricator came up and grinned. "The bombs did not bother us—we have very deep foxholes."

KILLING TIME

The Mad Bomber didn't come back for a while. He didn't bother us at Christmas or New Year's. This Christmas wasn't as elaborate as the first—no star—but they did have a special meal for us. New Year's Day we had chicken and rice, fried in Prevaricator's can of butter.

We'd been really worried about that butter—the can was starting to get rusty. We worried about it every day. Anus had it stacked on his little shelf everywhere we went—just looking at it and swearing. We didn't want to ask him for it—afraid he'd lose his mind.

We ate at a little picnic table that Camacho and I had built in front of our house. The bars from the slammers were still lying in the grass where they'd thrown them after we moved away from Auschwitz the first time. Rather than serve us individually, they'd have Roraback and McClure come over and eat in front of our house. We were getting a lot of vegetables from the little gardens at this time. The eggplant was always delicious. Boiled, fried, whatever, it's a pretty good vegetable. We demanded eggplant.

There was fruit, too. Once they brought us grapefruits tied around their waists like bandoliers, but the other fruit came from the jungle. One was something they called a *buoi* that tasted like a cross between a peach and an orange, really a delicious fruit. They had to climb eight-foot trees to get it. Husky was one of the best climbers, and he was always very generous. He'd bring us a whole gob of *buoi*.

They brought Camacho and me a whole sack of hot peppers one time, since we liked them better than McClure and Roraback. Roraback finally started eating them because he felt he was missing something. Camacho and I were enjoying them—he couldn't stand that and wanted his share, even though it just about killed him every time he ate one.

Camacho decided to start a pepper patch. I told him I thought you had to do something to the seeds before you planted them, but he just took a whole core of seeds out of a pepper and planted them. Not long after that a little thing came up where he had planted the seeds. I told him it was a weed, and he said it was a pepper plant. He had planted it where the sun came through in the morning, so it did get a little sun. And he watered the damned thing every day, cleaned the debris away from it, and generally nursed it along. Thing only got to be about two inches high. The one or two weeds that came up were the extent of the pepper patch.

Troll gave us a little water turtle he had caught someplace. He told us to keep it until it got big enough to eat. We figured it would be fifteen or twenty years before it got big enough to eat, but it was a novelty. We built a stockade for it with little bamboo stakes—"a strategic hamlet built by genuine mercenaries." We put the turtle in, and of course it tried to escape, just like the people who lived in strategic hamlets did. It'd get itself up sideways and try to wedge itself through the stakes we had driven. We'd let it get about half-way through and we'd throw it back and repair the wall. We'd scold it and tell it it was supposed to stay in there and behave itself and be pacified, that it was a belligerent turtle.

We gave it rice and Camacho tried to capture insects for it, but it wouldn't eat anything. It was obviously on a hunger strike. It was just like a damned Vietnamese turtle to do something like that.

In the midst of our depression about not being released, up

popped a big healthy Vietnamese in black pajamas who must have been in his thirties. He was Chinese-looking, with very wavy hair. Many Vietnamese let their hair hang in their face, but he had his combed back. Camacho named him Alex.

Prevaricator brought us down all at once rather than separately to one of those little jungle gazebos to meet with Alex. He was jolly and spoke excellent English. He brought us the news of the day: the war goes on, the U.S. is losing— and he'd go on to list this camp overrun, that unit ambushed, so many helicopters shot down. He had a cup of tea but didn't stay long. He was coming to check our attitudes, I think—how did we respond, were we smiling or glaring at him, did we drink the tea, did we agree with him.

Almost as an afterthought, as he left he told us, "You will be released—as soon as your government recognizes us." That hurled us into gloom. "They won't even recognize Red China—and they're six hundred million people," I thought. "How the hell will they recognize this bunch of clowns." I almost felt like laughing. I figured it would take five or ten years before the United States would allow them to hold their elections. Then there would be a coalition government—there had been one in Laos—and the United States would recognize them and withdraw. There would be no victories. The Vietcong weren't going to be defeated, and of course the Vietcong couldn't defeat the United States. "We cannot conquer *your* country," they told us. "But we want you to get out of *our* country." They knew damned well that they weren't going to blow up San Francisco or New York.

Whenever Alex visited us after that, he'd always ask us, "What do you think about the war?" We'd tell him, "It's lousy—we wish it would end so we could go home." The litany ended with, "We agree, and as soon as your government recognizes us, you'll go." Gloom.

Occasionally Harry or Prevaricator brought us a radio so we could listen to the news. We had a choice—Radio Peking or Radio Hanoi. I think Radio Peking lasted about an hour, and Radio Hanoi about half an hour. Hanoi's English-language broacasts told their side of the story—propaganda. They weren't directed at anybody in particular. They read letters they got from ham operators in San Francisco and Alaska and Australia. But it was mostly news. Sometimes they would take a position on something like the U.S. bombing of North Vietnam, condemning it. Radio Peking was broader. The Chinese were airing their fight with Russia. They were taking off on people that they didn't like, as well as giving their version of the news of the day. They talked about the Johnson-Goldwater race, comparing them with rival motorcycle gangs.

We were taking what they said with a grain of salt. Later, when they announced that they had shot down five hundred planes, it sounded unbelievable. I didn't realize that there were enough jets going into North Vietnam to have shot down five hundred. They were saying militiamen were shooting them down with rifles. "Well, this is obviously exaggerated," we would say. All this was after they said they'd sunk that aircraft carrier in the Saigon River. Of course, that incident turned out to be true, and even the U.S. government admits now that the North Vietnamese shot down nearly a thousand planes by the end of 1968.

They never said why the North was being bombed. We thought the United States had just arbitrarily started bombing North Vietnam. But one night Prevaricator left the radio in the charge of a guard who started fiddling with the dial. It came to rest on an Australian news station, and for the first time we found out that the Gulf of Tonkin had something to do with it. They were supposed to have attacked a couple of U.S. destroyers with motorboats. When Prevaricator came and found what we were listening to, he almost had a fit.[9]

While I was recovering from getting shot in the leg, Camacho decided it would be a good opportunity to teach me Spanish. I went along with it, and Camacho would give me twenty words a day to study while he was off milling rice and test me on them when he came back. When I had about a thousand-word vocabulary, we started on sentence construction. He wrote me a version of the "Three Little Pigs"—"Los Tres Moranitos." What he couldn't remember, he made up. "The Big Bad Wolf" came out "El Lobo Malo," and the way Camacho described the three little pigs wasn't quite as they were in the original story. He made them a little more hilarious.

Camacho wrote the story in my notebook, in keeping with our tradition of putting only nonsense in it for Prevaricator. Prevaricator saw us laughing over it and came over and picked up the book. When he saw the thing was written in some language he couldn't read, he really looked puzzled. That plus our laughter convinced him we were in on a plot— perhaps developing a code. He took the book to Oil Can, but since nobody in the camp could speak Spanish they would have had to send the book to the Central Committee to break the "code." Finding a Spanish-speaking Vietnamese in the middle of the jungle would be only the first problem. Once they'd translated the thing, they'd be sure it was a code. How long would it take before they found someone who would recognize it as a bastardized kid's story?

Camacho and I talked and talked about it until we had spun an elaborate fantasy: Prevaricator runs up to Oil Can all out of breath. "Harry, I have discovered Smith writing a secret message. It is in a special code."

"How do you know it is a secret message?"

"It must be devious, because Smith was laughing."

Oil Can puts the book in an envelope labeled "SECRET" to send it to Man With Glasses. But he has difficulty finding a volunteer to travel the forty miles of bad road to the Central Committee. Finally he decides to bribe Big Dumb.

"Big Dumb, I want you to deliver this package to Man

With Glasses personally. Tell him that I, Oil Can Harry, have uncovered this document which is obviously a very important breakthrough. As a reward for having to travel forty miles of bad road, when you get back you can make Smith cut down a tree with lots of ants in it."

With that kind of motivation, Big Dumb makes good time. Of course, there are no planes bombing him or mortars shelling him, because the forward observers are only watching for Man With Glasses. At Central Committee headquarters he delivers the packet and message to Man With Glasses and is told to wait.

Man With Glasses is as puzzled as Prevaricator and starts showing the notebook to other people at headquarters. "I have uncovered a plot by prisoner Smith at Auschwitz. It is all here in this book, but it is in secret code." Twenty men are assigned to break the code, but finally Nguyen Huu Tho, President of the NLF, takes a look at it.

"Man With Glasses, you are an imbecile. The writing is in Spanish. Go to the Liberation Language School and get it translated."

Man With Glasses summons Big Dumb and asks angrily, "What the hell kind of message is this?"

Big Dumb hopefully repeats his original instructions.

"It is not in code, it is in Spanish!" yells Man With Glasses. "Goddamn you, you smart son of a bitch, you know I can't read Spanish!"

"Don't apologize, sir. I cannot even read Vietnamese."

"That's it, wise-ass! Get down in the push-up position and stay there until I get this translated."

Four hours later, when Man With Glasses returns red in the face, Big Dumb was paralyzed, bow-legged arms. Man With Glasses helps him to his feet with a well-placed kick in the ass. This results in a sprained toe and more profanity because Man With Glasses has forgotten he is wearing his Ho Chi Minh sandals.

"Big Dumb, go back and tell Oil Can Harry he is the dumbest ass in the whole damned war. And if he ever sends any more stupid shit like this to headquarters, tell him I will take his pistol away and put him in Anus's guard squad."

Big Dumb dutifully repeats the message to Oil Can and gets thrown in the brig for disrespect to an officer. Prevaricator is summoned to the Orderly Room and reports to Harry. "Stand at attention, you multilingual son of a bitch. You are the dumbest ass in the whole damned war. You tell Smith and Camacho not to write any more bullshit in their goddamned notebooks and that I'm giving them a bad mark on their record. And after you do that, report to Anus. He has a tree full of ants that he wants cut down."

My leg healed, and another Tet came and went. Coburn put on an even better feast this year than the last. They killed a big hog and served it with an endless variety of succulent goodies and heaping bowls of rice and vegetables. Even Roraback had more than he could handle. But except on very special days, the food after Tet began to deteriorate. The belt was being tightened. The milk disappeared. The dried fish fried in soybean oil began to disappear. They didn't give us vegetables anymore. We began getting less and less of things like these—it seemed that Tet marked a turning point and the beginning of an austerity program.

Shortly after Tet the whole camp started packing up for another move. Work parties had been leaving camp for as much as a week at a time to build a new camp, and it seemed they were going to abandon Auschwitz once and for all.

We spent more time at Auschwitz than any other camp, but it was typical of them all. It didn't have any definable center like a collection of buildings or a meeting place. But it was itself the center of a whole bunch of trails. Within its own perimeter was a series of paths like spokes of a wheel connecting the various buildings. The two places where we stayed at Auschwitz seemed to be at the opposite ends of the camp about half a mile apart.

All the camps we saw were located near a stream. The stream at Auschwitz was a source of fish, not drinking water. We drew our own drinking water from the wells—there were at least four of them. Everybody's living quarters were built like our slammers (without the bars) and they were scattered throughout the area with no particular pattern.

Having everybody scattered like that reduced the time it took for people to get to their posts in an attack and kept their casualties down if they got bombed—unlike Hiep Hoa, where a few well-placed rounds could have wiped out most of us and most of the strike force. Other than the slammers and the guard house, the only grouping of houses was the kitchen and the mess hall along with a building I imagined was some kind of classroom. It was the same as any other building, except it had rows of benches. I never saw it in use.

You couldn't walk anything like a straight line between most places—say from our slammers to the volleyball court or from the volleyball court to the mess hall. They did this to make it difficult for attackers. The paths were always under cover, and at most they were only wide enough for two people to walk side by side. They'd cut halfway through the saplings along the way and bend them over, then intertwine them and lace them with the heavy, sharp briars that grow around the base of giant bamboo. They were more effective than concertina wire: you'd just touch them and they'd slice like a razor blade. All in all, the thing made a good barrier—a tangle of vines, thorns, branches, and briars. You couldn't just walk through it, you'd have to cut through it if you didn't want to go down the path.

The camp perimeter was guarded by this type of barrier too, with openings only for the entry paths leading to the camp proper. Ground troops coming upon it would see only one more impossible tangle of thicket. Everybody, friend or foe, was channeled down what looked like natural paths, and coming down a path like that, enemy troops would come to one—and only one—little shack. They couldn't go around it because of the brake and bamboo barbed wire. If they tried to go through it the whole camp would be warned. Besides, since they didn't know the camp layout, they wouldn't be able to overrun the thing by surprise even if they decided to go through the guard post. All this assumes that they could sneak by the outer defenses.

If a troop commander recognized the camp as a camp, he could probably surround it—but he'd have to spread his troops around something like a two-mile circle. They'd still have to advance along these narrow little paths that one man with an automatic rifle could defend easily. If the guy wanted to go ahead and take the losses he'd have to take to be successful with that kind of attack, he'd have to start with a force so big that he certainly couldn't sneak past the outer security. Even if he did, he'd have a hostile force to his rear. And if he did alert the outer security force, he probably wouldn't find anything but a bunch of empty bamboo shacks when he got into the camp. He would probably be so mad he'd burn the damned things down and get bombed by the Mad Bomber when the smoke rose.

We were taught all this at Fort Bragg. You make the base camp so that if you're attacked you can defend it. You don't set it up in one area, where it can be surrounded. You break it up, run trails different ways and criss-cross them, so that if it is bombed they won't get all of it. They'll only get part of it, and you'll still have some escape routes. You set it up so you can serve many areas from different directions. With different shacks all over the camp, it's less likely to show up as a definite outline on an aerial photograph.

Bombing might have been one way to do some damage to the camp, but I was amazed at how little damage a five hundred or seven hundred fifty pound bomb did in the jungle. Bombs that exploded on contact exploded when they hit the treetops. They tore the hell out of the trees, but they didn't do any damage on the ground. There might be fragments flying, but as far as tearing up anything, there was only very light damage. Delayed-action bombs would crash through and bury themselves in the soft floor of the jungle, and when they exploded most of the force went straight up. Somebody could be standing fifty yards from one of the things, and the concussion could pick him up and slam him down again, but he'd still be out of the way of the shrapnel. So a bomb pretty much had to hit in somebody's hip pocket to do any damage. The load the Mad Bomber dropped the second time in Auschwitz could have wiped out a city block, but it didn't do any real damage to the camp.

Since the camps were so spread out, a ground commander would have to call for saturation bombing over maybe a couple of square miles for it to be effective. He'd have to pull his troops back quite a distance, and the Vietnamese would probably just walk out of the camp and out of his trap. Or run out of it, more likely, carrying all their weapons and Coburn's pots and pans, and their sacks of rice, and whatever else they could lay their hands on. One time when we had to move camp hastily I saw them carrying heavy sacks of rice along with all the equipment they usually carried. I don't see how they did it. A well-trained American unit wouldn't have been able to sustain the pace they did all night long.

It was early morning when we moved out of Auschwitz. Anus blindfolded us for a while and then took off the blindfolds, but at certain points along the march they put them back on. Perhaps we were passing something they didn't want us to see—other camps, some landmark we might identify, fortifications, caches of supplies—or perhaps they were just trying to confuse us. We passed through a lot of open fields, and then late at night we arrived at our new camp.

It was like Auschwitz, including new slammers. But they were barred and locked. That was very disappointing. We'd been living without bars at Auschwitz, and here suddenly we had bars again. We didn't really understand their reasoning or their purpose—I suppose they wanted to make it easier for the guards. We had worked our way from barred cages and chains to being allowed to walk around practically at will. With Alex telling us we wouldn't be released until the U.S. recognized the NLF and now their putting us behind locked bars again—we were back where we started. It was a real letdown.

We began to speculate that they locked us up because they were going to bring more prisoners in. They took us out on work details to help them build more slammers. We could hear a lot of helicopter activity in the area—they were making rocket strikes a good way off—but we didn't pay it any mind. We had hardly started work on the extra slammers—we hadn't even had time to give the camp a proper name—when suddenly Anus came running in one morning. "Roll 'em up, move it out!" They must have received information that the camp had been seriously compromised and that an air attack was imminent. In a matter of minutes, we were out and on the trail again.

"SHARPEN STAKES"

After a day-long march, we arrived at another campsite. The only thing they'd built before we got there was our cages, and they put us to work helping build the rest of the camp. We got our name for the camp from our first day digging foxholes—Iron Mines. Every other place we had been, the soil was sandy or loamy, but here you'd go a foot below the surface and you'd run into this heavy red rock that seemed like iron ore. It even knocked sparks out of the hoe.

You couldn't go very deep in that damned rock. We even had to modify most of the foxholes because it was so hard to dig. Instead of digging down and then tunneling back in, we dug shallow L-shaped trenches ten by six, covered one end of them with saplings, then piled dirt on top of that. They weren't a great deal of protection, but they were better than nothing at all.

The work was hard, but one of us would dig while the other shoveled the dirt out of the hole. Anus never pushed us; we usually worked in thirty-minute shifts. I felt better than I had since my capture and didn't mind the work, and McClure felt the same. Anus had us working together because they had decided we were about the two best workers they had. Camacho had another touch of the gout and Roraback was playing his usual game of trying to do as little work as possible, throwing as much as he could on us. One time McClure climbed out of a hole that was especially difficult digging. It was Roraback's turn to go back in and dig. He told McClure, "You realize of course that NCOs don't have to do this kind of work—how about getting down in there and

212

digging it for me." McClure just blew his top and was going to throw Roraback bodily down the hole, but the guard stopped him. Roraback just decided, "Well, actually, a sergeant first class doesn't have to do this kind of work, McClure, you understand that." But McClure didn't understand.

I had the impression that Anus respected us, with the possible exception of Roraback. He seemed to realize that we were trying to do the best we could under the circumstances, that we were members of the United States Army and had been through a whole lot of nonsense in the States. He seemed to respect the fact that we weren't being complete asses and that we sometimes tried to do things.

As long as he could see that we were trying, he tried to encourage us. I'd drill a good hole in a piece of bamboo, and he's say it was a very good hole and then get me a drink of his white lightning. But when somebody really screwed up, he was just as quick to criticize, especially with Roraback.

Roraback just seemed to fuck up on purpose, and he got it from everybody, guards and prisoners alike. When he wasn't sick or didn't have sore feet, then he said he couldn't see to work. But he could see what he wanted to.

He was just leaving the work for the rest of us. Every time he fucked up, they'd get somebody else to do it. That didn't seem to trouble him at all. He just went back to his slammer and rolled up the biggest piece of horseshit he could get hold of—he usually got mine if he could get his hands on my sack. He lay there and puffed it while the rest of us were out there sweating.

Xuan didn't like me, but he hated Roraback with a passion. He'd go to his cage and lecture him every day. *"Bac! Bac! Con duc!"*—"You're no good, Roraback. You're a rotten bastard. You don't work. You eat too much. You smoke too much." Then he'd come over and tell me, "Roraback, *bac*, no good." And I'd tell him, "You're damned right he's no good—the bastard burns up all my tobacco on me." We understood quite well what they were talking about.

What really got Camacho mad was Roraback's taking the biggest share of food. There'd be four portions of meat and he'd reach clear across the other three to get the biggest one. When Camacho protested, Roraback would tell him he didn't notice the difference. "God damn," Camacho would say, "you can tell other people you can't see, but you can't convince me." And they'd get into one of their arguments.

Because Roraback was the oldest, the Vietnamese thought he was senior among us and would take command under the Code of Conduct. We never bothered to tell them differently, but actually Camacho was senior, and I finally convinced him to exercise his authority and divide up the meat every night.

The hunting was very good around Iron Mines, and we had plenty of meat. There was more game in this area; maybe it had been driven in or maybe this was virgin territory. They had a hunting party out most of the time and they brought in several deer. And there was an abundance of wild boar—they seemed to bring boar in every day or so, and we had all the boar we wanted for quite a while. One was so big they had to cut it in half to carry it—not lengthwise, like a butcher would—they just cut it in half in the middle and slung each half on a pole. They had two men on each end, and they were still struggling.

One time Coburn came up to my slammer and walked around *dung, dung, dung, dung,* imitating an elephant, making a trunk and tail with his arms. Did we want some elephant for dinner? Sure enough, that night we had elephant meat. It was very tasty, but the fiber was so tough you had to chew and chew and chew just to soften it enough to swallow it. McClure's gums were sore and he wouldn't have anything to do with it. "Hey, Camacho," I asked. "How do you like your elephant?" "Tell you in a while—I'm on a rest break from chewing."

Besides being larger than Auschwitz, part of Iron Mines was next to a large open field. It was a couple of hundred yards from our slammers, and when we took showers we could see open sky—the well was right beside the field. There was an ox herder who brought a couple of oxen from the ox pool by our slammers every day to the well, and he put them out to graze in the clearing. We'd passed the ox pool coming into Iron Mines—figured it was an ox pool like the U.S. Army might have a motor pool. It was night, and it looked like there were maybe half a dozen oxen there, but there could have been a hundred. We could smell the ox manure. Iron Mines was apparently on a network of intersecting trails. Where they came from, where they went to, how much traffic was on them, I don't know, but there was quite a bit of ox cart traffic in the area, judging from the many ox tracks and wheel tracks on the trails. Iron Mines might have been a central depot or a relay station straddling a main supply route.

But the ox herder we saw brought the same two oxen past every day to the well. One was a big healthy ox, and the other was a skinny one. Later on the ox herder knocked him in the head and we ate him.

They probably brought the generator for the movies in an ox cart. At his first meeting with us Man With Glasses had told us he was going to teach us more about his people, "and maybe one of these days you will see movies." Of course I didn't believe him. How the hell were they going to show us movies out there in the middle of the damned jungle? But one evening Prevaricator came and got us. "You go to cinema tonight." We thought that was ridiculous. "Hey McClure, can I sit next to you?" But Prevaricator took us to the volleyball court and there was a goddamn generator and a movie projector. Apparently this movie team traveled from camp to camp with their projector and their generator. They probably had to carry the damned things a hundred miles in an ox cart.

The first film was about Ho Chi Minh, a brief history of his life. Prevaricator sat beside me, telling us what was happening. They showed where Ho had been born in North Vietnam, and that he had gone to Europe and put out a newspaper in France, and that he had traveled to the United States. In the States he saw many jails—they showed pictures of banks of jail cells in some big prison. And he saw police beating the hell out of dock workers—they showed dockworker riots back in the twenties in New York, where the police were beating the hell out of them. And they showed his home—that he slept on a very plain bed and apparently lived a very plain, simple life.

The other film showed how the Vietminh had fought the French. It showed the French attacking villages with airplanes, and how they avoided the French and fought back. They were walking along roads where time bombs were planted, and people were disarming them. Some of them were blowing up, blowing people up. The film showed how hard they worked to defeat the French—how they pushed things on bicycles to supply the siege of Dien Bien Phu.

Interesting films. Really something to be sitting there in the middle of the jungle watching a movie.

I don't know whose idea it was, Harry's or the Central Committee's, but one day Anus came to give us a new work detail. He brought a pile of bamboo poles and threw them in front of the slammers along with a couple of machetes and told McClure and Roraback to sharpen them into punji stakes.

Punji stakes are bamboo sections two or three feet long, split down the middle and sharpened at both ends into extremely sharp points. They're stuck in the ground at an angle, directed outwards from the perimeter of the camp usually. Or they dig pits and fill the bottoms with these stakes pointed upwards to catch anyone who falls on them.

McClure and Roraback refused, so Anus asked Camacho and me to do it. We told him, "Absolutely not; under no circumstances."

Anus went and reported our refusal, and Harry came with Prevaricator. But Roraback persisted in saying no and told McClure he shouldn't do it either. We figured it was some kind of test. It was really a big issue, and I think they staged it not because they wanted punji stakes sharpened, but to see what our attitudes were. Camacho and I tried to be as diplomatic as possible about saying no. We told Harry we understood his position, and we didn't want to aid the war—from either side—but we could not in good conscience make weapons that might injure American soldiers.

Oil Can said he understood how we felt but that if we didn't sharpen the stakes he couldn't guarantee our lives. "If you do not comply with sharpening punji stakes, at the time this camp is attacked we will be in a dilemma. In a dilemma you will probably be shot." That seemed rather concrete. If we didn't do it, we were going to get shot if the camp was overrun—because we failed to help them protect the camp, thus failing to protect our lives. There was some logic in that. It wasn't the kind of logic I liked especially, but from their point of view I suppose it seemed *very* logical.

They went back to McClure, and Anus got him out and made a couple of punji stakes himself to show him what he wanted him to do, and this time McClure sat down and started making punji stakes. Camacho and I were mad as hell; if one guy did it, it weakened the position of the rest of us.

We told Harry we were willing to take the risk, and they accepted that for the time being. We were banking on the chance that the camp wouldn't be overrun. They sent us out to dig, and we dug and dug all day. They had us digging big, deep ditches, and they didn't want to give us breaks as often as before. They shouted and pointed their guns. It was the worst we had ever seen them act, including the night we were captured. Meanwhile, we weren't talking to McClure.

The next day McClure got a letter from his wife. It was the first letter any of us had had in the jungle. We joked about it—"Guess it took so long because we forgot to leave a forwarding address at Hiep Hoa." But the letter had a profound effect on us all. I got the feeling they had the letters and were holding them—if we sharpened the stakes, we would get the letters.

But even though Oil Can was in the position of power, he still had a pretty good argument: They weren't going to carry the stakes to some American base camp and hurl them as spears against the soldiers; if they were going to be used to defend the camp, they would only hurt American soldiers if they attacked the place. When we said we'd just as soon take our chances, we were as much as saying we didn't care if they got killed, as long as no Americans were hurt. And of course, they were going to sharpen the stakes whether or not we helped them. When we dug holes or did other work, we were in fact freeing the Vietnamese to do other things—including sharpening punji stakes.

The next day they took Roraback and Camacho out to dig holes, but they left me in the cage. After they were gone, Wild Bill (who got his name from wearing tight pants and cowboy boots) came over with his machine gun. He gave me a machete and motioned me over to where McClure was already sharpening away. I went over and sat down but refused to sharpen the stakes. He started jumping up and down and carrying on, pulled the bolt on his MAT-49, and told me to sharpen or he'd shoot me. All the while, McClure was hacking away; I felt like strangling him. I gambled that Wild Bill would have to get permission to shoot me even if he wanted to, so I told him I still wouldn't sharpen the stakes.

Mad as hell, Wild Bill ran off and got Huskie with his BAR. Huskie came down, and he started yanking the bolt on the

BAR and aiming it, saying he was going to shoot me. I was telling him, "Go ahead, if that's the way you feel about it—I'm not sharpening the stakes." So they ordered me into a ditch we had dug, and Huskie told me, "Close your eyes—I'm going to shoot you." I told him that I wasn't going to close my eyes, because I didn't believe that he was really going to shoot me.

Maybe I did believe it; I don't think so, or I would probably have sharpened the stakes. Anyway, I called his bluff, and they were frustrated. They mumbled about it between themselves and they kept telling McClure I was no damn good. They would come over every once in a while and tell me, "If you want to get out of the hole, you go and sharpen the stakes." But I said, "No, I'll just stay in the hole." So they got disgusted with me and took me inside Roraback's house and put me in his air-raid shelter and put the top on it. They told me to stay in there. I asked if I could go out and go to the toilet, but they wouldn't let me out. They made me stay in until Roraback came back that night with the others after their work detail.

The next day Oil Can Harry came with Prevaricator and told us he had received orders from the Central Committee. "You will sharpen punji stakes—otherwise you will be forced into your shelter and not fed until you do."

How much harm would the stakes do, anyway? Unless somebody stepped on them, they couldn't do anything. Besides, we were convinced it was merely a show, a test of attitude. We looked to Camacho, the ranking man, and he said, "Sharpen stakes." So we all sharpened stakes. The next day we got our letters.

That was probably the most unfortunate and unpleasant episode of the whole captivity.

We had been at Iron Mines about two months when Grandpa showed up. He was from the Central Committee and he seemed to be a replacement for Man With Glasses. We never saw Man With Glasses again. Maybe forty miles of bad road finally got him.

Grandpa was much older, a frail little man with white hair. He didn't speak English as well as Man With Glasses, but he knew what he was talking about, even though he had to use Prevaricator at certain points. He had learned his English working for Shell Oil Company, he told us, and had become acquainted with American imperialism at the same time.

Grandpa made a big push for us to tape a statement. "What you have written us is very good, of course, but maybe you would like to record it."

"Well, you know, really I *wouldn't* like to record it, because—what's going to happen to it?"

"We consider it more effective if it's recorded rather than just written. Things written are often not believed. The recorded voice is then again something else."

"Yeah, that's a good reason for me not to do it."

McClure agreed to do it immediately, I believe. But even though I felt I was against the war, I was very opposed to the tape. This was very serious, I thought. If I made this tape I'd be in all kinds of trouble. Of course, if I didn't make it I might be dead. Grandpa went on to explain: "We cannot force you to do this; we cannot require you to do this. This must be strictly up to you. Of course, if you don't, you must realize that we can no longer guarantee your life. If the camp is attacked, what happens to you is not our responsibility."

For the first time the offer of release wasn't being waved in front of me, and it caused me to suspect that they were testing me to see how I'd react when I wasn't offered that possibility. "I cannot promise that you will be released," Grandpa told me. "Perhaps you will not be released until the end of the war. But we can guarantee your life."

Since the early days of my capture I had been very cautious not to be inconsistent. Refusing to sharpen the punji stakes had almost formed a contradiction, which I was trying to erase. As I thought about it, it seemed reasonable to make the tape. My life would be guaranteed—as far as they were concerned, at least—and I didn't have any hope of getting out any other way. By this time I didn't give a shit about the Code of Conduct, Eisenhower, Uncle Sam, or any of that bullshit. I'd lost all loyalty to the U.S. Army. I decided I had to look out for myself. And I couldn't see much point in going through the bluffing game only to end up doing it anyway.

"Tell your thoughts," Grandpa told me. "I do not want to tell you what to write. You go back to your house and think very deeply, and then you write what you feel and come back and we will record it."

The tape was generally along the lines of the last statement I had written. What I said seemed very strong at the time, very potent. Very likely it was, for a POW at least. But if I went out and said it now, standing in the biggest crowd in the country, people probably wouldn't pay a bit of attention to me because it's all been said so many times, even on the floor of Congress. Basically I said that I was opposed to the war and I felt that we should get out.

It took two days before Grandpa had a tape that satisfied him. If an airplane went over, he stopped the recorder. If a chicken cackled—"No, we must do it again." I wondered what they were going to do with it—broadcast it, probably. I understand that later on they did broadcast at least parts of it over the radio—Peking or Moscow.

McClure and I both agreed to make tapes. Camacho and Roraback refused. I think they were inconsistent. You couldn't write a statement and then refuse to make a tape, I figured. What they had said before became invalid after they refused. But Grandpa said they would treat everybody the

same, no matter what. And they didn't treat them any differently because they didn't do it. They fed them the same as
they did me; Camacho continued to live with me.

Camacho was very angry with me for making the tape.
"They're going to court-martial you when you get back,
man—just think of all those coins you're going to lose." He
wasn't thinking about dying in the jungle; he was thinking
about getting out and buying that car he daydreamed about.
He based everything on his back pay. "You've got to think
about that money when you get back—they're not going to
pay you your back pay, they'll just throw you in jail." Jail
was so remote—why think about jail when there's a bomb
over your head?

Making the tape recording was probably just another progression in the step of changing your mind about everything.
Probably a more binding type of thing, because if you went
to the trouble to record it, it must mean that either you
really mean it or you're really bullshitting somebody. What I
recorded I honestly meant. It was nothing I wouldn't be
willing to repeat now. In fact I have repeated it many times—
and much stronger.

McClure had been in good health. He and I had been working together digging the well. We were very healthy and
strong. But before McClure got the chance to make the tape,
he got so damn sick that he couldn't. I had made my tape
before he made his.

A few weeks before McClure fell ill, while Grandpa was
talking with us the helicopter activity in the area increased
and seemed to be moving closer to the camp. Late one afternoon, a few days after I completed my tape—McClure was by
now a complete invalid—what sounded like three or four helicopters flew into the open air in the clearing. They hovered
for a couple of minutes and then pulled up quickly. Anus was

running and jumping and carrying on, so we assumed that the helicopter must have spotted something. If the light was behind the 'copters, slanting into the jungle, the pilots must have seen something among the trees.

The Vietnamese held a series of meetings and the following day they told us to pack our gear. We were to abandon the camp. It must have been hard to decide to leave, considering how much work they'd put into building the camp. They probably didn't know if the helicopters had spotted anything, but they couldn't take any chances.

We were really under pressure moving out. They gave us a bicycle and told us that Camacho and Roraback and I would have to make sure that McClure got to where we were going—wherever *that* was. It was a forced march with only a few short breaks. We had to carry not only our own gear but McClure's as well, and at the same time push him along. Most of the burden fell on Camacho and me, because Roraback would quit after a few minutes.

We marched all day and all night. Everybody was agitated at everybody else. The guards were angry and disgusted. Anus was yelling and telling us to hurry up with McClure, and we were telling him that we were tired. Pushing McClure on the bicycle wouldn't have been that bad, but he wouldn't even balance himself. We had to hold him on the damned thing. Trying to push him along a teeny little trail at night while he was flopping around was worse than carrying him. I got so disgusted with him that I let go of the handlebars and the whole bicycle doubled up and he fell off on his ass.

Finally Anus saw that we were exhausted from carrying McClure and we camped until daybreak. After breakfast we started marching again and in a few hours we arrived back at Auschwitz. We walked past where we'd stayed the first time and on through the camp to the slammers near the rice mill. Auschwitz was really dilapidated. In the short time we'd been away from it, it had almost gone back to the jungle.

We only stayed there a couple of weeks. As far as I could tell, the only reason for staying there was to give McClure a chance to recover. He had been strong, and then he went down suddenly. There are waves of depression that can be really overwhelming if you let yourself fall into them. They can kill you in a matter of days.

I thought McClure's illness was psychosomatic. When we got to Auschwitz I started harassing him. He stumbled over one day and hung his clothes up to dry in the sun on the line in back of our house. I went and washed my clothes, and I just slid his all the way to the end of the line in one big blob and then hung mine up very neatly where his had been. He came back. "Who did that?"

"I did, you son of a bitch. You're lucky I didn't throw them on the ground."

"You better watch what you're saying."

"What the hell are you going to do—kick my ass?"

"Well, I just might."

"You're too goddamn weak to sit up—how the hell are you going to kick anybody's ass?! You better watch what *you're* saying!"

He went back to his house and started going into training—eating like a horse, shadow boxing. He got better immediately. It seemed to prove that his problems were more psychological than physical. I was proud of myself for curing him. I thought I was a great psychiatrist after that.

When McClure got well, Grandpa came back and McClure made his tape.

ESCAPE

We named the new camp Paradise. Our slammers were slightly different—a little smaller, with the eaves extending over the door to make a rain shelter for the porch. The Vietnamese were well along with building it by the time we got there, but we helped dig the wells.

There was something about the camp that made us like it better than the others. We had been through all the rigors of being prepared for release and then not released. We weren't going to be released, we realized; we would just have to adjust to life there. We were taking everything at face value. The camp seemed comfortable. We were all healthy again, the food wasn't too bad, and the mailman knew where we were. The well was close by and we could take showers when we wanted to. There was bombing in the distance, but not right over our heads. "It's pretty good here, why raise hell?"

We were doing little things we hadn't done before—fixing the place up a little bit, if you can imagine that in the middle of the jungle. Camacho wanted to build a little table and have our own patio in front of the slammer. The guards were easygoing as long as we were cooperative. If they asked us to dig a well and we did it—rather than carping about it and breaking the spade handle—they let us move about between the cages pretty freely. We were locked in only at night. We played cards and visited each other from cage to cage. Roraback was constantly needing a light for his horseshit, and Big Dumb would get tired of getting him one. So he'd tell him to come across the clearing and get a light from us, and Roraback would come over and bullshit with Camacho and me for an hour or so.

They brought us a teapot then, and gave us a bag of tea, and let us build a fire to brew tea whenever we wanted. I'd ask Big Dumb if I could fetch some kindling, and he'd let me go out in the woods and ramble around for bamboo. Nice Guy showed us how to make a fire without too much smoke. When Big Dumb wanted to show you how to do something, he'd just stand there, point his carbine, and grunt. But Nice Guy would squat beside you and show you how to do it; and if you did it right, he'd smile.

We'd build a little fire and brew a pot of tea and just sit around and drink tea and smoke shit, and bullshit far into the night. And finally when they realized we were going to be up all night they'd tell Roraback to go home.

After a while they had us build a third and then a fourth slammer. We were sure it meant they were going to separate us again. But when they had us start on a fifth cage, we began to speculate that there were going to be more prisoners. Then Prevaricator showed up with Grandpa one day to tell us that indeed more prisoners were coming. He told us their names, but we didn't know any of them.

They told us that they would be there in a short time, but it was almost a month before they arrived. It was the beginning of the rainy season. One night when it was pouring, Prevaricator came to borrow a set of dry clothes from me. The prisoners had just come in and they were soaking wet. I gave him a pair of black pajamas.

In the morning we saw that there were men in two of the three cages we had built. The guards let one of them out to draw water from the well to wash his clothes, and they sent me along to show him how to use the rattan vine and bucket. So I showed him how to draw water with that damn vine, just as we had had to learn it. He had a hell of a time with it. We had a moment to talk, but he didn't tell me much. I asked him what outfit he was in and he told me, "the Army."

"Oh," I said. "Where were you captured?"

"Down south." I went back to the slammer talking to myself and told Camacho I thought this new guy was some kind of damned fool. But he was just suspicious: later on he told me he'd wondered why they'd let me come to the well without a guard.

Little by little we did exchange information, but it wasn't easy. Even though our own cages weren't locked up during the day and we could visit back and forth, the new men were locked up and weren't allowed to talk to us. But Camacho got word to one of them—through singing, I believe—"Look under the leaf at the well." We set up a "dead-drop" letter system. We wrote notes and put them in a medicine bottle and took them down to the well and carved out a hole in the ground and put a leaf over it. We communicated very well with that bottle.

The man I had met by the well was a private by the name of Crafts. The other was a Marine captain named Cook. Crafts was locked up within sight of us, but Cook was farther across the jungle and couldn't see us unless he came out of his cage to go to the well. If Cook had a message for us, he carried his towel on his right shoulder on his way to the well. No message, left shoulder. If we had a message for him, we hung a towel on the outside of the slammer.

The limitations on our communication almost finished Crafts. Coburn sent along a cup of *mam* with dinner one night. Crafts thought it was tea and swallowed it in one gulp. It nearly choked him to death—he gagged and hacked. "Damn," he told us later. "I thought I'd die."

Crafts was a radio operator. He looked like a big hick from Maine, which he was, and I could hardly understand him when he spoke because he had a heavy Down East accent. He'd been captured just before Christmas with a sergeant named Bennett. The Vietnamese unit they were with had abandoned them in a pitched battle. They'd been captured in the Delta around Cap St. Jacques, and Cook had been captured in the same general area on New Year's Day. He was directing a group of South Vietnamese marines, and they got in a hell of a battle and left him standing there like Crafts and Bennett. He was wounded very seriously in the leg and the Vietcong had to carry him off the battlefield in a litter.

When we got together later on, Cook said that the Vietcong were extremely fair with him, even after he and Bennett had stomped the shit out of a guard trying to escape. The three of them had been put together, and once when Cook and Bennett were taken to the toilet they jumped the guard. They almost beat him to death, but he bit Bennett's thumb and held on long enough to foil the attempt.

He thought they would shoot him after that. One of the officers had put his pistol to his head and threatened to, but they didn't. They didn't do anything more to them than lock them in leg irons so they couldn't move.

Apparently the Vietnamese blamed Cook for everything bad that had happened from the time of his capture until he reached Paradise. They accused him of trying to command the other prisoners, and they didn't like that. They were afraid he would try to do the same with us. "Do not listen to him," Prevaricator told us. "He is an evil man." We were not to associate with him for any reason.

It had taken them almost two months of walking to reach the camp, and apparently it hadn't been pleasant. It must have been a couple of hundred miles, and they'd had to pick their trails. The Vietnamese had prodded them along, but Bennett had decided he didn't like that shit and refused to eat. Cook said he had refused to eat for several weeks and was so weak he couldn't walk. They had had to carry him sometimes, which delayed them considerably. Finally they had to leave him.

Prevaricator told Cook they had shot Bennett. But we had

no way of knowing whether Bennett died from refusing to eat or if they really had shot him. Executions had been going on for some time in Saigon, and the Vietcong had been warning that they were going to retaliate.[10]

One day, as Camacho and I passed our usual nonsense back and forth, I noticed a baby chick standing in the middle of our cage. In Paradise, Anus was in charge of the camp chicken coop, so baby chicks were no rarity, but this was the strangest creature we had ever seen. It was black and brown and had uncommonly long legs, like stilts.

It stood there solemnly checking us out while we speculated that its mother must have had a wild affair with some jungle bird and it had come to us as one member of a minority to another. I picked it up, and the thing didn't try to get away like the little peeps usually do. Then another one walked in through the bars, this one wobbly on its thin legs. Close behind it was Anus looking here and there and going *cluck cluck*. When he saw us with the birds he unlocked the cage and came in; across his dour face was that rarest of things, a smile.

Apparently Anus and his gang had caught the birds out in the jungle somewhere and brought them into camp. He had developed the habit of wanting to know the English word for anything new, and he asked us what the bird was called. "Baby chicken," we told him. But he knew what that meant, because we'd told him before. He shook his head. "Ga-Loi," he said. "Yeah, baby chicken, right?" Each time he said "Ga-Loi," we would repeat "baby chicken." Finally he got disgusted with us and went off after Prevaricator. Great, I thought, that should make everything clear as shit.

Anus came hustling back with Prevaricator, and through him he gave us an explanation in great seriousness. "These are not baby chickens," he said. "They are Ga-Lois. Ga-Lois are very rare and extremely hard to catch. In fact, you can hardly come by a Ga-Loi anymore. I was only able to catch this one with much skill and luck. Ga-Lois are very intelligent and when they grow up they are very beautiful. But they are delicate and require expert care. You and Camacho have demonstrated sincere kindness to animals and if you promise to take the best of care of the Ga-Lois, you may keep them for me."

Besides Troll's turtle, they had given us other animals as pets, and for the most part they had been a pleasure. The exception was a baby monkey that got into everything; it didn't like rice and died within a week. Roraback didn't have a pet so they had given him a racoon-like animal which they called a *chom*. But Roraback stepped on its head, and from then on the *chom* couldn't do much more than run around in circles. This had upset Anus no end.

We assured Anus we would lavish the greatest care on our Ga-Lois and would do everything we could to protect them from evil spirits and Roraback. That got us another smile. Despite his long speech, I still didn't know what the hell a Ga-Loi was. When Anus left, I asked Prevaricator. "It is the son of a savage hen."

Camacho's Ga-Loi got weaker and died, and he got a stern lecture from Anus. But my Ga-Loi thrived on the termites I fed it, and it was a great source of enjoyment. Such an intelligent little chicken—I was really fascinated with a little bird being that bright. When I talked, it listened with great attentiveness. I'd go to the well and it would go with me, following like a little dog. It would come when I called. Anus brought me little termite nests, and I'd take a machete and chop them up and shake out the termites for the Ga-Loi. It'd be scratching someplace; I'd call it and it'd run over and look up at me, as though to ask, "What you got?"

"Termite." *Gulp*, and it'd run back and start scratching again. I became attached to the Ga-Loi. It liked to sleep in my shirt pocket, and I took to bragging about all the things it could do. Anus was proud of me.

Camacho and I were digging a hole one day and the Ga-Loi was nearby scratching for grubs. I got in the hole to dig for about fifteen minutes, and when I came up the Ga-Loi was gone. Camacho said Troll had come by and the Ga-Loi had followed him to the well for a drink.

Then here came Troll with a mournful look on his face, holding the Ga-Loi in his hand. He was very sorry, but he didn't know the Ga-Loi was following him. When he drew a bucket of water, he'd stepped back on it and killed it. Anus came up and offered his condolences. It was almost a wake.

Losing the Ga-Loi hurt. Anus promised to look for another, but without any luck. As he said, I guess, you can hardly get a Ga-Loi anymore.

A few days after the new prisoners arrived, Anus called the four of us together and took us to see Alex. Alex was beaming as usual. After greeting us he gave an order to Prevaricator and Prevaricator went off for a few minutes. He came back carrying four large boxes. He was smiling and looking very proud. We almost fell over. The boxes were International Red Cross parcels.

They had got the Red Cross packages in Phnom Penh, Alex said, and carried them all the way through the jungle. It was most difficult and they probably wouldn't be able to do it again. We were dazzled that they had done it at all. The boxes weighed about ten pounds apiece.

We walked back to our huts opening the packages. We were smiling even more broadly than Prevaricator. There was underwear, soap, cigarettes, raisins, corned beef, cookies, vitamins. Roraback was admiring the chocolate bar. I was digging the coffee—espresso, enough for umpteen cups.

The fruit had a few worms in it, but we ate most of it

anyway. Crafts and Cook didn't get a box, so we made up some packages for them and conned Big Dumb into taking them down the trail. I guess he got royally chewed out for it, because he wouldn't even take Cook a drink of water after that. They told us we could give things to Crafts, but not to Cook. If you don't count eating, Cook was being one hundred percent uncooperative, to the point that he wouldn't tell them his symptoms when he wasn't feeling well. They wanted him to write them down, but he'd refused to write anything since his capture, even his name. In his view, writing violated the Code of Conduct. They asked him just to write requesting treatment, and he refused. "Well, Mr. Cook, you can be sick," they said. And he was sick.

But we were startled one day to hear Cook bellowing out the Marine Hymn. At first we thought he'd flipped, but it turned out that on his way to Paradise, like Camacho he had learned that if he sang they'd give him candy or cigarettes. Maybe the guards found out what the words meant, or maybe it was his attitude, but they wouldn't give him anything when he sang in Paradise.

I figured that by singing for favors Cook was contradicting his stand about not writing anything because it violated the Code of Conduct. Either you live by the Code or you don't.

A couple of days later the fifth cage received a guest, an Army captain named Schumann. He had just recently been captured and he had on a complete fatigue uniform, including jungle boots. He was a huge man, at least six feet six and proportionally heavy. When we got together later on he told us that on the way to the camp they kept taking him across little footbridges, and he was so heavy he'd crash right through and they'd all fall into the stream.

Northeast of the camp there was what sounded like a 155 howitzer that fired intermittently almost every night; to the southeast there were almost daily bombings by jets. They were both five to ten miles away; it was the first time we had been in an area with so much activity nearby. The jets were a new thing. We saw some of them through the trees—delta-wings, probably F-101s. It sounded like they were hitting the same spot every day, probably a road junction or something like that.

We had been talking about escape ever since Auschwitz. We agreed that we could get away very simply—walk away when we were on a work detail or when we went to the well, and then run like hell. But that didn't solve the problem. We had no direction to go in, and without direction the jungle seemed impassable. We agreed that this was the thing that kept us there: the jungle, rather than the trouble of getting away from the guards.

At Paradise we had a direction for the first time—that cannon firing. We knew that there had to be a semi-permanent artillery base there. The intermittency of the firing reminded us of the cannon at the sugar mill—it sounded like the ARVN just pissing around. We didn't think the Viet-cong had artillery pieces; if they did, they wouldn't be firing them into the jungle.

We'd always known that escaping was the thing to do, the chief responsibility of a POW. Besides, we thought it would be a feather in our caps—nobody had done it since World War II. Besides being heroic, we could show Oil Can Harry that we could do something by ourselves. Roraback and McClure thought we were full of shit: Roraback said he couldn't see and McClure said he was too sick, so we excluded them even from the planning. We talked and talked about it, and we finally worked out a plan.

It would have to be at night, during the rainy season. We'd have to use the paths to put some distance between us and the guards before they discovered we were gone, and there would be less traffic on the paths at night. Unless we stumbled right on top of somebody, our black uniforms would make it difficult for them to see us, and the guards on the outer perimeter would only be watching for people coming in, not going out. In the camp the guards would be under shelter while it was raining, and the drum of the downpour would cover any noise we made as well as keeping others off the paths.

The perimeter of the camp might be three or four miles out, and we would at least have to get out of the camp before they began looking for us. If they started after us before we got out of the camp, they could probably cut us off. They knew the trails; we didn't. If we could get out into some wild country and get off the trails, we would lose ourselves for a while, but they wouldn't be able to find us either. They couldn't travel any better off the trails than we could.

Going through the jungle would be a pain. The undergrowth was very heavy—briars and little bushes, bamboo. You couldn't walk through it, and we wouldn't have a machete. Camacho still had his boots, but I had only shower sandals. It would be a life-and-death situation; we thought about it a long time before we considered it seriously. Leaving at night, all the things we would run into—leeches, snakes, lizards, scorpions. Being lost, having nothing to eat, having to drink out of streams, wandering around, maybe getting lost in the jungle and starving to death, or having to give ourselves up, being captured, or just stumbling into them coming down the trail.

The only thing we really had going for us was our ability to recognize an encampment immediately—we had a year and a half of experience. But if they caught us they would certainly shoot us.

Two days pushing through the jungle without food and water would be exhausting but not impossible. Longer than that would mean having to drink from streams, and then it would become a race to reach safety before illness set in. We estimated that it was two to four days' traveling time to the cannon.

I figured we probably had about a fifty-fifty chance.

By now we had decided that we weren't ever going to be released. Grandpa had said, "You will be released when the war is over," and Alex had told us, "We will release you when the United States recognizes us." But there didn't seem to be any end in sight to the war. At Paradise we were preparing for a long haul, and we just decided that we didn't want to spend that much time there. Besides, it would be a great adventure to have been captured and then escape—if we could make it.

The guards were being fairly lax with us at this point, and we were just finishing our Red Cross packages. We'd gobbled up the vitamin pills, the corned beef, and the cookies. We were in the best of health. The rainy season was in its early stages, and what we had left from our Red Cross boxes was the beginnings of a survival kit. We made up a kit that included a jar of rice, some vitamin pills, and a mirror for signaling to a helicopter if one came close enough—and if the sun was out. We wrapped it in a piece of plastic sheeting and kept it hidden where we could get it and go immediately if the chance came.

Camacho even went to the trouble of writing a letter to be left behind when we escaped. We thanked them for their hospitality. We didn't mean them any harm, we said; we just wanted to go home. Since we couldn't wait until the end of the war, we were taking this opportunity to escape.

Through the dead-drop we told Cook of our plans, and he approved. We were going to try to bring it off on the Fourth of July and get our pictures in the *Saturday Evening Post*, just like in *Catch-22*.

Then disaster struck. Anus decided that we should sharpen some more punji stakes—it was optional this time, optional to the point that we could be stubborn. They came for McClure and started him sharpening stakes. Then they took Roraback and he looked over at us to ask what we were going to do.

"We're not going to sharpen punji stakes. Don't look at us. Hell, you're a sergeant—you know the Code of Conduct."

So he didn't sharpen them and they put him in the hole inside his house. McClure got shook up and he quit sharpening them too. And they put him in the hole with Roraback. They were in there about an hour, and then McClure came out and sharpened stakes again. Roraback didn't come out for another two or three hours, and then he sharpened stakes.

Anus came over and asked Camacho and me if we'd sharpen stakes. We told him no, but he didn't even try putting us in the hole. It was merely a show. Roraback and McClure only sharpened a dozen stakes, and that was it. The next evening they brought a lamp and hung it up in our slammer. They didn't put one in with Roraback and McClure. Camacho and I were suspect again.

The lamp hung a few inches above my mosquito net. They could see me in my bed, and its glow was sufficient to expose anyone moving around inside the slammer. But Camacho's bed was at least four or five feet from the lamp and his mosquito net just reflected the light.

They blew the lamp out only when a plane flew over. Then in about fifteen minutes they'd come back and ask me to hand the lamp through the bars so they could light it again. So our escape would have to coincide with rain and a plane flying over, and they didn't often come at the same time. Besides that, if both of us were going to go we would have to gamble that the guard would wait a couple of hours before relighting the light, or we'd have to accept only a fifteen-minute head start. Or Camacho could go alone, while I stayed behind to hand out the lamp. Camacho didn't want to go without me any more than I wanted to stay behind, and we almost scrapped the whole idea. But it was one man or nothing.

It was July 10 before everything clicked. The plane flew over, Little King came and blew out the lamp.

And then it started to pour.

"Camacho, you want to try it?"

"You going?"

"Un-uh, I've got to light the lamp. You've got the boots."

"Okay, man." He fiddled around for a few minutes, and then he was on the outside. "Wish me luck."

And he took off. Little King was sitting there on the bench, puffing his horseshit—I could see the glow at the end of his cigarette. Camacho was very quiet. Little King didn't see him go. I started kicking myself mentally for not going too. But in about fifteen minutes, Nice Guy replaced Little King. He came over and asked me to hand out the lamp.

Sleep for the rest of the night was impossible. I kept thinking of Camacho out there trying to find his way through the dark and the rain with nothing but the occasional noise of that damn cannon to guide him. Walking at night in the jungle is bad enough, but alone and off the trails it must have been a nightmare—with the constant worry of stumbling into a hammock or dropping into a punji pit.

I had a few worries myself. I was awake all night preparing my reaction in the morning. I had to convince them I didn't know anything about Camacho's escape or they'd blame me and probably take some action against me for helping him. If he was successful, it would compromise the whole camp, and they would certainly be more than pissed off at me.

It was daylight when Big Dumb relieved Nice Guy and came over to wake us up. With my heart thumping, I got up as casually as I could, rolled up my net, and blew out the light. Normal routine. " 'Macho, yi. 'Macho, yi." Camacho didn't get up of course. Big Dumb told me to get him up. I went over. "Camacho, get up." He didn't answer. I lifted up the net and gasped and my eyes got big. I looked at Big Dumb. "We haven't got any 'Machos."

His eyes were bigger than mine. He couldn't believe it. He was thunderstruck that there wasn't any 'Macho. He looked at that bed, and he looked all around the cage. It suddenly dawned on him that Camacho really was gone. Then he exploded in a torrent of yelling and screaming.

It was like poking a stick into an ant hill. Anus came running so fast that he almost ran through the bars without opening the door. When he started yelling, it completely blanketed Big Dumb's chatter. Oil Can Harry came running down the trail, his pistol out. People were running in every direction, yelling and hollering, jumping up and down. Oil Can was standing outside the cage, holding his gun on Camacho's sack, while he went through it.

I was sitting there trying to act scared and shook up and surprised. I wanted to laugh so bad. It was the funniest goddamned thing I'd ever seen.

Anus came into the slammer with a lamp. It was daytime. The sun was up. He was looking all over the house with a lamp. He kept darting here and there, always returning to stare at Camacho's bunk as if he could make him appear by sheer will power. He gave me the lamp and told me to look in Camacho's foxhole. I got down there and said, "Anus, he's not here." He wouldn't believe me; he had to crawl in to see for himself.

They couldn't believe that Camacho had escaped. When they figured out that he wasn't there anymore, they couldn't figure how the hell he did it. They tried to squeeze through the bars from the outside in and from the inside out. They found his tracks going down to the well. His boots had lug soles, so they could track them in the damp ground until he got into the underbrush. They tracked him, and they backtracked him. They went around the house trying to find tracks on the other side, to see if he'd jumped out of both sides of the house. They went around stomping on the ground, poking at it, to see if he'd tunneled out.

They searched his belongings and found that some things were gone—the mirror, a razor blade. That shook them up even more; it finally dawned on them that he was really gone. Oil Can finally got things organized and sent people running down all the trails. They went over and took Schumann's boots—he was the only other prisoner with boots—and they put us all in chains. Poor Schumann hadn't been in the camp for more than two or three days, and he didn't know what the hell was going on.

Camacho had an eight- to ten-hour start.

Oil Can Harry told me that he was holding me personally responsible for Camacho's escape. A can of corned beef was missing from our cage, and Harry accused me of giving mine to Camacho. But Big Dumb said he had seen me throw my can away. Roraback had neither corned beef nor empty can, so he was accused. His vitamins were missing, too. Harry figured that Roraback was somehow in cahoots with Camacho, but since he wasn't in the same cage. . . .

"You!" he had Prevaricator tell me. "You were friend to Camacho. He could not have done this without you knowing about it."

"Please tell the camp commander that since I made the tape recording Camacho has not confided in me. He doesn't trust me anymore. He has spoken nothing of escape to me."

They discussed that for a while with Harry looking thoughtful. "The camp commander says he will take your position into consideration."

I started to breathe easy again. That seemed to satisfy them; I was never again blamed. They never interrogated us. Apparently they decided they weren't going to find out, at least not from me. Roraback would surely deny it if they asked him. He ended up getting blamed as Camacho's co-conspirator. They were convinced that McClure wouldn't do it, and if I didn't do it either, then it must have been Roraback. He had refused to make a tape, he had tried to indoctrinate Man With Glasses—and because of his age they still thought of him as the senior man.

Security really tightened. Except in the very beginning at Auschwitz, we had never been chained inside our cages; but now we were chained twenty-four hours a day and let out only once, to empty the urinal can they gave us. It looked like they were going to keep this up until they figured out how Camacho had got out of the cage.

The day after Camacho escaped, Nice Guy came and told me he had been captured and shot. He might be telling the truth, I thought. Camacho and I had planned that if he made it he would have a jet fly over the area and make a sonic boom. There had been no jet, no sonic boom, and the Vietnamese didn't appear to be making plans to break camp. If they haven't caught Camacho they would surely have to move the camp, I thought.

But I still didn't believe Nice Guy. I couldn't believe that the Vietnamese would shoot Camacho. If they found him it seemed likely they would bring him back to find out how he had escaped and who, if anyone, had helped him. I had the impression that some of the search parties were still out. Some of the camp's company were still missing; things had not gone back to normal.

After four days there were still no plans for moving. I figured he hadn't made it. He was either wandering around lost or had been killed by a booby trap or was in the bottom of a punji pit.

That morning the guards chained us wrist to wrist and took us to where Alex had given us the parcels. Alex was there, but this time he wasn't smiling. He was really mad.

"I told you and told you to be patient," he said, pounding on the table. "And you do this thing. We treat you too well. We bring you boxes. Now you do this thing—you run away." The letter Camacho had written them thanking them for their kindness had been in the plural, so he had taken it with him, rather than leaving it as we had planned when both of us intended to go.

"We must be more severe. We do not like to do this, but we are obliged to. You force us to put you in chains. We are obliged to take away privileges. We have been too kind." *That's right, Alex, that's how it happened—you were too kind.* We were getting to be friends with them, being trustworthy. They trusted us to the point that it was possible to escape.

"We must change our policies. We do not want to do this, but we are obliged to do so. Two more prisoners have been executed in Saigon. The Central Committee has decided that two American prisoners will be shot."

McClure looked stricken, and Roraback almost swallowed his mustache. I was in shock. "We've warned them and we've warned them and we've warned them. The Central Committee can no longer allow the murder of our people to go unchallenged," Alex went on. "And so two prisoners have been executed." And he got up and left.

It was such a relief. He had sat there and pronounced a death sentence on us and then reprieved us in the next breath and walked away. When I thought it over, I realized that Alex had just wanted to inform us of the executions and he had got his tenses confused. Then I felt guilty at being relieved that two others had been shot instead of me.

Four days later the camp was going about its usual routine, when everything suddenly stopped. In a few seconds the camp exploded with activity. Prevaricator came running up to our shacks with Anus and two other guards. They were yelling and shouting and completely out of patience. "Roll up your shit! You've got a minute to do it!" They were furious, glaring and scowling. "Get out of the damned cage! Line up! Get going!"

Within an hour we were on the trail and the camp was deserted. It could mean only one thing—Camacho had made it. I don't know how they found out he had reached safety, but it was clear that they had, and the shit had hit the fan.

We'd made out that Paradise was supposed to be a model POW camp. They weren't cutting any corners; the camp was going to be as permanent as things could be for them. They had brought in new prisoners and told us there would be more. Now everything had changed.[11]

EXECUTION

We walked all day and most of the night. It was a forced march, and this time the guards were hostile. They blamed us for having to leave the camp in a hurry when they nearly had it finished. They had us chained wrist to wrist, McClure, Roraback, and myself in one group, Crafts, Cook, and Schumann in another. Crafts was having trouble with his legs—some kind of vitamin deficiency—and he kept falling down. Anus booted him a couple of times. It was the only time I ever saw them physically abuse a prisoner. Anus wasn't trying to hurt him, just to get him up and moving; but I don't imagine Crafts noticed the difference.

Crafts really couldn't walk, so they cut a big pole and made a hammock so that two of us could carry him. He was like a pendulum—every time he swung, he threw us off balance. We were staggering all over the jungle. Finally they left him with Husky and Loudmouth, a guard who yelled at us even when he was trying to be friendly. He caught up with us a couple of days later; they pushed him all the way on a bicycle.

We made camp just before daybreak. They told us to sling our hammocks and they chained us to the trees. We were traveling with Anus's guard squad, but there could have been any number of other people moving with us, even other POWs. At Paradise we had just been living in our own little area, but the damned camp could have had another fifty POWs in other cells scattered all over the jungle. It would all have been disrupted by Camacho's escape.

One of the spotters must have seen something; he dropped a flare. Suddenly a roar and an explosion brought me to my feet—one of which was chained to a tree. An F-105 came in at treetop level and dropped everything it had. I got my belly to the ground. There wasn't a damned thing else I could do; there wasn't any hole to crawl into.

Four or five other F-105s joined the attack. The bombs and rockets were exploding no more than a thousand yards from us, and the noise was deafening. The exploding bombs were only slightly more terrifying than the roar of the low-flying jets. We were shaking and cowering, belly down at the base of the trees we were chained to, hands over our ears. The Vietnamese were shook up too. I yelled at one of them, "How about unlocking me from this tree!" and he just gave me a real nasty grin. "How do you like it now, you son of a bitch? You're the one got us into this shit!"

After they dropped their bombs, they strafed until they ran out of ammunition. They made five or six passes; the attack went on for ten or fifteen minutes. I thought the spotter had seen us, but apparently it was a column down the road a little way. If he had seen us I'm sure they would have got us, because they seemed to be firing accurately. I hoped to hell they weren't going to try to rescue us. We had enough trouble being bombed, without somebody trying to rescue us. You don't stand a chance if they start that bullshit.

When the attack ended, we moved off a short distance. After nightfall we started marching again. Now we were moving along little roads with about six inches of mud on them. I wasn't having much trouble keeping up, but we were chained together—Roraback, McClure, and myself—and Roraback kept falling down and pulling us after him. We were carrying all our stuff, and we weren't on friendly terms with the guards anymore. In the past they would say, "How are you doing—you want to take a break?" But it wasn't anything like that now, just "Move out! Keep marching!" They gave us a break about every four hours. In the daytime they blindfolded us.

At one point we crossed a big stream on a bridge large enough to handle light trucks. When I peeked under the blindfold I could see boat traffic on the stream and even a motorcycle parked near the bridge. It was a corduroy bridge, about a hundred feet across, hidden by overhanging trees. Then we were on a hard-top road, and I could hear the steel wheels of an ox cart grinding in the distance. They moved us off the road until it passed.

When they got us back on the road we moved along it for about a mile and then they turned us off onto a trail. No sooner were we in the underbrush than Prevaricator came and put his hand over my mouth to show me that I wasn't to talk or call out, and we heard this *stomp, stomp, stomp*, another column moving by very fast. As soon as the column had passed they took our blindfolds off. I presume there were other POWs in the column, or something we weren't supposed to see.

We walked all night again. Then during the day we rested and ate. They still kept us chained, but the guards seemed more relaxed. Some of them were digging around for cicadas. They thought cicadas were a real delicacy—fried them up in salt and soybean oil—and we had learned to like them too.

They had to dig a foot or so for each one, but they shared them with us at lunch. I had five or six.

The guards were talking in normal voices but they told us we had to whisper. This started us speculating again about there being other prisoners nearby.

We had always suspected that they had other prisoners with us there in the jungle. We knew they had at least three or four more somewhere. Many months earlier, Man With Glasses had asked me if I knew a Sergeant Pitzer, and of course I did—he and Rowe had been captured in an ambush a few months before we were. Man With Glasses said he had talked with Pitzer—"He feels very much the same as you do." I asked him if he had seen Rowe. "I have talked with an officer," he said. "He is a very stubborn person—he talks very much about his flag." Apparently he was doing a Roraback.

But we didn't know where they were keeping Pitzer and Rowe. Camacho said one time that he had seen lug marks from jungle boots on the trail, but he could have been imagining it. Back at Auschwitz the Vietnamese had given us Christmas presents of commercially made mess kits—separate plates and pots stacked together and carried by a single handle. Only the prisoners had mess kits. The guards ate at the mess hall. One day the four of us were sitting eating dinner when Little King came in with a fifth mess kit. He caught hell from Anus, who tried to explain it away, but we knew damn well he was bullshitting. He even looked guilty. He wasn't as good a liar as Prevaricator.

Walking down the trail that night we came to a stream that we had to cross by balancing on a little foot-pole. When we got out on the middle of it, I was convinced that if Roraback could fall in the middle of the road he was surely going to fall off that pole—and pull us in with him. Roraback didn't fall off, but the Troll behind him did—with a big splash, cursing and complaining, and all the other guards laughing at him.

We made camp at about two in the morning. When the sun

came up it was apparent we were going to stay there for a while—Anus cleared the area around his hammock and immediately built a little table.

Anus was the most disgustingly hard-working sonofabitch I ever saw in my life. The first thing he did when we moved into a goddamned camp was build one of those tables. He'd tie a bunch of twigs together with rattan vine and set it on some legs driven into the ground. As soon as he'd finish his, he'd come over and make me build one. I'd be really beat, tired, just wanting to lie down someplace. "Anus, I don't want a table, I don't need a table, I don't even *like* a table." But I'd have to build that goddamned table, even if he had to call in Prevaricator to give the orders.

He made everybody build one, but he always came to me first. "If I get White Wise Guy to build one, I'll get everybody else to build one, because it will scare them." It always seemed to work—by the time he and I had got done with our hassle, everybody else was so frightened they already had theirs half-started.

As soon as the table got built you had to start clearing the area. They gave you a machete, and you'd have to clear all the sticks away, and then make a broom out of all the sticks you cut down, and then sweep away all the debris. "Jesus Christ, Anus, there's an airplane coming to bomb us." Didn't make any difference to him—"You must clear your area."

Energetic bastard—always building tables and washing his goddamned hat. Everybody else's hat was all beat up and mangy-looking, but Anus's hat was always neat and clean. He insisted on wearing a clean hat all the time, like someone who likes to shine his shoes. It started out being sort of a khaki color, but now it was almost white because he'd scrubbed it so many times.

They didn't begin to dig any wells, so apparently we were just staying here until they built a permanent camp nearby. When we weren't out on work details, we were all hammocked in a circle. I was surprised that they allowed Cook to be with us. I thought they didn't want him contaminating the rest of us. He was really hard-nosed. I believe he would have stopped shitting if he had thought "Charlie" was using it for fertilizer.

This was really the first time we had been able to talk to Schumann, and the first time he had been able to communicate with us. He hadn't been in Paradise more than two or three days before they took his boots, threw some chains on him, and marched him through the jungle. "What the hell happened?" We told him about Camacho's escape.

Schumann had been a MAAG advisor to a village chief, and they had been riding down a road in a car and got ambushed. He jumped out of the car and started running, and the village chief turned the car around and left him stranded in a rice paddy. He got mired in the mud and they caught him. "I was standing there with my rifle, and they were all around me. I felt like a damn ass."

Despite his size, Schumann was very soft-spoken and gentle. He said that the Vietnamese had treated him very well on his way to Paradise, that they were very kind to him. He wasn't really interested in the war, he said; he had been a victim of circumstances—and not too happy ones at that. He had been with the Transportation Corps in a depot in New York City. If you are going to be a career officer in the U.S. Army you have to put in a certain amount of combat time, and so they sent him out as an adviser to that village chief. So the innocent guy ends up a POW. "Oh, Jesus, I never imagined I would get into a mess like this. I ain't pissed off at anybody."

Schumann, as the most recently captured, was a source of information to the rest of us. He told us more or less how the war was going—that it was being expanded and we weren't doing any better, in fact maybe a little bit worse. I asked him about that aircraft carrier they said they had sunk in the

Saigon River, but he didn't know anything about it.

One day the guards unchained McClure and took him away and when he came back he had a letter from his wife and a message from Oil Can Harry that Camacho had been caught and executed. This time nobody believed it.

After about ten days we packed up our gear one afternoon after lunch and Big Dumb put the blindfolds on us. Then they turned us around and around about six times to disorient us. Of course, it only made sense to do that if we knew where we were to start with. I hadn't been oriented for almost two years. In about an hour we reached the new campsite, and they took the blindfolds off.

Once again we began building a permanent camp. This one was close enough to a road that we could occasionally hear traffic. One time we heard what sounded like a two-and-a-half-ton truck start up and change gears. Anus tried to tell us it was an airplane. "No, Anus, airplanes don't shift gears."

Something, maybe the road, sure as hell attracted airplanes. They bombed and bombed around us. Spotter planes hovered over the area, sometimes all day. We seemed to be in the dive path of jets and Skyraiders—a Navy prop plane that carries more than its weight in armament. They never dropped their loads more than a mile away, and many hit within three or four hundred yards. Every time they dropped their shit, it nearly threw us out of our hammocks. They weren't aiming at the camp, but if they pushed the button a second early, it was good-bye.

Nothing is more frightening than being in the dive path of a jet. I tried to explain to the guards that when you hear him diving, he's already *done* it. He's already released the bomb and he's on his way back up; you don't have *time* to jump in the hole anymore.

They couldn't believe that. They'd wait until they heard him dive, and then they'd tell us to jump in the hole. It really was frightening to have that jet dive right at you, and know that he's either going to drop a bomb on you or strafe you—or napalm you, which is even scarier. At Fort Bragg they showed us color films of jets napalming villages along canals. "Charlie don't like that stuff. Charlie usually moves out after a couple of times like that." Then they took us out and dropped some napalm about five thousand yards away. *Whomph*—you could feel the fire taking the oxygen out of the air. They say it doesn't burn you, it takes the oxygen away long enough to suffocate you.

There must have been a hell of a target further away, because it drew several B-52 attacks. They were fearful and awesome. The B-52s would fly so high that you could barely hear them. They'd drop tons of bombs that would explode with the rapidity of machine-gun fire. Later on, when I figured out where we must have been, it seemed certain that they were bombing in Cambodia.

You could hear the Skyraiders coming from miles away—that slow, heavy engine sound. They carried such tremendous loads that they could bomb for more than an hour. They would bomb and bomb and bomb. After they'd dropped all their bombs, they'd strafe for an hour or so.

The bombing got more and more intense. First they were coming a couple of times a week, then every morning, then twice a day, three times a day, sometimes all day long. One sortie would be replaced by another, then another, then another, until three would come together. Three Skyraiders would come and drop heavy stuff, then three or four jets would come and drop some lighter stuff and strafe, then more Skyraiders. They'd have a spotter plane flying overhead all day. They'd fire the spotting flares into an area, and that area would be attacked.

It really began to wear on me. Every day! Every day! I'd get up and try to eat my breakfast, and the first bomber would arrive before I'd finished. I became very nervous about the whole thing.

McClure was going into another one of his moods. Cook and I were discussing it, and he said McClure appeared to be a classic case of combat fatigue. He would get up in the morning and sit on the side of his foxhole in his shorts, waiting to jump in as soon as he heard a propeller. Of course, he was usually right—they usually came—and the rest of us would jump into those muddy foxholes, *splash, splash*, fully dressed. McClure was one up on us—with only his shorts on, he didn't have to wash his clothes.

I wasn't quite that bad, but I started getting that way after I'd been there a while. When we were first prisoners the planes would fly over and Big Dumb would come and take my plate and cup out of the sun so they wouldn't reflect, and I would yawn and say, "Oh, man, they won't bomb us anyway." But it was a wearing sort of thing. Finally I started getting shaky. I started hiding my things even if the sun wasn't out, and I would jump in my hole when they even just sounded like they were going to dive. I'd jump in even if I heard a reconnaissance plane—"Well, he's going to mark the area, and there's going to be a bomber come and bomb us." I really began to suffer a little bit from combat fatigue myself.

Roraback didn't seem too worried about it, and Cook with his usual style kept telling me to keep a stiff upper lip. But I got a phobia about airplanes. It still bothers me sometimes. I wake up at night and hear a plane—"Shit!"—and then, "Oh, hell, I don't think he's going to bomb me." It's such a relief to be able to stand out in the open and watch a plane go over, and not have to worry about it bombing you.

It scared the shit out of Anus, too. He used to jump in his damn hole pretty regularly. This was unusual for Anus. He'd jump in it almost reflexively, before he knew what he was doing. Then he'd pop up, looking around like a tank commander trying to find out where he was. "Where am I? How'd I get in this hole?"

If it was bothering him, it was bothering a lot of people.

The guards seemed less happy than they had been, a bit edgy all the time—maybe not as much as we were because they could run away more easily. If the plane began zeroing in on where we were, they could zoom off to some other part of the camp. We were stuck. If we started getting hit heavy, nobody was going to save our ass. We were just going to get splattered.

Every day! Every day! I *hated* the planes. When I'd hear them coming, I'd begin to hate—hate the people flying them, hate the people who sent them, hate the fact that I'd got myself into such a situation, hate the war.

We'd spend half a day in a foxhole. It made me believe we had a very dim future. They seemed to be closing in, and these guys were going to have to run. I doubted that they would want us to run along behind them. It became obvious that the bigger the war got, the less chance of survival we were going to have. Under pressure, they would neglect their prisoners rather than neglect their war effort.

Everything was in short supply. Sometimes they didn't have any tobacco; other times, no kerosene. Vegetables were practically nonexistent. Then there would seem to be another supply run, and things would be a little better.

It was obvious that the war was increasing at a tremendous rate. We were getting reports on Radio Peking and Radio Hanoi that there were more troops coming, Marines and Marines. "Where is it going to end? They're not doing us any good. They're certainly not changing the situation in South Vietnam. Why don't they stop, and take the planes away? This is not helping a damned thing."[12]

It was just like we were right in the middle of a combat zone. We relaxed when it became clear that they weren't after us, but we were right in the middle of it nonetheless. Every day was unnerving. Your adrenalin was constantly flowing. I could never figure out why they'd construct a camp at ground zero of a bomb range, unless they felt that because it was about two feet away it was safe. Nobody would ever suspect anybody of building a camp at the end of a dive path. On those terms I suppose it would be safe. It made me nervous as hell, but we never got hit.[13]

I named the place Camp Baffle. Except for its general layout, nothing seemed to follow normal practice. Usually our slammers were built before we got to a camp or shortly after we arrived, but at Baffle they didn't seem to be in a hurry to get a cage built. They hauled in the poles for the slammer and just stacked them up and left them there.

We dug the usual foxholes, and the guards started on a well but hit rock at twenty feet. They detailed us to dig another, and we hit water at thirty feet. If we had waited a few days, the guards' well would have been sufficient. It was still the rainy season, and the water table was steadily rising. After a while any hole deeper than six inches was a well—including our foxholes. Jumping in our foxholes to escape getting killed by a bomb was risking death by drowning.

Cook didn't do much work. If the guards took Cook out to do something, they usually ended up shouting at him. They'd try to show him how to do it, and he'd just stand there and watch them. They'd get disgusted and chain him up again and get somebody else to do the job.

As at the temporary camp, they hammocked us all together so they could watch us more easily, but they ordered us not to talk to Cook. We all violated the orders, of course, but only Roraback did so openly and deliberately. They told him time and again not to talk to Cook, but he ignored them and kept right on talking. He was trying to show Cook that he wasn't being influenced. He was a dedicated soldier, even if the rest of us weren't, and never compromised with the enemy on any score. I told Cook that he was a phony sonofabitch, but I don't know whether he believed me or thought I was a bigger liar than Roraback.

They repeatedly told us not to talk to Cook, but Roraback

continued to talk and talk and talk in long conversations. Finally it got to be too much for them, and Anus went for the camp commander. Harry brought Prevaricator with him. "You have been told many times not to talk to Cook and yet you continue to do so. Because of this your life can no longer be guaranteed."

Maybe Roraback had heard the speech too often to take it seriously; maybe he wanted to impress Cook. He barely waited for the translation before laughing in the camp commander's face. I thought Harry was going to hit Roraback— his nostrils flared and his face flushed. But he spun on his heel and walked away.

For several days on Radio Hanoi we'd been hearing that Saigon was preparing to execute more prisoners. Hanoi was warning that if the executions took place the U.S. must bear responsibility for the consequences. I told Roraback he'd better play it cool. Since Camacho had escaped, all our asses were in danger—most of all Roraback's, since they thought he was an accomplice, and senior man besides. But he just laughed at me and kept right on talking to Cook.

The next evening, while we were sitting in our hammocks smoking our after-dinner horseshit, Prevaricator came for Roraback. "The camp commander wishes conversation with you." As soon as Roraback was gone, the guards took down his hammock and awning and packed up all his gear. They even took away his half-wit *chom*. The following morning we heard a couple of shots.

It could have been anything—a hunting party, somebody shooting at a monkey swinging through camp. But I told Cook I thought they had shot Roraback. That's what they wanted us to think, Cook told me, but they'd never really do it. If they were going to shoot anybody, he was the more likely candidate. "Maybe so," I told him. "But you didn't laugh in the camp commander's face."

They kept the radio from us for a couple of days, as if

something had happened that they didn't want us to hear about, and that seemed to confirm my suspicion. But if Roraback had been executed for disobeying orders, why would they keep it a secret? They hadn't been bashful about telling us they had shot Camacho.

I didn't know what to think. All of a sudden Roraback was gone. The guards never again mentioned his name.[14]

PART FIVE: RELEASE

RELEASE

While the guards built a bamboo and thorn barricade around our hammock area, Anus had us build a big slammer in the middle of it. Anus invariably chose me to drill the peg holes in the bamboo—he said I was the only one who drilled them straight. He'd got some more of that white lightning, and when I did a good drilling job he'd give me some. I kept fighting it, but in spite of myself I was getting to like the bastard. I had to respect the sonofabitch for his industriousness, if nothing else. He was tough, but fair—he wasn't petty like some of the other guards. I really couldn't criticize the guy, except for his power over me.

Rather than build a guard house outside the barricade, they put a bamboo ceiling on the top of our slammer and then built an attic for the guards. Eight or ten of them lived up there. They'd climb up the ladder and bullshit all night long—kept us awake.

One day we saw the guards going up to their loft with loaves of French bread. "God damn!" Since they had bread, we should have bread. We sent for Prevaricator, and we told him we had seen the guards with bread, so why didn't we have bread.

Prevaricator climbed up the ladder and talked to the guards. He climbed back down with some of them and told us that the guards had saved up and bought the bread with their own money. We countered that Schumann had money

259

when he was captured and they had confiscated it. If they couldn't afford to buy bread for us, could they please draw a sufficient amount from Schumann's fund to buy some?

That embarrassed them. They didn't say another word. They just went and got us some of their bread.

Eventually we built a second, smaller slammer for the officers, and Cook and Schumann were separated from McClure, Crafts, and me. By then it was October. With only three of us in the cage, there weren't enough people for hearts, so Crafts taught us to play cribbage. He showed us how to make a cribbage board, and McClure made one. We became pretty good cribbage players.

It was a time for visitors, too. Once it was Alex, "just passing through." Maybe he came by to see if we had died of fright, camping at the end of a bombing range. He was no longer angry with us. We had a casual conversation, and he didn't stay long. He said he was going to come back, but he didn't. We never saw him again.

One morning Prevaricator brought Cook, Schumann, and Crafts the fatigues they'd been captured in and told them to put them on. He told McClure and me to put on our clean "blacks." Then they brought us some coffee—with cream and sugar—and a pack of ARAs. With that preparation, we weren't very surprised when they marched us out to meet visiting VIPs. They were all sitting behind one of the little tables in the usual jungle gazebo. There were a few photographers and several well-dressed Vietnamese we had never seen before. In the center sat two Latin Americans, a man and a woman, who introduced themselves as Cuban journalists. After some speeches, they took us back to our cage.

Later on, they brought us back individually for interviews. Mine began with the customary tea and cigarettes and the customary questions. "Where were you captured?"—"Hiep Hoa." "When?"—"A couple of years ago." "How have you been treated here?"—"Very fairly." "Do you have enough to eat?"—"Seems to be." "Do you like living in the jungle?"—"Not especially."

The Cubans could speak a little English. I said a few things to them in Spanish, but they spoke too fast and they lost me. They had a Vietnamese translator with them who spoke both English and Spanish. I couldn't help but smile. Was this the man who had broken the secret code of "Los Tres Moranitos"? It was a strange setup. If the Cubans asked a question in English, it was translated into Vietnamese. My answer was translated into Spanish and Vietnamese. But if Oil Can had a comment, it was translated into Spanish but not English.

What did I think about the war? I was opposed to it. Did I expect to be shot when I was captured? "At first, yes. Later I expected that I would be released because I knew the Front's lenient policy toward people who they feel can see the truth. But as you can see I am still a prisoner two years later."

That caused quite a stir—they were babbling back and forth. When you're in a situation like that where you're depending a great deal on facial expression, you *feel* your way. You can almost tell by the way a guy shapes his face what he's saying, even if you can't understand him. When I made that statement, the immediate reaction was not, "Yeah, he's been a prisoner for two years, and he's been a *bastard* all that time." It seemed something like, "That's true, he's one of the men we're going to release." That's what I speculated they were saying, but I kept it all to myself—it was my own wishful thinking.[15]

Things settled back to normal: bombing all day with chopper strafing runs during the lulls. Otherwise, things seemed to level off. Even the horseshit seemed to be a better grade. They had either put Prevaricator on permanent detail or told him to stay away from us; at any rate we didn't see much of him. In fact, we had much less contact with the guards than before.

One regular visitor was a little lizard that used to come and sun itself on one of the poles. "Damn," said McClure. "I'm going to get that sonofabitch and cook him." Every day the lizard came, and every day McClure chased it. Finally one day McClure swung at it as hard as he could with a piece of firewood. He hit the lizard's tail and broke it off.

"By God," said McClure. "I'll just eat the tail." He built a little fire, toasted the tail, and ate it. "This guy's nuts," I thought, and the guards thought he was even crazier. Hungry, too. Big Dumb must have told Anus what he'd seen. That night they brought us a large pot of cassava root, and when we had gobbled it up they brought us some more.

The lizard came back a few days later without the tail. "Damn," said McClure; "son of a bitch came back." He immediately set out to try to catch the lizard again. In the end he gave it a terrible blow and killed it. By this time it had become a game with the rest of us too. We prepared the lizard. I was a medic, I took a razor blade and cleaned it out. I did a very neat job of it. Big Dumb wouldn't let us build a fire until night, but as soon as it got dark we built the fire. As soon as we got the fire going, a plane came. We had just started the lizard cooking, and we had to blow the fire out. It was the third time around before we got the lizard cooked, and then I burned it.

We tried to get the guards to take a leg over to Cook and Schumann, but they just laughed and brushed us off. It wasn't as big as a good-sized frog's leg. They were sure we were nuts, and they weren't going to be any part of it.

That dumb lizard came back after it lost its tail, and it ended up getting eaten. There's some sort of moral in that.

We were listening to the news one night on Radio Hanoi when we heard that large groups of people in the United States were demonstrating in the streets against the war. It created quite a stir among us.

"Crafts, what the hell is going on?" Crafts said he didn't know much about it. Demonstrating in the streets in the United States? About the war? This was a new turn. It sounded interesting. Maybe something was going to happen.

We kept hearing more about demonstrations and something called the peace movement. They talked about a big demonstration somewhere—in New York or Washington.[16] Maybe something *will* happen. They're going to start dealing with the American people. If anything gave us hope, it was that. This was a new outlet. Since the United States government wasn't going to recognize the Vietnamese people, the peace movement was going to recognize them.

One broadcast talked about two people who had immolated themselves to protest the war. I couldn't understand what had made the Vietnamese burn themselves in 1963, let alone an American getting that upset.

We had had a newcomer in camp for a while. He was a neat, fair-complexioned Vietnamese who carried himself well. He had curly hair and spoke in a soft voice; he was a little bit feminine. We named him Pussy. He showed up wearing a pistol one day, and we concluded he was an officer. He didn't seem to take orders from anybody in the camp; he just walked around and observed.

One morning Husky and Little King marched McClure and me to the interrogation shack. There was Grandpa—and Pussy. Pussy, it turned out, must have outranked even Oil Can. And he spoke better English than McClure or me.

They caught us up on the news and we chatted about irrelevant things—the effect of nicotine on the system, the fact that I liked the heavy French coffee better than the American kind—and then it came. We should help bring an end to the war by making another tape, Grandpa told us. This would hasten our release. I figured we were being set up for another round. We told him we'd consider it and waited for the conditions. But there weren't any. Strange.

Two days later, Pussy came and told us they were having a memorial service for Norman Morrison and Alice Herz, the two Americans who had burned themselves to death.[17] He explained that when the Vietnamese had a memorial service, they wrote the names on a board or a piece of paper and posted them. Then there were a couple of minutes of meditation in honor of the people, and if someone wanted to say something about their merits, they could.

"You don't have to do anything if you don't want to. But if you feel like saying something, we'd appreciate it, because we feel that these people have contributed a great deal. Especially since you are Americans and they were Americans, we feel that you should be present if you want to be. But it's not compulsory that you attend."

Four of us decided to go—maybe out of curiosity—with Cook holding out. I had no idea what kind of a guy Norman Morrison was. He could have been some fanatic who just burned himself. We all did attend, finally, even Captain Cook, and we all had some little thing to say. I said something like "If Norman Morrison has truly given his life in the cause of peace, then he has contributed a great deal and should be honored accordingly." Cook said something along the same lines—"If he has done this in the interest of peace, then good, I praise the man, respect his memory."

They seemed to be very pleased. It was very quiet, informal, didn't last long. If Norman Morrison didn't get any other recognition, he got that—in the middle of the jungle in South Vietnam.

The next morning, after McClure and I were through brushing our teeth, the guards ordered us outside to do calisthenics. Exercising wasn't that strange, but why us and not the other three? Then at mealtime Coburn brought shrimp and fresh fish and all the rice we could eat. Again, just for the two of us. After three days of this they took us back to the interrogation shack.

Grandpa told us that the Front would release us if the Peace Movement—it was in capitals now—requested it. He suggested we write a letter to something called the Vietnam Day Committee stating our feelings about the war and the Front and asking them to make the request. He seemed to assume that I would know what the Vietnam Day Committee was, but of course I didn't have the slightest idea.

We felt it was certainly an interesting twist on an old game, if nothing more. Cook was the ranking man now. Schumann was actually senior, but he had informally relinquished command to Cook. Cook told us we shouldn't write the letters. He said we shouldn't even accept release if it was offered—it was against the Code of Conduct to accept parole. Professional soldiers get it into their heads that the Code of Conduct is God's Word, and that if you go against it you end up in Hell. But after two years my qualms about the Superman Code were nil. I would have been more impressed by it, maybe, if Eisenhower had ever been a prisoner of war.

They had dangled release in front of us so many times, but now I could see that our situation was changing. We were obviously being favored. There was little doubt that something was up—what, we didn't know. McClure and I felt it was worth the gamble. We went ahead and wrote the letters—told them that we opposed the war and that our treatment by the Front had been humane. I didn't know what the hell this Vietnam Day Committee was, but if they could do what the United States government couldn't—get us out of the damned jungle—they had to have something going for them.

Even so, when we gave the letters to Pussy it all seemed too easy. Maybe they would take us to another part of the country, maybe to North Vietnam—remove us from the war zone and use us for propaganda. Release still seemed to be a little bit out of our grasp.

The next morning Pussy took us some way from our

slammer and asked us to dig a couple of air-raid shelters. Then he walked away. The guards came by to check on us from time to time, but for the first time in two years we were working without an armed guard standing nearby. It felt strange. At one point Oil Can came by for casual conversation. Pussy brought some tea out to the hole and gave it to us when we took breaks. Very strange—we were digging holes and they were serving us tea. Then Pussy began singing American pop songs—and whistling, something I'd never heard a Vietnamese do before.

We didn't finish the holes the first day, so they brought us back the next morning. When we arrived, Harry was sweeping a path they had just cut to the shelters. "Christ," I thought, "this guy must have been trained at Fort Bragg." I always equated sweeping the jungle with raking the North Carolina sand. Then I remembered that Oil Can was the camp commander—and colonels don't do the sweeping at Bragg.

When we finished the holes, Oil Can said that McClure and I were very good hole-diggers—we dug holes as well as they did. We did many things nearly as well as they did, Pussy said. It surprised him because of the culture we had come from. We took it in the spirit in which it was offered—as a compliment. It was an encouraging sign, we felt. Maybe we *were* being prepared for release.

After the first wave of bombers had come and gone the next morning, Little King and Husky came to get us. McClure had on a raggedy shirt, and Husky stopped him and told him to put his good shirt on. They took us down to the volleyball court, where Oil Can, Grandpa, and Pussy were waiting. Pussy was wearing his pistol for the occasion. Oil Can said a few words, and we waited patiently for Pussy to translate. It was simple and to the point.

"You have been released. You are now our guests."

I exhaled so violently I thought I would damage my rib cage. Two years is a long time to hold your breath.

"ON THE WAY OUT"

"There'll be a few days' wait while you get your stuff together and we make plans to move you out of here," Grandpa told us. "So you can make yourselves comfortable. You'll move into new lodgings; you can travel around the camp."

Walking back to the slammers was a heady experience. We were strolling through the camp without a guard. The jungle seemed beautiful. Big Dumb was watching over Crafts while he built a new chicken coop. We said hi to Big Dumb, just to test out our new status. He just waved and smiled.

We told Crafts the news. It must have been difficult for him, knowing he would be staying and we would be going home. But he said he was happy for us, that we had been here a long time and deserved to be the first to go home.

We packed our things and Pussy came and took us over to our new house, which turned out to be the interrogation shack with the table and benches removed and two beds put in their place. "You will sleep here while you are waiting. You may go where you please. You are our guests." Then McClure and I were alone.

No guards, no bars, no doors. It was a strange feeling. We unpacked our gear, made our beds, but after that we didn't know what to do. I felt like the GI who has one more patrol before he rotates home—I was afraid to think too far ahead for fear it would bring bad luck. We still had a long way to travel.

I think both McClure and I were waiting for the catch. It

had been implanted in our minds that you just can't make deals with the enemy; they were going to expect something in return. "If you make an appearance in Hanoi's Red Square. . . ." They don't let you go home in the middle of the war—obviously there had to be something that went along with it. As it turned out, there was nothing.

One thing was certain: they weren't serious about the peace movement having to request our release. Only a couple of days had passed since we gave Pussy the letters to the Vietnam Day Committee, so they must have just been an attitude check. I got a chill thinking about what might have happened if we had taken Cook's advice and been hard-nosed.

Pussy came back and asked us to come down to the volley-ball court with him, the ceremony was about to begin. They'd built benches and a lectern for the occasion, and they sat McClure and me front row center. The entire camp company was there, and the guards brought Crafts, Cook, and Schumann and sat them further to the rear.

Everybody stood at attention as a Front official dressed in khaki walked to the lectern. Then everybody sat down and he read the proclamation of our release. Pussy translated: We were being released on behalf of the many people in the U.S. working for peace. Our return would help repay America's great loss in the deaths of Norman Morrison and Alice Herz. The NLF wanted the American people to know that they understood that loss and mourned with them.

They took Crafts, Cook, and Schumann back to their slammers after the proclamation, and then McClure and I were asked to make some response, which they taped. Our statements were brief. I told them that I supported their cause, and that I could see that the war was not for me and not in the best interests of my people. I thanked them very much for the kindness they had shown me, and expressed the hope that some day soon both our peoples could live in peace. McClure said about the same thing.

Then the whole group sang "Giai Phong Mien Nam." This time we didn't hesitate. After it was all over, the Vietnamese came up and congratulated us, shaking our hands and patting us on the back.

Alone again, we wandered around the camp aimlessly, not really knowing what to do with ourselves. We went by the holes we had dug the day before and discovered that they were shelters for the shack where the officials were staying. We watched Charlie's Mother cooking for a while. Then Coburn told us to go see Pseudo Doc, the camp medic, and get some shots. After that we went back to our house and sat around wondering when we were going to leave.

Dinner was a diversion. Coburn gave us all we could eat and told us if we wanted anything else to just let him know. We didn't know what the hell to ask for.

The next morning I was smoking an after-breakfast horse-shit when Grandpa came by and told us we should get as much rest as we could, we'd probably be leaving the next day. We lay around on our beds, but sleep was out of the question. Pussy, Harry, and Coburn dropped by for casual conversation. It was awkward. I just didn't know what to talk about; I hadn't thought of these guys before as friends.

The following morning they put us to work again. Somebody had evidently been bragging about us. They got a photographer with a movie camera and McClure and I showed how we could chop wood with the Donald Duck ax, drill straight holes through poles, and split rattan vines—I still couldn't do that worth a damn. Anus stood by with a big smile on his face, like a teacher showing off his star pupils.

At noon they brought us to the mess hall near the kitchen. What a feast! It was like a big family get-together—more like a reunion than anything else. I sat at one table with some of the people; McClure sat at another. Oil Can Harry was walking around joking. Everybody was smiling. Lots of noise and chatter. They had just about every dish you could imagine the Vietnamese would serve—chicken, all kinds of little vegetables, sausages. There was even wine. We ate with chopsticks. It was really an outstanding meal, even better than Tet. I congratulated Coburn, telling him what a wonderful cook he was.

After the meal we all sat around talking and laughing, putting a real strain on Prevaricator and Pussy. Everybody was coming around with congratulations. It was like a big party. The conversations were brief—you don't get a hell of a lot out of a big party, except a little joy. But I talked with Little King. He'd been with them about as long as I had. I asked him why he'd joined the NLF.

He said that his family had been very poor, but that didn't prevent the Diem regime from coming and taking away every damned thing they had. He knew that his family was just one of many, and so he had decided to fight with the NLF. He felt that they were the people who should be in control of the country, that they were *his* people. He seemed very sincere. Nobody was forcing him to stay there. He was very pleased with the life he had taken up and was very definitely motivated to winning the war.

By this time I wasn't feeling too comfortable with the names we had pinned on the Vietnamese. They were still the same people they had been a week ago—we'd known some of them for nearly two years—but after they announced our release I began to realize that most of the names simply didn't apply. After you've called a guy an asshole for two years it's hard to sit down and smile at him, and be honest, look him directly in the eye. I felt a little guilty about it. At the time I named them I'd thought the names were appropriate, but now they didn't seem so right. I had been just a little bit nasty.

I regretted not knowing more about each of them. They'd never told us much about themselves, but then we'd never asked. We just lay on our beds feeling superior. "You silly bastards, here you are giving me stupid rice and sardines and I'm making something like eight hundred dollars a month—I'll be eating steaks when I get out of here, and you guys will still be living in shit. Even if you do win the fucking war, what have you got—nothing."

This was a holdover from being an American—that you're superior to Asiatics—the thing they teach you at Fort Bragg and in high school and in grade school.

Gradually I had changed. I had learned humility, I believe. It's something I had to learn; I hadn't had it before. I was really a nasty bastard when I was in the Army. I didn't have any consideration for anything or anyone. But I was taken out of my arrogant environment—where the Americans were always telling someone else what to do—and then *I* was being told what to do. Being in an extremely difficult situation myself, I could understand how other people in a difficult situation feel.

I changed from my arrogance and nastiness to liking people, from my superiority to feeling that the Vietnamese were pretty good people. Some of the honest culture of an oppressed people must have worn off on me.

Back at our house, Harry came by to talk again. He pulled a picture of his sister from his billfold and asked if I thought she was beautiful. She was, and I told him so. "If after you return to your home you are a good fighter for peace, when the war is over I would like you to come stay in my village. If you so wish it, I will give my permission for you to marry my sister." He said it simply and sincerely. He wrote down his address for me, shook my hand, patted me on the back. Prevaricator and Anus also gave us their addresses. Anus told me, "I would like for you to be guest in my home in my village. My village is very beautiful and grows much fruit.

You will enjoy it and will do me honor."

I was very deeply touched. I told them when the war was over I would come visit them. I still mean to visit them, even though the Army later confiscated the addresses. People who would sit down with you after a bitch of a time like that and invite you to their village were pretty extraordinary—I just have to get to know them better. It would be really good to go talk to Anus, sit and drink tea with him, puff on horseshit. He'd probably talk about his rice crop, his chickens, get his bottle of white lightning out. I only hope they will be there to greet me.

In the afternoon, it was time to go, but first they brought Crafts to say good-bye. He had a letter for his mother. They told him he could write a letter and I would take care of it for him. They asked me, "Could you speak with him for a few minutes." It seemed like Crafts was going to be the new candidate, and they wanted me to clue him in. When they brought him to us, I told him something like, "You can get out of here, if you use your head." The Front had kept faith with us, even if it had taken two years. I wanted to tell him to be patient with the Vietnamese, to try to see their position, that the party least interested in his release was the U.S. government. I told him I hoped he'd be released soon.

Apparently he got the message—they released him about a year later. Whether he was sincerely opposed to the war I don't know. He was a gentle person, and like Schumann he'd got caught up in something he really wasn't prepared for.

We didn't see either Schumann or Cook before we left. Being an officer and under the hand of Cook, Schumann wasn't presenting himself as a potential releasee. He'd been a captain for fifteen or twenty years; I suppose he was in his late thirties. "What would I do? I've devoted my life to the Army, I don't know any other jobs." He's still there as far as I know—with that fanatic Cook.

The whole camp company came to the gate to say good-bye. It was like when you're leaving home, going off to college or the Army. "Well, good-bye, take care of yourself." They shook our hands and gave us gifts, things that were really parts of themselves. Anus took off his hat and gave it to me. It was like taking off the watch you've worn for the last ten years, something that really means something to you. Somebody else gave me his Liberation Lamp. Another kicked off his Ho Chi Minh sandals. Coburn and Charlie's Mother gave me some small towels for my mother. Oil Can gave me a big bag of horseshit and asked if there was anything else I'd like. I asked for a packet of Tiger Brand Tea. Oil Can was slightly incredulous, but he fetched it right away. But the Army confiscated that, too.

We were on our way out. It was two years to the day. Our escort consisted of Pussy, Husky, Gidget, and a man so new I hadn't had time to name him. I wished I'd given Pussy some other name. He looked fragile, but he was obviously very tough. He had a tough time—he fell down, he struggled—but it didn't slow him down. He was doing better than I was, and I considered that pretty good, because I'd been living there for two years and I was in as good condition as anybody.

We walked through the afternoon and evening and into the night. It was hard going. During the night we walked knee-deep through some swamp or flooded area. Once there was a sudden, terrible thrashing and carrying on in the water. Husky had stumbled on something and was wrestling with it, and the others hurried to his aid. Finally I could see that it was a snake—a ten-foot boa constrictor that must have weighed fifty or sixty pounds. They finally wrestled the damned thing into a sack. They were just jubilant—they were going to eat the damned thing. But I was glad as hell when we got out of that swamp.

We stopped long enough that morning to eat and rest for an hour, and then we walked on again until late afternoon. We went through some clearings; we were gradually coming out of the jungle. There would be a rice paddy here and there and fields with just a few trees. At one point an old guy appeared along the trail, probably going to gather some firewood. I suppose he'd seen the Liberation Army hundreds of times along that trail. But he caught sight of me and McClure and just couldn't believe his eyes—a couple of Americans in black pajamas walking out of the jungle with the Vietcong. He probably didn't dare tell anybody after he got home. Afraid they'd think he was crazy.

We came in sight of a village, but we camped half a mile outside in the brush. Pussy went into the village and came back half an hour later with some tobacco and curry and a couple of peanut bars for McClure and me. They curried up the boa. It was tough as hell, but quite tasty. We had warmed-over boa ribs the next day.

When it got dark we walked through the village. The people were in their straw houses cooking rice, kids were running around here and there. Some chickens were pecking in the road. On the other side of the village was a river, and waiting for us there was a fairly large motor launch with a long propellor shaft and one of those *chug-chug* motors. We climbed aboard and settled down.

I discovered that it was a beautiful experience riding along a Vietnamese river in the moonlight. We were on our way out. That was a great thrill in itself. Things that hadn't seemed beautiful before now became beautiful. The moon was in a clear sky—we could see the sky again. We hadn't seen it for a long time. We're going down a very wide, peaceful Vietnamese river. The guards aren't pointing their guns at us anymore; I can light a cigarette whenever I feel like one. I'm sitting there puffing a cigarette, and the boat is chugging along. It's calm and serene. There are trees along the banks, and now and then you see a little house, smoke curling up, and there are some kids yelling and maybe a chicken cackling, a dog barking here and there. You see outcroppings, and the river gets narrower, then wider again, very wide, and then I get sleepy and just go to sleep, and whenever I wake up the boat will be wherever it's going, *chug-chug-chug*, down the river.

To have all this given back to you after it had been denied forever as far as you could tell. . . . And the same guys that had kept me all that time, they're running the boat now, taking me somewhere, rather than forcing me to go someplace; they're doing things for me. Beautiful scene. You could never appreciate it unless it had been denied to you.

We left the boat at dawn and made camp in the trees by the river bank. In the early afternoon we were joined by a group of rag-tag guerrillas, much like Walter Brennan's crew. They must have been local irregulars detailed to help carry us on to the next point. We were far south from where we had been, out of the jungle in rice country. The sun was bright overhead—it hurt our eyes, they smarted and watered a lot—but the rice fields were green and beautiful.

I looked over and nudged McClure, and he grinned. There was the Black Virgin Mountain. Apparently, the Vietnamese hadn't moved it after all.

At night we kept moving, crossing endless inundated grasslands. The area might have been paddy once, but now it was just very heavy grass. The water stood six inches to a foot deep in some areas. There was moonlight. It was very bright, almost like a dream. You could see the horizon, but when you got there you were nowhere. You were still walking in the same watery grasslands and everything looked the same. It was like walking on a treadmill. I would see what looked like trees way out on the horizon, and when we'd get there, there wouldn't be anything there, and there'd still be trees on the horizon. Occasionally we would pass a village or hear people talking or maybe singing or children laughing in the distance.

The leeches nearly did us in. They were really bad where

water buffalo had been, where the water was a little stagnant. If you stood still they would actually stalk you. There were big ones—as big as your finger—horrible-looking creatures. I got one on my foot. I slipped three fingers under it and yanked it off, and blood poured everywhere. I still have a scar from the damned thing.

By morning we were in paddies, and before noon we finally stopped at what looked like an abandoned machine shop in a clump of trees. It wasn't too old, but it was made with thatch and poles and the termites get to that pretty fast. There was a hearth and bits and pieces of things lying around that looked like they might once have machined something. They might have made weapons there.

That afternoon an English-speaking Vietnamese in khakis joined us and introduced himself as Le Van Diep. It was so unusual for a member of the NLF to tell us his name that I suspected it was a pseudonym.* He told us he would go with us to our final release point. Arrangements were still going forward, but they were not quite complete.

We rested for the remainder of the afternoon and were preparing to bed down for the night when somehow a message must have arrived. I still had to marvel at how people and boats would show up at the right time and the right place—at the damnedest times and places. I hadn't yet seen them use either a compass or a radio.

We rolled up our gear and walked about four hours to another bivouac area. South, always south, bearing slightly west. We camped in an abandoned cluster of small shacks in a clump of trees. We slung our hammocks and went to sleep, but it seemed that I was no sooner asleep than someone started shaking me. First light was in the sky, and Pussy was trying to wake me up.

---

* Le Van Diep probably gave his name freely because he worked openly and was known to a wide range of people outside Vietnam.

"Hurry, the cars are waiting."

"Cars?"

"Yes, you must hurry and shave."

Cars were waiting? It was unbelievable. We were still out there in the middle of the rice paddies. Ox carts, maybe—but cars? Compared to the month it took us to get into the jungle, we had been walking just a short time—a few days. Wherever we were going, we couldn't be anywhere near *there* yet. My mind boggled at the idea of McClure and me driving around in cars with the Vietcong.

I must have cut myself shaving sixteen times, but I really didn't give a shit. If there were cars out there waiting somewhere, I sure as hell didn't want to miss my ride.

We had a hell of an escort by then—the guards from Camp Baffle, the irregulars we had picked up after the boat ride, Pussy, Le Van Diep. We were joined by still another group, led by a big jolly Vietnamese with a red shirt and a large grin that revealed large gold teeth. He just smiled to greet us. I don't know if they were a security patrol, or if they just happened to be friendly guerrillas living in the area who wanted to walk along and bullshit with the guys from the jungle.

Our guides set a fast pace. McClure had worked himself into one of his moods just before they started giving us the better food and exercise, and he was still weak. He would keep lagging behind, and I would keep saying, "Come on, McClure, I want to go home." He'd struggle along, bitching as he went. But this morning he had no trouble keeping up, evidently inspired by the promise of a ride.

They took us across field after field, with no road in sight, and I began to have my doubts about the cars. The country was completely open and we could hear intermittent machine-gun fire no more than a mile away. The Vietnamese didn't seem overly concerned, but they weren't fiddling around. They weren't going to sit down and take a break or anything like that. They apparently knew what the firing was—maybe an ambush, maybe sniping—it could have been somebody just playing around in one of those ARVN camps.

I felt terribly naked. I had the awful feeling that a Skyraider was going to zoom in and blow us all to hell. I was sure I would get bombed or strafed. I was feeling those .50-caliber rounds going *splat, splat, splat* in the water right beside me from the time the B-26 strafed us in that village. You're right out in the open—they're up there and they can see you and they will shoot you. They can't hear you yelling, "No, no, not me." You can't just pull your hat off and show your yellow hair. Bullets don't discriminate.

Another hour and a half and we were in another field. The area was flat and level. I nudged McClure. "See that flag! Man, we're going to Cambodia!" It was like a new life. We started moving a hell of a lot faster. I kept waiting for the Skyraider, but we made it. At the border Husky shook hands with us, and then he and the rest of the escort started back across the field to begin the long trek back to the jungle.

Le Van Diep and Pussy crossed into Cambodia with us. There was a little fort with mud walls and the headquarters of the Cambodian border police. We sat down in the courtyard and the Cambodian sergeant gave us a pack of ARAs. We barely made it with our ass intact. While we were sitting there we could hear the Skyraiders coming, and then they started raining all kinds of shit over the field we had just left. Husky and the rest of the column that had brought us were out there somewhere—they would really have had to hurry to get out of that field. I sat there and drew on my cigarette and wondered once again why some die and some don't in Vietnam.

When the cars finally came they were Land Rovers. They brought Cambodian officials—national security police—who asked McClure and me to sign a request asking permission to travel in Cambodia. Pussy said his good-byes and went back

into Vietnam. The Cambodians took some pictures, and then
McClure and I climbed into one of the Land Rovers with the
interpreter they had brought, a Cambodian educated at
Oxford. We were going home.

It was like the end of one life and the beginning of
another. The situation was so strange, so completely and
utterly changed, that it was almost bewildering. As we swung
onto Highway 1 toward Svay Rieng, I thought of all the
Vietnamese we had met in those two years. Already the
rough spots were fading. What could I say—they let us go
home and sent themselves back to the war.

"AIDING THE ENEMY"

Le Van Diep rode with us to Phnom Penh in the other car.
The Cambodians took him to one of the big hotels, while
they took us to national police headquarters to take our
pictures. We were still in our pajamas, and they went out and
got us some civilian clothes—a pair of grey slacks and plaid
shirt for me. When they took us to the hotel to change, Le
Van Diep was waiting for us. We shared a large room with
three beds.

That night Le Van Diep treated us to something like a
sixteen-course meal. They brought it up to our room. The
hotel featured lobster, but we featured bread—loaf after loaf.

The waiter just couldn't believe that two people could eat as much bread as we did. We ate about a dozen loaves apiece, besides the fish and all the entrees. We just gobbled up ungodly amounts of food.

A real bed, hot showers, electric lights, ice in a glass, sleeping without a mosquito net, glass in the windows, the bustle of traffic outside in the night. I ordered a Coke.

The next day Le Van Diep showed us a Cambodian French-language newspaper with our pictures in it and the story of our release. It was in the paper so it must be real. But there was a sobering note. The story said Roraback had been executed. That was real too. Le Van Diep read it to us.

They brought a doctor to look at the leech bite on my foot. While he was there Wilfred Burchett dropped by for a moment to congratulate us. "Really good to see you again, under somewhat different circumstances, I might add. You're feeling fine now, I suppose." I was a little friendlier than I had been before. We joked about his advice to try to eat the rice. "Under the circumstances it was the only advice I felt would do you any good."

Le Van Diep's English was halting. He didn't talk to us much. But he told us there was going to be a press conference the next afternoon. "All that we would like for you to do is tell the truth." Of course we assured him that we would. Then Mike Mansfield was coming down the street in a motorcade, and he took us out on the balcony to look. There he was, going by in a black Continental, waving to all the people. He knew we were in town—it was in all the newspapers—but for some reason he didn't come to see us.[18]

The next morning the Cambodians took me around town in a frantic search to find a pair of shoes big enough to fit me. I wanted to wear my Ho Chi Minh sandals to the press conference, but they said, no, no, it just wouldn't be appropriate.

The press conference was in a big room at the Ministry of

Information. There was no member of the U.S. press present, but everybody else seemed to be there. A Cambodian official made an introduction, and Le Van Diep read the proclamation of our release to the reporters, the same one they had read at the camp.

Then for half an hour McClure and I took turns answering questions. How were you treated? Were you well fed? How long were you prisoners? Burchett was there and asked if we had seen any damage done by the bombs. "Yes, they blew the tops out of a lot of trees." That got a laugh.

Then a woman reporter with a French accent asked me, "What do you plan to do when you get back to the United States?"

It came as an abrupt question, a shock. Well, I will be getting back pretty soon, won't I. People are going to ask what it was like. I've got to make a decision right here, I thought. I've got to tell people; this is what I have to do. I had some purpose after all.

"I want to tell people the truth about Vietnam."

"How will you do that?"

"I will join the peace movement."

I wasn't too sure about the last answer—I still didn't have any idea what the peace movement really was. But they had somehow influenced my release, so they sure as hell weren't the bad guys.

Le Van Diep came up to us afterwards with a pleased look on his face. "You told the truth." [19]

We left the Ministry with the Cambodians. There had been a couple of men at the back of the conference hall taking notes but asking no questions, and one of them came up to me. "Congratulations, I'm from the Australian embassy." Since the U.S. didn't have diplomatic relations with Cambodia, they represented the U.S. there. They invited us to lunch, but there was something strange about their approach. We weren't too sure about our status with the

Cambodian government, so we told them no thanks, and the Cambodians hustled us off.

That afternoon we moved from the hotel to a room at national police headquarters. We saw Le Van Diep only one more time. He brought us some grapes, about $150 spending money, and some advice. The Australians would turn us over to the U.S. military, he said. "You are free to choose, but it is my opinion that it is better to go home some other way than with the military. Any government that would send you to Vietnam. . . ."

But officially we were still in the Army, and we didn't want to go home through China—we didn't want to get involved in all kinds of international politics. We asked the Australians to make the travel arrangements, and a few days later we flew into Bangkok. As we got off the plane we were met by an Army colonel, who greeted us with, "Welcome back, soldier." Our Australian escort, John McNally, had promised us a night on the town, but we weren't going to get it. The colonel just walked us across the runway to a waiting C-47 for a short hop to the U.S. base at Korat. While I tried to read *Stars and Stripes,* our Army escort read us Article 31—the military version of the rights against self-incrimination under the Fifth Amendment. A real friendly homecoming.

We stayed at Korat for a day, just long enough for me to call my mother and tell her I was okay and would be home in a few days. They gave us a physical, and orders promoting us one grade, retroactive to August, the time of Camacho's escape. That sounded a bit better than the Article 31 reading.

The two CIC men were with us everywhere except in bed, and when we boarded the four-passenger Lear jet for the Philippines, they were our escort. The Philippines would be the first leg of our journey home.

As the little plane passed over Vietnam, one of the CIC men turned to me—"Take a look down. This is the last time you'll ever see that piece of real estate."

Maybe you're right, I thought. But I felt sad—I hoped he was wrong. The mood passed quickly. As we flew over the South China Sea, I became greatly elated.

We were going home.

EPILOGUE

George Smith's elation at the prospect of being home in a few days was short-lived. The Army flew him and McClure from the Philippines to Okinawa for "debriefing." The change was as much a surprise for the CIC men with them as for Smith and McClure. Indications are that it was a last-minute decision by the Army based on Smith's press-conference promise to join the peace movement and tell the truth about the war.

Since neither of them knew much about the peace movement they could have had no idea that, as far as the military was concerned, George's statement was the worst thing he could have said. They would be in Okinawa six months.

The two had had a short debriefing in Korat. Senator Stephen Young of Ohio, there on other business, had made an abortive attempt to talk with them. He had been allowed to introduce himself, but when he began asking questions about the statements they had made in Phnom Penh, the CIC hustled Smith and McClure away.

In Okinawa, Smith and McClure were turned over to Army intelligence agents who told them they would be kept out of sight. There were people on the island who would bring harm to them, they said. The agents accompanied them wherever they went, usually two at a time; and they slept with them where they were quartered, at separate ends of an otherwise unoccupied Quonset hut.

They were debriefed separately by three intelligence officers, a map expert and two interrogators who took turns questioning them and running the tape recorder. "They started with Day One, the day we were captured, and had us explain what happened that day and then every day thereafter for all seven hundred and some days we were prisoners of war."

Their debriefing lasted three weeks. When Smith complained and said he thought he was going home, he was told he might not make it for Christmas. He didn't. He requested his back pay and got a partial allotment of five hundred dollars for both himself and McClure. He used it to buy a watch, a wallet, and some civilian clothes. They were issued phony identification cards to use at the officers' club— McClure was "Gerald Rook," Smith "William T. Knight." Smith thinks the names were "picked from a chess game— maybe that's what they thought it was."

They were not allowed to talk to anyone without prior clearance by the intelligence men. Their mail was read and censored.

"Tell us everything that happened that's important," the interrogators told them at the outset of the debriefing. "It will be helpful for Americans who become prisoners of war." Smith remembered that Man With Glasses had once warned him that "a government that will send you to Vietnam will certainly put you in jail after you get back for saying the things against U.S. policy that you have." But he didn't believe it. The Army had taken them back, he thought. Both of them were cooperative; they wanted to get it over with and go home.

Two-thirds of the way through the debriefing one of the interrogators read Smith a statement informing him that he was suspected of violating Article 104 of the Uniform Code of Military Justice—aiding the enemy. Without offering him legal counsel, they asked if he wished to continue the debriefing. Smith said he had promised to tell them everything and would continue.

When the debriefing was finished a few days later, they were transferred to headquarters company at Fort Buckner, Okinawa. Without knowing it, they had been removed from Special Forces. When they were introduced to their new company commander, he informed them that they were to be court-martialed and read them the charge—aiding the enemy. According to the specifics of the charge, they had made writings and statements "inimical to the United States."

Aiding the enemy carries the death penalty. Treason, which also carries the death penalty, must be tried in a civilian court and conviction requires corroborating witnesses to the crime. Aiding the enemy can be tried by a military tribunal without witnesses. The military would use as evidence the testimony given freely and openly by the defendants themselves during their debriefing.

Only after the debriefing had been completed, the charges made and read, and the specifics released to the press, were Smith and McClure assigned legal counsel. Their lawyers were military lawyers under the command influence of the judge advocate at Fort Buckner, whose office was preparing the case against the two.

The Army's duplicity came as a tremendous shock. Smith just couldn't believe that they would set up a debriefing under the pretense of getting information important to the welfare of American soldiers and then turn it around and use it for court-martial charges. McClure, too, was flabbergasted.

While it kept Smith and McClure from the press, the Army issued press releases intimating that Smith and/or McClure had turned official papers over to the Vietcong. Accepting the Army's allegations without checking the facts, one national news weekly referred to the men as "turncoats." But any documents Smith and McClure might have had access to had been consumed in the flames of the team house that night in November 1963.

The number of their agent escorts increased. One of them was Major Thomas C. Middleton, who in August 1969 would be implicated with Colonel Reault in the supposed Special Forces assassination of a Vietnamese national.[20]

As they were now prisoners, the senior intelligence man told them, they could be put in the stockade for pre-trial confinement. But that wouldn't be necessary as long as they were cooperative and didn't try to escape. A more comfortable site had been found for them, he said, where they would have greater freedom of movement and would be assigned some duties. In supposed secrecy a convoy of blue military Plymouths carried them through gawking Toyotas to the northern end of the island and a small, isolated Special Forces post in the jungle, Camp Hardy.

There Smith was ordered to construct jungle trails and keep in repair a simulated Vietnamese village used for Special Forces training. "Dig some foxholes, some tunnels, maybe some punji pits—make the thing look authentic." He had a detail of Okinawan civilians to do the heavy work, but McClure was assigned to clean and maintain weapons in the camp arms room—a detail usually reserved for a private.

The whole camp was sworn to secrecy about their presence there, and the issues of *Time* and *Newsweek* that had carried their pictures were removed from the reading room. They had to ask permission to go to the beach; a trip to town required an okay from headquarters.

Their terms of service had long since expired, and their defense counsels suggested that they apply for discharge, just to see what would happen. Through their counsel they began corresponding with civilian lawyers in Washington, preparing to go to federal court on the grounds that their constitutional rights were being violated because they were being denied their own choice of legal counsel by being held on Okinawa and because they were being tried in a military court for a capital offense even though their terms of service had expired.

In the United States, they heard, their case was becoming controversial. Organizations within the peace movement were asking where they were and what had happened to them. "Two GIs Disappear Behind Army Shroud," the *Army Times* headlined. A rally demanding their release was held in New York, and the organizers sent them a button—"Release Smith and McClure." *Time* and *Newsweek* did sporadic stories wondering if they would ever be brought to trial. Their counsels told them they thought the government would try to offer them a deal.

One morning early in April, Middleton told Smith that they wanted him at the hospital at Fort Buckner for an examination. Smith thought it odd that McClure wasn't coming, too. They left Camp Hardy, and Middleton drove him down a narrow coast-side back road to Fort Buckner— not to a medical examination but to an audience with the judge advocate.

"Would you testify against McClure?"

"Well, if I was called to testify, I'd tell the truth."

"That's not what I asked. Would you testify against McClure?"

"I think I'd like to talk to my defense counsel."

Their counsels weren't at Fort Buckner, Smith was told. They had been decoyed to Camp Hardy that morning by a call from the intelligence officer there, who said that he was going to interrogate McClure and that if they wanted to be there they'd better hurry. Naturally, they had taken the main highway and missed Smith and Middleton on the back road.

Smith, McClure, and their counsels were scandalized. Of course, Smith refused to "testify" against McClure, and the judge advocate made them a second offer—they could demand a general court-martial, or accept "something less than an honorable discharge, something more than a dishonorable discharge." A court-martial would take as long as eighteen months to convene, they were told, and the government thought it had at least enough evidence for a dishonorable discharge.

Their counsels said they thought the government was bluffing, but Smith and McClure decided they had had enough—they wanted out. They took the deal and the discharge.

The Army probably was bluffing. Washington had decided that there would be no court-martial—it would have become a *cause célèbre* for the peace movement and just one more black eye for the administration. But Smith and McClure had no way of knowing that, isolated as they were.

To Smith and McClure, the interrogators kept harping on the statements they had written and the tape recordings they had made. The press conference in Phnom Penh was never mentioned. But almost no one in the U.S. except the Army knew anything about the statements, while almost everybody had read or heard about Smith's promise to join the peace movement. The Army's reason for attempting to court-martial them was generally assumed to be the press conference. Smith feels that it was a threat to other GIs not to join the peace movement.

The story Smith told the military is the one you have just read. The military could not turn him loose with such a story. He had had the bad grace to come away from Vietcong captivity in reasonably good health, with no tales of torture or beatings and no rancor toward his former captors.

Camacho, of course, was treated much differently from Smith. His debriefing took days, not months. And he was quickly reunited with his family, with much media hoopla. Court-martial was never considered. Instead, President

Johnson made a special trip to Texas to pin the Silver Star—the nation's second-highest award for gallantry in action—on the sergeant's chest. Camacho remains in Special Forces with either a "secret" or "top secret" security clearance.

For one man the threat of court-martial and death, for the other an award for bravery. Camacho probably could not have made his escape had Smith not stayed to cover for him, knowing that if Camacho was successful life was going to be most unpleasant for him. Prior to his escape Camacho had dug holes, milled rice, sharpened punji stakes, and *written the same statements as Smith and McClure.*

Two weeks after accepting the government's deal, Smith and McClure were told to pack their bags for a weekend in town. Again they were taken, not to town, but to the judge advocate. They had been given a "general discharge under honorable conditions"—better than they had expected—and were being sent home that afternoon. There were hints that the decision had been made at the highest level—in the White House.

But the judge advocate wasn't through with them yet. They were forbidden to describe their captivity and specifically warned not to discuss such things as the B-52 raids and the Red Cross parcels. These things were "secret information"—secret, not to the Vietcong of course, but to the American people. They were forced to sign papers acknowledging that they had been warned. Any violation would put them *in flagrante* of national security—a federal offense. Having branded Smith and McClure "turncoats," the military then denied them the right to clear themselves publicly.

They were put on a Northwest Orient airliner with escorts. Touching down briefly in Tokyo, they were not allowed to leave the plane. They flew to Seattle, then changed planes for Indianapolis, where Smith was taken to Fort Benjamin Harrison, Indiana. There he was issued his final pay and his discharge papers. "In two hours I was discharged from the Army and in civilian clothes. They took me to the Indianapolis airport and told me, 'You're on your own.' And there I was after all those years." Smith went to a friend's in Columbus where he called his mother and asked if she could pick him up that night without letting the press know.

That night the Army announced their release. They had told Smith and McClure that they would never divulge what type of discharge they were given—an empty gesture. What the Army *did* make public was that they had not been cleared of the charges against them, that the charges had merely been dropped.

A few days later at his mother's home in Chester, West Virginia, I met and talked with George Smith for the first time. The meeting only lasted three hours, and in terms of gaining information for the feature article I was planning, it was a bust. He was wary, if not outright suspicious. Was I an agent passing as a reporter checking to see if he would talk? He was polite but unwilling to talk to me or anyone else. I thought at first that he felt guilty and was hiding, but one doesn't try to hide in a town the size of Chester, where everyone is known by his first name. No, he was too soon out from under the gun and hadn't yet reoriented himself sufficiently to know that he was free. My article was reduced to a piece of marginalia (*Ramparts*, July 1966). Like all those of the media who made the trek to Chester, I left my card and asked him to call if he ever decided to tell his story, believing as I did so that I would never hear from him again. George Smith had been traveling a long time to reach freedom—but he hadn't traveled quite long enough.

Three years later George Smith wrote saying that if I was still interested he wanted to tell his story. In a subsequent phone call, I had two questions: Why had he waited so long, and why had he contacted me rather than some other journalist? To the first he replied that he had long decided to tell the story but had felt there was no longer any interest in it. Now he felt that the Navy's harassment of Commander Bucher of the *Pueblo* was similar to his harassment by the Army. That and disillusionment with what were passing for "peace" talks in Paris prompted him to tell his story.

His second answer came in the form of a compliment that journalists thrive on. "You were the only reporter willing to reserve judgment. You reported our last meeting just like it happened. I want you to do the story because I trust you to write what I saw, not what you think."

As I traveled across the country for the interview, I felt happy. Perhaps George Smith had at long last found his freedom. This time my trip took me through Chester and over the frail bridge that separates the town from East Liverpool, Ohio, his new home. George was married now, with two babies. A member of the local Veterans of Foreign Wars, he was living in a VA-financed house, working for the post office (where his Army service counts toward retirement) and drawing an Army pension for his leg wounds. He told his story and told it well, but it was apparent that despite three years he still had some distance to travel. When we parted that day, I asked George, now that he had had some time to think about it, what his impressions were of the peace movement.

"Well, it's hard to say. You don't hear much about them these days. Fact is, I wouldn't know where it is or where to look for it."

I waited until the article appeared (*Ramparts*, September 1969) to phone and tell George that a publisher wanted him to write a book. If he was interested, would he come to Los Angeles to discuss it? His visit coincided with a rally in MacArthur Park November 15, 1969. Those participating were people who had not been able to travel to San Francisco for the huge peace march that day but who wanted to show their support.

As we watched the proceedings, approximately forty young active-duty Marines marched onto the stage. As they stood there holding peace signs, Sergeant Jack Anderson, a black Vietnam veteran, stepped forward and spoke against the war and its causes and articulated why we had to get out.

George stared unbelieving, almost in a trance. The roar of the crowd at the end of the speech broke the spell, and before it subsided George was at the microphone. He started by describing his treatment at the hands of the Vietcong and comparing it to how prisoners had been treated at Hiep Hoa. Then he compared the Vietcong treatment with the way the military treats its own in the stockades and brigs. He went on to make a series of statements about the war and the role and responsibility of the United States in that war. The audience had no way of knowing, but George Smith was making public the statements he had written for the NLF, the statements for which his life had been held in jeopardy by the United States Army. It wasn't a confession. It was a statement of purpose. George Smith was free at last.

That night George Smith joined the young Marines at a party, and for the first time I saw him completely relaxed, smiling and joking. George Smith had found the peace movement—and he took it home with him.

DONALD DUNCAN

NOTES

1. Rogers' Rangers was an elite company of mercenary bush fighters that fought for the British in the French and Indian War. Under the command of Robert Rogers, the Rangers' most famous exploit was an eighteenth-century My Lai—the virtual extermination of a small tribe of Indians forty miles south of Montreal. The Rangers later joined a contingent of British troops in the Carolinas in methodically burning the crops and villages of the Cherokees.

2. Contemporaneous news accounts of the Hiep Hoa attack differ somewhat. The *New York Times* story the day after, derived primarily from the first military reports, said that two to three hundred Vietcong guerrillas had "slipped past government defenses" and were inside the camp before opening fire. Thirty-seven strikers were killed, most of them in their beds. According to the *Times*, Colby was "critically wounded" and the ARVN troops in the sugar mill were pinned down by a "diversionary attack."

Neither *Time* nor *Newsweek* was so kind. Colby's wound is not mentioned, nor the diversionary attack on the sugar mill. According to *Newsweek,* some three hundred Vietcong, "admitted to the camp by traitors," began to blaze away when a bugle blared. After forty minutes of firing, they withdrew with "300 weapons, 20,000 rounds of ammunition, and $13,000 of Special Forces' funds." *Newsweek* quoted one U.S. officer as saying that Hiep Hoa was "one hell of a beating."

Time had the Vietcong knifing a sentry, then slipping into the compound "evidently in collusion with a spy inside." The ARVN at the sugar mill heard the battle but "fearing ambush, dared not go to the rescue." It took Saigon more than a day to mount a helicopter-borne assault.

3. The same week as Smith's capture, the National Liberation Front released a five-month's prisoner, Arthur Krause of Onarga, Illinois. Krause, twenty-nine, was a civilian engineer working for the Army as an adviser in military airfield building. "I was never mistreated or tortured," he said. *Newsweek* reported December 9, 1963 that "for the most part he was treated as a comrade, not as a prisoner. When he fell sick of malaria, the guerrillas found a French-trained doctor for him, and since hunger was the common lot, Krause joined his captors in hunting monkeys and dining on barbecued lizard." They moved deeper and deeper into the mountains. "It was a grim life," *Newsweek* paraphrased Krause, "but . . . the Vietcong were quick to laugh."

4. Disturbed by the conduct of American POWs during the Korean War, President Eisenhower ordered an investigation into its causes. As a result of the investigation a code was established to serve as a guide for U.S. servicemen who became POWs. High sounding and idealistic, it is worthless as a guide to individual survival, primarily because it is based on the premise that the state is paramount to the individual. Besides, Special Forces teaches that a skilled interrogator, given the time and determination, can extract whatever he desires from a subject.

5. On May 2, 1964, NLF frogmen blew a hole below the waterline of the U.S.S. *Card*, a 9800-ton "baby flattop." Loaded with a cargo of old helicopters and fighter bombers, the *Card* settled on the bottom of the Saigon River with its flight deck and superstructure above water. Military spokesmen said that the hole in her hull was "very big" and would take "weeks" to repair. (See *New York Times*, May 2, 1964.)

6. Burchett reported his visit with the four prisoners in his book *Vietnam: Inside Story of the Guerrilla War* (New York, 1965). The camp Smith calls "Auschwitz" was, according to Burchett, "doubtless the beginnings of the first camp for U.S. POWs to be established in Southeast Asia." Past NLF policy was to "give captured Americans a few weeks of 'explanations' as to what the struggle is about and then set them free." But it seemed from the organization of the camp that many more POWs were to be cared for "and release in the future may be a matter for negotiations."

As Smith says, it was Roraback who seemed to have the most to say to Burchett. Talking about the attack on Hiep Hoa, he told him, "They called our place a training camp. . . . In reality it was just a sitting target to be wiped out at any time." He had been writing a letter to his wife before the attack; when the assault came, he ran for the trenches without a weapon. "My captors were considerate from the moment I was taken. I expected to be shot right away." When Burchett asked why he expected to be shot, Roraback "looked a little confused." Guerrillas couldn't look after prisoners, he explained. "But they saw I was afraid and did everything to calm my fears. . . . They patted my back, waved their hands in a sort of friendly way in front of my face . . . and generally made signs that I shouldn't worry." Roraback told Burchett that he kept occupied at Auschwitz by building radios and model airplanes in his head. "My wife was mad with anxiety when I left," he told Burchett. "So many friends and acquaintances of ours had been killed, badly wounded, or just missing once they left for South Vietnam. The first word she got about me was that I'm wounded [at Can Tho]. And four months later that I'm captured."

The four prisoners' surprise at seeing him come out of the jungle "could not have been greater than if I had dropped down from Mars," Burchett wrote. But he was astonished at their lack of interest in what was happening in the outside world. The interests of the guards and the camp's company at the evening meeting were very different. "Questions ranged over the whole world and discussions lasted far into the night. They were especially interested to know what the outside world knew and thought about their own struggle and to know about national liberation movements in other parts of the world. They may often have been hazy about geography and the status of many of the countries they named, but they knew what they were interested in, and it was not the world heavyweight boxing championship that was on the top of the list."

7. On November 1, 1963, three weeks before the NLF overran Hiep Hoa, Vietnamese dictator Ngo Dinh Diem and his brother Ngo Dinh Nhu were assassinated in a coup led by General Duong Van Minh ("Big Minh"). Three months later, before Smith's first interview with Man With Glasses, Minh himself was ousted in a bloodless coup headed by General Nguyen Khanh, who kept Minh on as a figurehead "supreme adviser" to his Military Revolutionary Council.

In mid-August Khanh dropped Big Minh and then had himself elected president by the Military Revolutionary Council. Buddhists and students, protesting that Khanh's government was "dictatorial," rioted in the streets, and Khanh was forced to resign and form a triumvirate of generals including himself, Minh, and one other. When the rioting continued, a coup against Khanh by generals advocating a hard line on dissent was narrowly put down through the intervention of air force head Nguyen Cao Ky. In late September 1964, amid rumors of yet another coup, Khanh formed a civilian High National Council to write a constitution for civilian government, appointing Phan Khac Suu council chairman. A month later, the military council elected Suu chief of state, and Suu named Tran Van Huong to replace Khanh as premier— leaving Khanh with the real power as chairman of the Armed Forces Council.

In June Quat resigned and handed over formal power to a military triumvirate, including Ky and Nguyen Van Thieu.

8. Nguyen Van Troi, an electrical worker, was executed on October 15, 1964. He had been arrested on May 9, then quickly interrogated, tried, and sentenced to a public execution by firing squad.

Through radio and third-party diplomatic channels, the National Liberation Front warned the U.S. not to permit Nguyen Van Troi's execution, indicating it would jeopardize the lives of their American prisoners. At first the U.S. authorities refused to intervene, on the grounds that they could not interfere in the internal affairs of the Saigon government and that as a "terrorist" and member of an outlaw organization Nguyen Van Troi was not entitled to treatment as a POW.

But on the same day that Troi was arrested, Venezuelan guerrillas kidnapped Lt. Col. Michael Smolen, deputy chief of the U.S. Air Force mission in Caracas.

The U.S. requested a delay in Troi's execution to see if there was any connection between the announcement of Troi's execution and Smolen's kidnapping half a world away—not out of any consideration for U.S. POWs a scant few miles from Saigon. When Smolen was released on October 12, Nguyen Van Troi's execution was allowed to proceed.

9. The "Tonkin Gulf incidents" of August 1964—supposed attacks by North Vietnamese PT boats on U.S. destroyers some eight to ten miles off the North Vietnamese coast—took place in a context of increasing aggressiveness by Saigon and Washington toward North Vietnam. In late July, France, the Soviet Union, and UN Secretary U Thant proposed that the Geneva Conference be reconvened to negotiate an end to the war. North Vietnam agreed and the NLF was "not opposed," but Johnson rejected the proposal and increased American troop strength in Vietnam by twenty percent. General Nguyen Khanh called for a "march to the North" and Air Marshal Nguyen Cao Ky revealed that South Vietnamese commando teams were already operating there.

As anti-Khanh, anti-U.S. demonstrations in South Vietnamese cities persisted through January 1965, the Soviet Union continued to press for a reconvening of the Geneva Conference. Johnson waited until Soviet Premier Alexei Kosygin was visiting Hanoi on February 7 before unleashing the first wave of air attacks on North Vietnam. They were supposed to be in retaliation for an attack on a Special Forces camp at Pleiku in South Vietnam, though the attack had certainly been mounted by local guerrillas.

With a few short pauses, Johnson continued these attacks until November 1, 1968, dropping more tonnage of explosives on agricultural North Vietnam than had been dumped on industrial Germany during the whole of World War II. The cost, even to Johnson, was high. By the end of the bombing in 1968, the North Vietnamese claimed more than three thousand planes shot down (including reconnaissance drones), and the Pentagon admitted to 915 lost and a consequent shortage of flyers. Pilots shot down over North Vietnam constitute most of the American POWs in the war, with North Vietnam listing 368 captured and the U.S. reporting 378 captured and 405 missing.

10. The NLF announced June 24, 1965, that Army Sergeant Harold C. Bennett had been shot to death in retaliation for the Saigon regime's June 22 execution of an NLF cadre, Tran Van Dong. Dong, accused of trying to blow up an officers' billet in a Saigon suburb, was executed publicly in Saigon's central marketplace. The Ky regime vowed to hold more such public executions in other South Vietnamese cities. Bennett was the first American POW shot in retaliation for executions carried out under Ky's June 16 decree.

11. Camacho reached an allied camp on July 13, 1965. Within days he was home with his family in El Paso. In an August 24 interview with UPI, he said that the NLF had treated him "good sometimes, sometimes bad"—good treatment, he said, was three meals a day, bad treatment forced interrogation and "brainwashing." Other than one letter from his mother there had been "no bright moments."

Though he had been removed from both American society and Army life for two years, Camacho chose to attack critics of the war. They were "very disheartening to the troops over there facing death today," he said. "This only makes matters worse for the American people. The President has more important things to cope with than those protests."

"I want you to know your President cried this morning when he read what a boy from El Paso said," Lyndon Johnson told newsmen after reading the interview, and on September 4, Camacho was presented the Silver and Bronze stars in El Paso. President Johnson sent him congratulations by telegram.

El Paso declared the day "Sergeant Isaac Camacho Day," and Camacho rode as grand marshal in the city's *Fiesta de Las Flores* parade.

12. American troop strength in Vietnam when Smith was captured stood officially at 15,500 and at the end of 1964 was only 23,000. By May 1965 it had doubled to 46,000. While Smith was at "Baffle" the first really large debarcations took place, and by the end of 1965 there were 125,000 American troops in South Vietnam.

13. Smith may have been lucky. The steadily increasing American air war in Vietnam has apparently taken as heavy a toll among American POWs as among the Vietnamese. According to the June 22, 1971, CBS documentary "Pawns of War," the NLF reports holding twenty American POWs currently, while the Pentagon estimates eighty-two captured and another five hundred five missing. A spokesman for the NLF delegation in Paris, Nguyen Van Thinh, explained to the People's Commission of Inquiry on November 24, 1970, "During the battle sometimes we capture American GIs, but the American planes come over and drop bombs and kill these American GIs. . . . If we can keep them for some time, maybe they will be released, but unfortunately they have been killed by American bombs."

14. On Sunday, September 26, 1965, NLF "Liberation Radio" announced the execution of Captain Humbert Versace and Sergeant Kenneth Roraback. After a series of warnings, the NLF had for the second time executed American prisoners in reprisal for the Saigon regime's execution of Vietnamese—in this case three fishermen.

Fishermen from the villages surrounding Danang had demonstrated in the city the previous Monday. They were protesting that Marines guarding the U.S. air base there had evicted them from their lands, that curfew regulations were interfering with their fishing, and that the government was shelling their villages. The fishermen carried anti-American and anti-government banners, but there was no violence.

The military regime of Premier Nguyen Cao Ky arrested three of the demonstration's leaders and gave them a hurried military trial the day after the demonstration. The court found them guilty and sentenced them to be shot the next day. Their execution was to be held in the Danang soccer stadium, but it was postponed briefly when newsmen refused to agree to the government's demand that no photographs be taken until the fishermen were dead. (Photographs of Nguyen Van Troi standing undaunted at the stake had brought him worldwide admiration.) The fishermen were shot later that night without audience.

A U.S. spokesman in Saigon denounced the NLF's retaliatory executions of Roraback and Versace as "acts of wanton murder." He upheld the killing of the three fishermen. They were "civilian, non-uniformed VC agitators," he said, who had been tried "in accorance with established Vietnamese law and judicial procedure" and convicted of "fomenting public violence."

Premier Ky told newsmen that despite the NLF reprisals he planned to continue his executions of agitators. But apparently he was prevailed upon to act otherwise. In another public execution held later that week in a Saigon square, three men convicted of murder and rape were shot, while the death sentence of a "VC agitator" was commuted.

In fact, the execution of Roraback and Versace seems to have accomplished its purpose. There have been no further public executions of NLF cadres by the Saigon government. The NLF, in turn, has announced no further executions of American POWs.

15. The Cuban journalists were Marta Rojas and Raul Valdes Vivo. Their book, *Vietnam del sur*, was translated into English in 1967 by Havana's Book Institute. Their description of the five prisoners is not complimentary. As soon as they get to a camp, the Cubans reported, ". . . they break their necks looking for a pick and shovel to dig a trench. . . . They are panic-stricken at the B-52s, terrified of the F-105s, the helicopters drive them mad. . . . They huddle in the trenches and bury their noses in the mud."

The Cubans' assessment of the prisoners is that Schumann was "an ultra-reactionary high-ranking officer," Cook a "cowboy-type captain," Smith and McClure "two sergeants who understood the situation," and Crafts "a simple fellow . . . who was taken prisoner a month after his arrival in Vietnam."

After talking with the prisoners, the Cubans talked with Oil Can Harry, who gave them "some spoons made out of scraps of U.S. rockets and inscribed with poems of his own inspiration." Oil Can Harry, they report, is Le Hoa, a "hero of the war against the French," separated from his wife and children for many years.

16. Widespread criticism of the Vietnam war began in the spring of 1965 with a wave of "teach-ins" on college campuses and the massive "March on Washington" on April 11, sponsored by the Students for a Democratic Society (SDS). In August, Berkeley's Vietnam Day Committee (VDC), which had sponsored a May teach-in that brought fifteen thousand to the University of California campus, made several widely reported attempts to stop troop trains believed to be carrying men en route to Vietnam.

Perhaps a hundred thousand were involved in the VDC's "International Days of Protest" in mid-October—simultaneous demonstrations organized by anti-war groups across the country and abroad. In New York more than ten thousand people demonstrated, while in Berkeley fifteen thousand marching on the Oakland Army Terminal were stopped at the Oakland border by phalanxes of police. Large demonstrations took place in London, Rome, Brussels, and Tokyo.

Announced by the Vietnamese as "a response to the friendly sentiments of the American people against the war in South Vietnam," the release of Smith and McClure came on November 27, 1965, the day of the "March for Peace" in Washington, which drew some fifty thousand. SDS wired Smith and McClure in Phnom Penh: "Millions of Americans support you. Help us tell the truth about Vietnam."

17. Late in the afternoon of November 2, 1965, as thousands of Pentagon employees began to stream out of the building, Norman Morrison soaked himself with kerosene and burned himself to death below the third-floor windows of Secretary of Defense Robert S. McNamara. That evening, Ann Morrison, his wife, issued a statement: "Norman Morrison has given his life today to express his concern over the great loss of life and human suffering caused by the war in Vietnam. He was protesting our government's deep military involvement in this war. He felt that all citizens must speak their convictions about our country's action."

Morrison, thirty-two years old and the father of three children, was employed as the executive secretary of the Stoney Run Friends Meeting in Baltimore. He was a pacifist. A native of Erie, Pennsylvania, he had graduated from Wooster College, Ohio, studied theology at the University of Edinburgh, Scotland, and in 1959 taken a bachelor of divinity degree at Western Theological Seminary in Pittsburgh.

Though more than fifty thousand American men would march to their death in Vietnam, the American press was bemused by Morrison's pacifist sacrifice. Loudon Wainwright in *Life* called it a "deranged act." The *Christian Century* labeled it "bizarre." But the Vietnamese, who understood it very well, venerate Morrison.

Mrs. Alice Herz also burned herself to death in an anti-war protest. She died on March 16, 1965 in Detroit at the age of eighty-two.

18. Senate Majority Leader Mike Mansfield of Montana was in Phnom Penh on one leg of a "fact-finding mission" for Lyndon Johnson that took him to Europe and Asia with four other senators. When Johnson initiated airstrikes against North Vietnam in February 1965, Mansfield had supported him, saying, "I think he is proceeding cautiously and carefully." He met with Cambodia's Prince Sihanouk on November 29, 1965 and on his return to the U.S. he reported to President Johnson that the U.S. could win the war militarily while losing Southeast Asia politically. He urged the president to seek a negotiated peace.

19. "Two Freed GIs Say U.S. Should Quit Vietnam," the *New York Times* headlined a UPI report on December 1, 1965. It quoted the two as saying such things as, "The United States has nothing to gain from the war in Vietnam," "The Vietcong treated us very well," and "I didn't have to submit to any brainwashing." According to the report in *Time* on December 10, Smith said, "I have known both sides, and the war in Vietnam is of no interest to the United States." It quoted McClure on how the Vietcong had treated his leg wound: "Had it been the Saigon government, I would have been tortured." *Newsweek* on December 13 quoted him as saying, "The Saigon government is not the government of the people. . . . The Vietcong are the people."

From his vantage point in Washington, General Wallace Greene, Marine Corps Commandant, immediately said he believed the two men had been brainwashed. *Newsweek* intimated that the men had collapsed under the pressure of Roraback's execution—without bothering to check if they were aware of it. One of the first to call them turncoats, *Newsweek* asked, "If it wasn't brainwashing, what then was it?" It concluded that as "typical enough Americans—of the underprivileged variety," they were "the men most likely to crumble under such pressures." The media, of course, couldn't dare believe that perhaps "typical enough Americans" were the men most open to the truth, and that the truth included a description of the "enemy" that didn't match that portrayed by the administration's propagandists.

20. The Army arrested Colonel Thomas C. Middleton Jr. and seven other Special Forces personnel on August 6, 1969, on suspicion of murdering one of their agents who was thought to have been working as a double agent for the North Vietnamese. When the CIA—said to have ordered the execution—refused to allow its personnel to testify at the trial, the charges were dropped. Senator Stephen Young said that the order to withdraw the charges came from the White House.

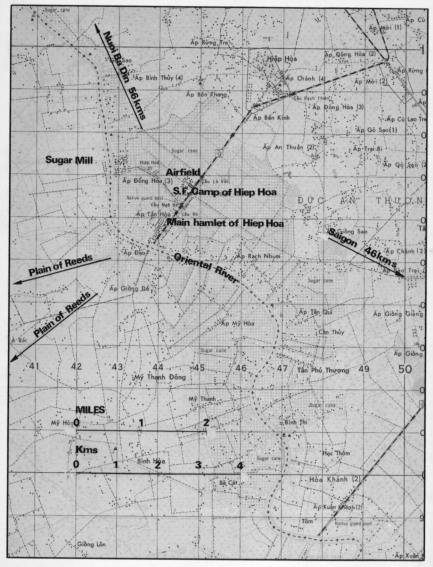

"Ap" is Vietnamese for hamlet; hence Ap Tan Hoa is the hamlet of Hiep Hoa.
"S.F." designates "Special Forces."